Conflict and Compliance

PENNSYLVANIA STUDIES IN HUMAN RIGHTS
Bert B. Lockwood, Jr., Series Editor

A complete list of books in the series is available from the publisher.

Conflict and Compliance

State Responses to International Human Rights Pressure

SONIA CARDENAS

PENN

University of Pennsylvania Press

Philadelphia

Copyright © 2007 University of Pennsylvania Press
All rights reserved
Printed in the United States of America on acid-free paper

10 9 8 7 6 5 4 3 2 1

Published by
University of Pennsylvania Press
Philadelphia, Pennsylvania 19104-4112

Library of Congress Cataloging-in-Publication Data

Cardenas, Sonia.
    Conflict and compliance : state responses to international human rights pressure /
Sonia Cardenas.
        p. cm. — (Pennsylvania studies in human rights)
    Includes bibliographical references and index.
    ISBN-13: 978-0-8122-3999-7
    ISBN-10: 0-8122-3999-7 (cloth : alk. paper)
    1. Human rights.   2. International relations.   I. Title.   II. Series.

JC571.C28 2007
323—dc22   2006051454

For Andy and Alex

Contents

Preface

This book has its origins in the streets of Cairo. As a visiting fellow there years ago, researching the Arab world's relations with European countries across the Mediterranean, I was struck by a prominent gap: the disparity between the numerous international cooperation agreements that governments concluded and the daily conditions of people on the ground. This contradiction led me to question more generally the sources of compliance with international norms and the conditions required for human rights protection. The result is this book, which has nothing to do with Egypt per se but focuses on the multiple and complex ways in which states around the world respond to human rights pressure.

Despite my attention to states as political actors, or the role of national leaders and activist organizations, the key protagonists are the victims of abuse. Their stories have both inspired and haunted me. And I do little justice to them here other than to use their full names whenever possible in the text, a small symbol of their significance.

In this book I seek, above all, to unify disparate fields of study, contributing to the growing volume of social science research on human rights. Theory and methods are therefore used in the book as tools to illuminate complex patterns of interaction. As such, I have cast my net broadly to benefit from the insights of international relations, international law, comparative politics, sociology, and history, as well as studies from other disciplinary perspectives. On the empirical side, the scope is also deliberately broad, presenting in-depth cases from Latin America in the 1970s and 1980s, a statistical survey of all the countries in the world in the 1990s, and a brief application of the argument to a set of prominent cases spanning the globe: Eastern Europe, South Africa, China, Israel, and Cuba. My aim is to bolster the argument's persuasiveness by submitting it to a variety of tests and circumstances. For example, although the Latin American cases compose the bulk of the book, they are intended to showcase the nuance and detail undergirding the argument, especially those aspects that may elude the rigors of quantitative analysis—such as state rhetoric, social demands, archival evidence of the institutionalization of ideas, and decision-making debates. The two chapters devoted to the region are thus structured analytically, one testing skeptics' assumptions and the other exploring the limits of human rights optimism; they reveal how the same events can be interpreted differently depending on one's analytical lens. Accordingly, the cases of Argentina and Chile serve as windows onto the world of human rights compliance, geared to regionalists and nonregionalists alike.

Though human rights protection is premised on the peaceful respect for human dignity and diversity, conflict and tension feature prominently in this study. I am most interested in the conflict engendered when international human rights norms clash with domestic rules of exception, or when national security and personal integrity collide. I am also intrigued by the competitions that ensue between pro-compliance and pro-violation constituencies. These tensions pervade real life but they remain surprisingly undertheorized. My assumption is that a more systematic understanding of these conflict dynamics is needed before we can comprehend the timing of human rights reforms, the persistence of state violations, and more broadly, the conditions under which human rights pressures will most likely succeed. All of these issues raise crucial policy implications, vitally relevant in a post–September 11 world in which national security ideas so often trump human rights norms.

Various people have supported me on the long trajectory leading to this book. It is no exaggeration to say that without the candid and intelligent advice of John Duffield the book would not exist. David Waldner's sharply critical eye guided early revisions, and Jeff Legro's support and insight proved invaluable. Moreover, my own approach to international politics has benefited immensely (even shamelessly) from the work of these scholars. On the human rights front, Jack Donnelly's encouragement at a crucial moment in the project led me to the cases of Argentina and Chile. Thanks are also due to Len Schoppa, who commented thoughtfully on earlier versions of the manuscript; Steven Poe, who offered insights into some aspects of the material in Chapter 5; Bert Lockwood, who kindly supported the project; and the anonymous reviewers who pushed me in important directions. I also appreciate the unique perspective that Indres Naidoo afforded me on the South African case. Peg Herman deserves thanks for supporting and disseminating key aspects of the argument. Portions of Chapter 2 appeared in "Norm Collision: Explaining the Effects of International Human Rights Pressure on State Behavior," *International Studies Review* 6, 2 (2004): 213–31; and the discussion of state rhetoric borrows from my article "Violators' Accounts:

Hypocrisy and Human Rights Rhetoric in the Southern Cone," *Journal of Human Rights* 5, 4 (December 2006). Blackwell Publishing and Taylor & Francis Ltd. kindly agreed to publish substantial parts of these articles. Last, I thank Peter Agree for his unflagging support and patience, no less than his sound counsel, as well as Erica Ginsburg at the University of Pennsylvania Press.

Several institutions further facilitated and enhanced the writing of this book. The libraries at Columbia University (especially its Law School), Harvard University, the American University in Cairo, and the Colegio de México offered memorable research sanctuaries. I also thank the Kennedy School's Carr Center for Human Rights Policy and Harvard's David Rockefeller Center for Latin American Studies, which provided me with institutional resources to revise and complete the book. My students in international law and human rights, especially those at Trinity College and the University of Notre Dame, taught me to articulate my claims more clearly. Moreover, participants at talks given at various forums, including national and regional meetings of the American Political Science Association and the International Studies Association, proved very helpful at critical junctures. The Political Science Department and the Human Rights Program at Trinity College also afforded an engaging environment as I shepherded the book through publication.

On a more personal note, a circle of people shaped my thinking and disposition. In particular, Tony, Rosemary, and Joe fueled my determination by reminding me of all that is important. My parents, Antonio Cárdenas and Pura Lerdo de Tejada, promoted my education and kindled my internationalism from an early age, for which I am grateful. Without the partnership of Andy, however, this manuscript would never have been completed. His wisdom, humor, and companionship made it both possible and worthwhile. Indeed, our long-distance hikes—across the Welsh-English border, the Mexican jungle, the French Pyrenees, and the Scottish highlands—have been a metaphor for the writing of this book. Alex's arrival near the end has only made the destination more remarkable than the journey.

Chapter 1

Introduction: Compliance Revisited

States are often subject to competing normative pressures. Will they comply with international norms or violate them in the face of countervailing national standards? If they comply, they risk a backlash from domestic opponents of international norms. If they resist, they could jeopardize their relations with other states. The trade-offs actually associated with compliance and noncompliance, however, are not so straightforward. I argue in this book that the choice between complying and not complying with an international norm is in fact a false one. State leaders caught in a normative cross fire have an arsenal of compliance choices available to them. They can increase their violation of a norm but engage in lip service, or they can comply with some aspects of a norm but not others. When norms conflict, compliance is not an all-or-nothing outcome; it takes different forms and occurs to varying degrees.

The multifaceted nature of compliance poses a challenge to policy makers and academics alike. How are we to interpret state responses to international pressure that are varied and complex? A common strategy has been to infer the influence of international pressure selectively. On the one hand, skeptics point to violations as evidence of the limits of international pressure while labeling instances of compliance as coincidental. On the other hand, optimists trace most improvements in compliance to international pressure and tend to overlook ongoing violations. Although it is difficult to refute the claims of either skeptics or optimists, the failure of each to examine critically all state responses has made it impossible to confirm either position. Consequently, we still lack answers to an important set of questions: What is the impact of international pressure on state compliance? Which domestic factors mediate this influence? More specifically, why do states respond as they do to international compliance pressures? In addressing these questions, central to both international politics and law, I do not attempt to offer conclusive evidence in support of the claims of either skeptics or optimists. My assumption is that although both sets of arguments may have some truth, neither perspective by itself is adequate to account for the full variance in state compliance.

The book therefore makes two overarching contributions to our understanding of human rights. First, it reveals the complex set of dynamics that can ensue when human rights and national security norms collide. The attempt is to bridge a prominent gap in the human rights field between the study of state compliance and the literature on state repression. Second, the book joins qualitative and quantitative methods to study human rights, two bodies of research that have not always engaged one another. The aim is to show—through a focused comparison of two Latin American cases from the 1970s and 1980s, a statistical analysis of all countries in the world during the 1990s, and a set of prominent mini case studies—the possibilities for conducting rich and nuanced political analysis alongside more rigorous testing of propositions in the still-emerging field of human rights.

The Compliance Paradox

Inconsistencies in compliance have perhaps nowhere been more dramatic than in the human rights arena, where competing norms so often clash. A well-known case from the immediate post–Cold War period illustrates these tensions. Following the 1989 crackdown by the Chinese government against student demonstrators in Tiananmen Square, the regime came under strong international human rights pressure. The Chinese leadership responded to this pressure with a mixed array of strategies. First, it rejected international pressure verbally, arguing that such pressure constituted interference in its internal affairs. At the same time, it complied symbolically in both its rhetoric and its gestures: for the first time, the Chinese government acknowledged the importance of human rights norms, while defending its rights record and promising improvements; it admitted foreign delegates to discuss human rights concerns; and it released some political dissidents. At the level of actual compliance, however, there was a *rise* in the level of repression, including thousands of political detentions, widespread torture by state agents, and a sharp increase in state executions.[1]

As these events unfolded in China, a parallel debate in the United States questioned whether most-favored-nation (MFN) status should be linked to human rights compliance.[2] One group called for short-term enforcement, arguing that China should have its MFN status revoked. Another group advocated a long-term policy of persuasion and claimed that withdrawing MFN status would harm human rights compliance by decreasing the prospects for economic and political reform and damaging important bilateral trade relations. Both sides of the debate could point to examples from recent Chinese human rights actions to bolster their positions. Who was right? Were human rights commitments a sign of willingness to change, as proponents of international pressure argued, or were they purely a case of norm manipulation, as skeptics of international pressure contended?

The Chinese case may be unique in the amount of international attention it garnered, but it exemplifies the manifold ways in which states respond to human rights pressure and outsiders construe state compliance. This is no less true today than it was during the Cold War. In fact, the two countries that perhaps sparked the most international human rights attention in the 1970s—Chile and Argentina—also responded in highly inconsistent ways to human rights pressure. Decades later, following a slew of human rights trials, truth commission hearings, and even Pinochet's notorious arrest, the exact role of international human rights pressure in the Southern Cone remains unresolved.

Indeed, the Chilean and Argentine cases provide a powerful venue for exploring a largely unexamined paradox: why states respond differently to similar compliance pressures. After the military coups in Chile (1973) and Argentina (1976) and a phenomenal increase in egregious human rights violations such as arbitrary killings, forced disappearances, and systematic torture, international actors applied immediate pressure on these regimes to curb their human rights abuses. Yet despite comparably strong pressure on the two countries, these cases contain three puzzles that are emblematic of state compliance.

First, it is not clear why human rights violations varied both over time and cross-nationally. The Chilean government initially responded to human rights pressure with greater compliance than Argentina. By the late 1970s, however, the situation was reversed although international and domestic pressure remained consistent. Second, while the Chilean government was led by a hard-liner, it responded to human rights pressure by undertaking extensive institutional reforms. These reforms included incorporating international norms into domestic legal structures and deinstitutionalizing parts of the repressive apparatus, changes that outsiders interpreted as evidence of a growing commitment to international norms. In stark contrast, the moderate-led Argentine government initiated virtually no domestic institutional changes. Third, it is not evident why state compliance varied so widely even across international norms that were subject to similar pressures. Both regimes, for example, reduced the use of disappearances but continued to engage in substantial torture. If international and domestic pressures were overwhelmingly influential, changes in compliance should have been far more consistent than they were.

Why does compliance occur when it does, to the extent that it does, and with some norms but not others? Existing approaches have not answered these questions adequately because they have taken norm violations largely for granted. Institutionalists have often treated non-compliance as a problem to be managed, realists as a choice to be punished. But most research has remained remarkably silent about why international norms are violated in the first place. The most puzzling aspect of state compliance may not be that it occurs voluntarily and in the absence of enforcement, as mainstream approaches contend.[3] What can also be surprising about compliance is that similar pressures on behalf of a norm can result in different compliance outcomes: over time, cross-nationally, and between norms. Even when human rights pressures are similar, their impact may not be uniform. This is the paradox of state compliance, and the central problematique of this study.

I focus empirically on internationally codified norms of personal (or physical) integrity and security.[4] These rights refer to a special subset of civil rights, recognized in the Universal Declaration of Human Rights (1948) and the International Covenant on Civil and Political Rights (1966), which addresses issues of physical harm or intimidation. They include rights to be free of unlawful execution, arbitrary arrest, torture, and forced exile, as well as positive rights to basic legal protection. According to international law, states are obligated both to desist from violating these rights and to assure their guarantee. Although almost all states violate personal security to at least some degree or engage in what is commonly referred to as state repression, these international norms enjoy strong legal and normative standing. Consequently, a wide range of actors—including states, international organizations (governmental and nongovernmental), and domestic nonstate groups—apply pressure on their behalf. Rights of personal integrity are not necessarily the most important contemporary human rights norms, but they are those most subject to international pressure.

Despite growing attention in the last three decades to these international norms, questions about human rights compliance remain far from resolved. Louis Henkin set the stage for this new generation of scholarship when he observed in the 1970s that the "forces that induce compliance with other law do not pertain equally to the law of human rights."[5] Even today, we do not know why states respond as they do to human rights pressure. If international human rights pressure is effective, why does noncompliance remain widespread? Alternatively, if international pressure is ineffective, why have a growing number of transnational actors increased dramatically their pressure on noncompliant states?

Skeptics, often more cautiously optimistic than pessimistic and representing a wide range of theoretical perspectives, remind us of the limits of international compliance pressure. For Jack Donnelly, international human rights pressure is constrained by national action; changes in human rights practices are ultimately the result of domestic—not international—politics. David Forsythe has cautioned that "calculations of relative power remain decisive" in how states respond to international human rights pressure, just as Julie Mertus has emphasized the prevalence of double standards in U.S. foreign policy. Legal scholar Lori Damrosch, writing on humanitarian intervention, has focused on the negative consequences of international pressure. Stephen Krasner argues that international human rights pressure is effective only when it is in the interest of a hegemon, something not likely to occur often. And Andrew Moravcsik's work on human rights regimes suggests that state compliance is in fact the product of self-interest and the prior convergence of domestic and international institutions.[6]

Optimists, while not naive about international influence, highlight the achievements of human rights pressure. In a review of state compliance, Abram Chayes and Antonia Chayes say that the "legitimating authority" of human rights treaties "was an important catalyst of the revolutions of the 1980s." Oran Young refers similarly to the constitutive power of international human rights institutions. Legal scholar Dinah Shelton emphasizes how even "soft" human rights norms can influence state compliance. Likewise, Kathryn Sikkink's seminal research on principled ideas and transnational networks, Martha Finnemore's examination of changes in the norm of humanitarian intervention, and Audie Klotz's work on apartheid all place the influence of international human rights norms at the center of their analyses. Other research canvasses the far-reaching influence of international human rights standards, whether promoted through Amnesty International, the momentum of the Helsinki process, or U.N. agencies and their peace-building initiatives.[7]

Given the continued polarization of many human rights debates, we must now grapple more deliberately with the tensions raised by skeptics and optimists. Understanding the complex ways in which states respond to human rights pressure can be one step in this direction. The subject has implications for what we know about the prospects for human rights reform, the impact of international norms, and, more broadly still, the nature of state sovereignty. We should not wait for human rights compliance to become the rule rather than the exception before studying it more systematically.[8]

Three Debates

The topic of state compliance has attracted the attention of a wide array of scholars reaching far beyond human rights. The landmark work in this area is Oran Young's 1979 book, *Compliance and Public Authority: A Theory with International Application*, which drew on interdisciplinary research to provide the field of international relations with a theory of state compliance. Renewed interest in the subject began wholeheartedly in the 1990s, launched in part by Abram Chayes and Antonia Chayes's book *The New Sovereignty: Compliance with International Regulatory Agreements*.[9] Empirically, scholars of different persuasions have moved to test competing theories of compliance across a variety of international domains.[10]

This book contributes to this rich field by addressing three focal debates, which together have characterized the research on state compliance (see Table 1). First, scholars have disagreed conceptually over what constitutes state compliance. In particular, analysts have debated what types of action (e.g., behavior versus discourse) are indicators of compliance. Challenging the dominant view, which I elaborate on later, I contend that compliance is a multidimensional variable comprising both violations and commitments. Sometimes these dimensions coincide and other times they do not. Consequently, we should not expect international compliance pressures to have uniform effects.

Second, and more widely disputed, is the question of explaining state compliance or determining why compliance occurs. The debate here is over the sources of compliance, especially whether compliance is the product of external, individualistic, and rationally calculated forces or of internal, social, and habit-driven ones.[11] Moving beyond this debate and its emphasis on international and domestic pressures for compliance, I also examine pressures for norm violation. My assumption is that only by being attentive to such cross-cutting pressures can we explain complex compliance outcomes and recommend more effective policy strategies.

Third, an ongoing controversy exists over the meaning of compliance, in particular what it signifies about an actor's internal commitments and future actions. Does a compliant action represent cooperation or an attempt to silence further pressure? And are commitments likely to lead

TABLE 1. APPROACHES TO STATE COMPLIANCE

Level of Analysis	Central Question	Dominant Assumption	Alternative Approach
Conceptual	What is compliance?	Unidimensional variable	Multidimensional variable
Explanatory	Why does compliance occur?	Two-level pressures (*international and domestic*)	Cross-cutting pressures (*commitment and violation*)
Interpretive	What does compliance signify?	Cooperation	Conflict and/or cooperation

over time to meaningful human rights reform? My view is that these are largely empirical questions that cannot be answered a priori one way or another. Ultimately, our interpretations of state compliance should be based on a careful assessment of the sources of norm violation.

CONCEPTUALIZING COMPLIANCE

Many students of state compliance have assumed that compliance is a relatively straightforward concept, although they have disagreed over its exact form. Even perspectives that rely on different measurements of compliance treat compliance as a unidimensional concept. This is true of both those who view the concept dichotomously, alternating between compliance and noncompliance, and those who treat it as a continuous variable wherein different values or degrees of compliance coexist alongside one another. Even for those who employ a nonbehavioral (or deontic) definition and introduce discourse as a dimension, compliance remains a single variable. The image still is one of a continuum, wherein rejection and denial gradually give way to lip service and treaty ratifications and perhaps eventual reform.[12] Although each of these measures adds richness to the concept of compliance, none captures fully its complexity and multidimensionality.

A close look at compliance—any action conforming to a norm— suggests that it can be disaggregated. Just as other institutional outcomes may be disentangled, compliance itself can be thought of as having two key dimensions: violations and commitments.[13] Violations consist of the degree to which an actor deviates from the central tenets of a treaty; this view is closest to conventional definitions of compliance. All norms and treaties can be violated, even "positive" norms calling on states to take (and not just refrain from taking) certain actions. Indeed, without the possibility of violations, compliance would not be a salient legal and political issue. Commitments, on the other hand, require that states demonstrate publicly their *intent* not to violate a norm. Human rights commitments can include a broad array of actions: ratifying treaties, permitting international monitors to visit a country, showing leniency, implementing international norms domestically, and being accountable for any abuses.[14] In fact, most international demands for compliance invoke this broad cluster of obligations, itself embedded in the major international human rights instruments.

At the same time, the two types of compliance should not be conflated because they can and do conflict with each other. States can converge with some international requirements while simultaneously diverging from others. As the China example illustrates, governments often commit publicly to an international norm, showing leniency in a particular case or even implementing international norms, at the same time that they proceed to violate these norms. In such cases, the gap between the two types of compliance is large and states are committed only hypocritically; commitment consists of token compliance. Alternatively, an actor can commit publicly even to norms that it does not violate. A state that does not practice torture systematically can nonetheless be held accountable for isolated abuses, just as it can incorporate international law into its domestic institutions and cooperate with international actors. Under these conditions, the two types of compliance converge, and states do not violate an international norm *because* they are committed privately—not just publicly—to the norm.

Today's international norms therefore create a bundle of obligations. They call on states to conform to an international norm both by desisting from violating the norm and by demonstrating their commitment to the norm. A state responding to international pressure faces a panoply of compliance choices beyond simply deciding whether to comply.

EXPLAINING COMPLIANCE

Explanations of human rights compliance are increasingly comprehensive, attentive to the role of both external and internal factors. External sources of compliance emanate mostly from foreign governments, international institutions, and international nonstate actors. Internal sources, as Chapter 2 elaborates, can include societal groups, domestic institutions, and national leaders. The tendency to treat the two sets of factors as mutually reinforcing now pervades the study of human rights. The assumption is that international and domestic pressures on behalf of human rights compliance interact more than compete with one another.

Although approaches to compliance that highlight the dual role of international and domestic pressures have contributed much to our understanding of human rights change, they remain difficult to disprove. It is tempting to attribute human rights improvements in South Africa, the Southern Cone, and Eastern Europe to international and domestic human rights pressures. In retrospect, after all, it is almost always possible to trace a decline in violations of a norm to support for the norm. But what explains all those instances when human rights pressure apparently fails?

International and domestic support for a norm may be only one side of the compliance story. Even when "compliance constituencies" are strong, domestic support for a countervailing norm can persist and even prevail.[15] Accordingly, compliance can be the result of cross-cutting—not just two-level—pressures. If this is true, then decision makers may be constrained by the systemic logic of these contending structures. Pressures on behalf of an international norm may have complex and unintended effects, belying conventional expectations of uniform change.[16]

Focusing on these cross-cutting pressures serves to bridge a traditional divide between studies of state compliance and those of norm violation. Indeed, two decades ago, Friedrich Kratochwil and John Ruggie warned against treating the " 'violation' of norms as the beginning, middle, and end of the compliance story."[17] Yet since then studies of compliance have often gone in the opposite direction. Driven by an overwhelming concern with the "pull" of compliance, the literature has focused almost exclusively on situations in which state compliance is relatively strong and violations are conspicuously absent.[18] Although scholars have disagreed about which sources of compliance matter, they have not always faced squarely the fact that actors are often pushed both to comply with and to violate an international norm. And if actors are subject to competing normative pressures, as they surely are by virtue of belonging to different groups, we should not expect any single norm to triumph over all others.

States, after all, have always engaged in many of the behaviors that we now label violations of international law: they have coerced their citizens, distributed resources unequally, stockpiled and disseminated arms, polluted and depleted natural resources, and traded unfairly. Insofar as these activities have been tied closely to the rise of the modern state, there may be historical and structural reasons why states break even costly international rules. Understanding state compliance may therefore require looking outside the traditional confines of compliance theory. Ironically, we may need to bring violations back into the study of compliance.

INTERPRETING COMPLIANCE

Most disputes over compliance also raise questions of interpretation. When does a state's compliance signal a change in interests and perhaps even identity versus a mere shift in strategic calculations? These controversies arise in almost all international conflicts wherein compliance is at stake, whether the target is Iraqi recalcitrance over weapons inspections, Serbian resistance to U.N. resolutions, or Singapore's use of caning. As parties to a dispute sling accusations of noncompliance back and forth, all the while insisting on their own compliance, interpreting compliance can become inherently problematic and turn into the very linchpin of an international conflict.

A common approach to resolving these dilemmas of interpretation has been to treat compliance as an indicator of cooperation and the precursor to even greater compliance. Yet as one important study shows, reduced violations do not always reflect greater cooperation.[19] Definitionally, moreover, compliance requires only that a state conform its actions to a set of external demands. As Jon Elster observes, compliance is the "*public* aspect of a norm."[20] In and of itself, compliance tells us nothing of a norm's acceptance or embeddedness in internal structures.

How then are we to interpret human rights commitments, which may appear at once to be compliant but hypocritical? When arbitrary killings and the systematic use of torture are at stake, the value of committing publicly to international norms may seem negligible. Even if we assume that such commitments confirm La Rochefoucauld's maxim that "hypocrisy is the homage that vice pays to virtue," the global prevalence of human rights violations is sure to make skeptics of international pressure question its significance. The evidence is in fact mixed. As Figure 1 shows, while both human rights commitments and protection have

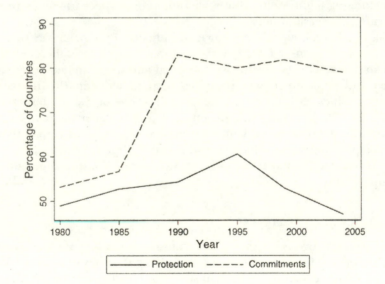

Figure 1. Human Rights Commitments and Protection: Global Trends, 1980–2005

Sources: Political Terror Scale #(http://www.unca.edu/politicalscience/images/ Colloquium/faculty-staff/gibney.html) and International Covenant on Civil and Political Rights, Office of the United Nations High Commissioner for Human Rights (http://www .ohchr.org/english/law/ccpr.htm).

Note: Scores for protection (or nonviolations) are derived from the Political Terror Scale, 1980–2005. They reflect the percentage of countries scoring one or two points on a five-point scale. In these countries, torture and extrajudicial killings are rare, and political imprisonment, if it exists, is limited. Scores for human rights commitments indicate the percentage of states having ratified the International Covenant on Civil and Political Rights.

periodically improved in the last twenty-five years, the percentage of countries adequately protecting international human rights norms remains low. Furthermore, substantially more states are willing to commit to human rights norms than are willing or able to desist from violating these same norms. What do we make of a trend whereby actors "talk the talk" of international norms more than they "walk the walk"?

Regardless of their origins or future effects, human rights commitments clearly can be significant. Some human rights commitments directly improve individual cases of violation, even if the overall level or pattern of abuse remains unaffected. This is certainly the case when political prisoners are released or prison and death sentences are commuted. Even from a strictly practical standpoint, human rights commitments cannot be dismissed.

Indirectly, moreover, human rights commitments can affect the future application of international pressure. For example, when states provide international monitors with access into a country, the information generated can be critical for mobilizing further international pressure. Even hypocritical state responses can serve as the basis of future international demands.[21] According to a prominent human rights legal scholar, human rights rhetoric and hypocrisy can unleash "forces for compliance, forces both official and unofficial, internal and external."[22] These potential benefits notwithstanding, human rights commitments can also have deleterious effects.[23] When states engage in high levels of commitment, outside observers may over-estimate the significance of these responses and declare a premature victory for international norms. In January 2001, for example, the Council of Europe interpreted President Putin's announcement that Russia would reduce forces in Chechnya as a concession forecasting an improved human rights climate. Only a few months later, it was all too clear that human rights violations against civilians in Chechnya were in fact mounting.[24] Whether directly or indirectly, beneficial or harmful, the effects of committing publicly to an international norm should concern all pragmatists.

The Role of International Pressure

If states respond in complex and often contradictory ways to international human rights pressure, how can those applying such pressures hope to enhance their influence? The conventional answer has been to increase the amount of human rights pressure, including by strengthening domestic proponents of international norms. The evidence presented in this book suggests that, although such efforts are significant, more pressure is not necessarily sufficient for combating a pattern of state violations.

International and Domestic		
International and Domestic	$\longrightarrow$	**Human Rights**
Pressures for Compliance		**Commitments**

+

Cross-Cutting Pressures	$\longrightarrow$	**Human Rights**
(e.g., national threats,		**Violations**
pro-violation constituencies,		
rules of exception)		

Figure 2. International Pressure and State Compliance: A Two-Tiered Model

Note: Commitments include ratifications, monitoring, leniency, implementation, and accountability.

The basic argument is as follows. International and domestic human rights pressures can have both direct and indirect effects (see Figure 2). On the one hand, human rights pressures can lead directly to human rights *commitments*. This is because human rights pressure alters a state's interest in appearing compliant, regardless of whether it actually violates international norms. Consequently, states will respond to human rights pressure by ratifying international agreements, acting with leniency in specific cases, providing access to international monitors, implementing international norms domestically, or even occasionally holding abusers accountable. On the other hand, human rights pressures tend to affect state *violations* only indirectly. As long as certain conditions exist—national threats, pro-violation constituencies, and rules of exception—states will continue to violate international norms even in the face of international and domestic human rights pressures. This two-tiered argument has important policy implications, discussed in Chapter 6. In particular, the argument suggests that the "ex-post" strategies that dominate the field of compliance may be most effective in eliciting human rights commitments, whereas the "ex-ante" (or preventive) strategies are ultimately needed to protect against norm violations.[25]

Indeed, states sometimes have an interest in violating an international norm, regardless of the cost of doing so. A broad body of research suggests, for example, that compliance with international norms of personal security ultimately hinges on national security concerns. Accordingly, as Chapter 2 details, armed threats can shape any decision maker's willingness to repress those under his or her rule.[26] Likewise, in countries where democracy is absent or relatively weak, pro-violation constituencies tend to have institutionalized access to decision making, and repression is deemed an appropriate form of social control. Governments in such countries will continue a policy of repression as long as they consider it domestically feasible. In some cases, of course, human rights pressures can play an invaluable role in eliciting democratization itself, but even these situations will tend to remain contingent on a country's national security environment.

Pressures to violate international norms, moreover, can explain why compliance often varies even across similar international norms. When states confront cross-cutting pressures, they are most likely to reduce only those violations that help them to evade responsibility for ongoing abuse. Disappearances in the Southern Cone, for example, declined only after local regimes had eliminated their opponents, and as bodies of the disappeared washed ashore. With pro-violation groups still in power, other violations of personal integrity (including torture) that were subject to comparable human rights pressure but could not be detected readily, or that helped to block state accountability, persisted.[27]

The different dynamics underlying state commitments and violations also manifest themselves in policy debates. Subsequent case studies show that policy disputes and regime splits in the Southern Cone revolved mostly around issues of human rights commitment, while both moderates and hard-liners supported the overall policy of state repression and violation. In fact, the cases reveal that varied structures of decision making led to different state responses. Chile was headed by a hard-liner but had a cohesive decision-making structure; this allowed the Chilean leader to control policy disputes and, ironically, implement international norms domestically. Argentina was led by moderates but had a fragmented system of decision making, which limited the capacity of its leaders to undertake controversial human rights commitments. Differences in state commitment can therefore reflect prior institutional capacities more than emerging state interests.

All told, domestic institutional configurations define national security threats and empower pro-violation groups, which helps to explain why the preferences of those who support international norms cannot always trump those of their opponents. Which actor wins a domestic battle over state compliance may in the end have more to do with who has the greatest institutional power than with who is committed most firmly to an international norm. Essentially, the book's argument moves what Judith Goldstein and Lisa Martin portray as "the contentious politics of compliance" to center stage and suggests that human rights compliance can be the product of national struggle as much as of international cooperation.[28]

Probing the Evidence

In a 1986 study comparing state responses to international economic crises, Peter Gourevitch noted that "Comparison allows us to stage a confrontation between competing explanations in the social sciences."[29] This book follows in that tradition by assessing the relative merits of two distinct approaches, those focused on the role of human rights pressure and those highlighting its limits. Because my interest is in understanding the intervening conditions that constrain the impact of human rights pressure, I have chosen to examine cases with similar levels of international and domestic pressure. This approach complements previous studies that have compared cases with varying levels of human rights pressure or undertaken single case studies. Those strategies have been necessary and useful for generating hypotheses in the early stages of a research program. Building on this solid body of work, I explore systematically the conditions under which international pressure can matter. My objective is to provide a "differentiated" and "policy relevant" explanation of how human rights pressure relates to state compliance.[30] In so doing, I test specific propositions about the relative role of, on the one hand, international and domestic pressures for compliance and, on the other, countervailing pressures for norm violation.

The cases of Chile and Argentina are similar in several important ways. Both countries faced comparable international human rights pressure during authoritarian rule and had active domestic human rights groups. Neighboring Uruguay, in contrast, was similar in many ways to these countries but was subject to very little domestic pressure during military rule. Additionally, Chile and Argentina had state elites who were concerned about their countries' international images, insofar as they pursued parallel monetarist economic policies that required attracting foreign capital and investment *and* enlisting the use of state repression. Both countries also shared similar national security ideologies and had comparable international power.

This method of comparison allows me to examine the role of antecedent conditions, namely armed threats and the domestic structure of decision making. Armed threats varied both cross-nationally and over time: in the mid-1970s, Argentina faced a higher armed threat than Chile; the reverse was true by the turn of the decade. The two countries also had very different decision-making structures; Chile's was cohesive while Argentina's was fragmented. Such differences in domestic structure, which scholars have used to explain varying national responses to international influence, also can have important implications for human rights policies. Although examining cases subject to dramatically divergent human rights pressures would normally appear sensible, such a strategy can also be counterproductive: because international pressure is partly a response to human rights violations, it is nearly impossible to isolate the effects of pressure while controlling for the sources of repression.

Various strategies can help to minimize the challenge of comparing cases subject to similar human rights pressure. For example, in addition to examining whether state compliance covaried with human rights pressure over time, I tease out the implications of the argument at the level of decision making. I look for evidence that international pressure both altered decision makers' calculations of state interest and shaped policy debates. Because decision makers' calculations cannot be observed directly, I examine several proxies for them, including diplomatic campaigns, internal government memoranda, and direct statements of policy intent. Policy debates, or intraregime disputes, also are important because they tell us about decision makers' definitions of the problems and options they faced. Only after detailing what human rights pressures can and cannot explain do I move to consider the role played by other factors, including armed threats. In the end, the argument is bolstered in the case studies most strongly through the use of process tracing.

The case studies are complemented with evidence from a statistical and global analysis of the 1990s. My primary aim is to see whether the argument is applicable across a wider array of cases and over time. In marshaling statistical evidence, I assess the role of human rights sanctions, interstate contagion, and domestic human rights groups, as well as armed conflict, democratic governance, and trade openness, among other factors. A detailed discussion of the variables and relevant statistical issues appears in Chapters 2 and 5.

Regarding documentary evidence, I employ a wide range of primary materials for tracing human rights pressures and changes in state compliance. I rely extensively on the records of intergovernmental organizations (IGOs), including official state responses to the United Nations, and the reports of international nongovernmental organizations (INGOs). I also examine publications by the Chilean and Argentine governments, including foreign ministry documents, as well as political memoirs and Chilean and Argentine newspaper accounts. Additionally, I use recently declassified U.S. government documents on both authoritarian Chile and Argentina. Secondary materials are extensive and reliable for these two historical cases.

This book, like all books in the social sciences, has had to overcome several potential obstacles. Perhaps the principal impediment to all human rights research is the availability and reliability of data.[31] To mitigate these limitations, I have measured most variables using general criteria. For example, in the statistical analysis, I consider the type of human rights pressure applied but do not assess its magnitude. In the case studies, in contrast, I can resort to greater specificity, detailing even changes in rhetoric. Nor do I account for the sources of international pressure, which are the starting point for the analysis. While understanding why international pressure is applied is an important question, it is one that has already been studied. More generally, the analysis is limited in scope to a certain group of human rights norms. By focusing on one subset of civil and political rights, I necessarily omit other human rights norms that are equally important but are not the subject of as much international pressure. Likewise, the emphasis here is on cases in which the state is both the principal violator and the guarantor of international norms. The argument may not be as applicable when societal actors are the principal violators of an international norm.

International human rights pressure and state compliance are inextricably connected in a globalizing world. Advocates of personal integrity, networking through a dense web of transnational activism, routinely challenge state sovereignty, whereas governments resort to a seemingly contradictory array of responses. Conventional views of state compliance may no longer be adequate to accommodate these political intricacies, yet the default mode for many observers is still to interpret state responses selectively. The stakes of such analytical bets are quite high: how we think about compliance and the impact of international pressure is essential for devising more effective human rights policies. The book links disparate theories and methods to offset these dilemmas, attempting to navigate between the Scylla of human rights optimists and the Charybdis of the skeptics to a more complex and satisfactory understanding of how international human rights pressure can shape state practice.

Chapter 2

Human Rights Pressure and State Violations

Louis Henkin observed over two decades ago that most states comply with most of their obligations most of the time.[1] Yet, as Henkin himself noted, human rights compliance can be exceptional while violations remain commonplace. Even if the costs of noncompliance rise, the incentives for complying become more alluring, or domestic support for international norms grows, states can continue to violate human rights. States may break international norms even when the conditions for compliance appear propitious.

Unraveling this puzzle requires understanding more fully the conditions under which international human rights pressure can be influential. I map out these conditions in the first part of this chapter. I then outline a complementary explanation for why states sometimes persist in violating international human rights norms and other times initiate dramatic reform. The chapter concludes with a brief discussion of the different ways in which states respond to human rights pressure, including a first-cut empirical test of whether human rights compliance is in fact multidimensional.

Mapping the Theory: International Human Rights Influence

Despite the clear policy implications and mounting consequences of international human rights pressures, we are only beginning to understand how such pressures affect state compliance. This is not as surprising as it may seem, because research on international human rights issues is relatively recent.[2] Studies of international human rights date generally to a mid-1980s "norm cascade," when international human rights mechanisms grew noticeably after the International Covenant on Civil and Political Rights and the International Covenant on Economic, Social, and Cultural Rights entered into force in 1976.[3] The first wave of researchers focused on explaining the emergence of international regimes and the application of human rights pressure.[4]

TABLE 2. INTERNATIONAL HUMAN RIGHTS INFLUENCE: EXISTING APPROACHES

Explanatory Factors	Power	Self-Interest	Norms
International/ regional	Hegemonic states; target vulnerability; coercive sanctions	Institutions (reputation, transparency, monitoring); legalization; and trade	Socialization; argumentation; persuasion and learning
Domestic	Governing coalition; bureaucratic politics	Regime type; (interest groups, uncertainty reduction); rule of law	Civil society; cultural match
Domestic– international interaction	Two-level bargaining	Institutional embeddedness	Transnational networks
Cross-cutting pressures	National threats	Pro-violation constituencies	Rules of exception/ exclusion

Only in the last decade have scholars begun to explore more systematically the impact of international human rights pressure.[5]

Explanations that link the impact of international human rights pressure and state compliance can be divided into three major groups. Two groups proceed from rationalist premises but differ insofar as one emphasizes the role of power and the other of self-interest. Another group adopts ideational concerns and sociological assumptions, often categorizing itself as "constructivist."[6] The debate mirrors a long-standing one in the study of compliance: what is the relative role of external pressures versus internal commitments?[7] Within each category, scholars have paid attention to international politics, domestic factors, and domestic– international interaction. Table 2 summarizes these theoretical, often mutually reinforcing approaches.

NORMS

Ideational-sociological approaches begin, at the broadest level of analysis, by emphasizing the *international normative context*. According to this perspective, human rights influence will be greatest depending on the strength of international norms. Martha Finnemore, for example, adopts such an approach to show how states have intervened with growing historical frequency to protect human rights abroad.[8] She argues that the growing willingness of states to use force on behalf of human rights reflects rising acceptance of international norms of humanitarian intervention. That is, as conceptions of who constitutes a full and equal human being have evolved over time, norms of humanitarian intervention have become increasingly institutionalized, shaping actors' goals and preferences in the international system. Similarly, Thomas Risse and Kathyrn Sikkink have emphasized how changes in "world time" may account for the growing visibility of human rights norms.[9] Accordingly, international human rights influence is greater now than during earlier historical periods. This set of ideational approaches, focusing on the international normative context, is especially well suited to explain the *global* expansion of human rights practices.

More specifically, Ann Marie Clark's work traces how Amnesty International has helped to transmit international human rights norms to domestic settings, while redefining states' interests and practices.[10] As the legitimacy of these norms and of Amnesty International itself has risen, human rights issues have shaped states' agendas. Remarkably, this has been true even of egregious abuses such as torture and "disappearances." Clark thus argues that an international nonstate actor can help to diffuse human rights norms, often leading to consequential changes in state practice.

Beth Simmons likewise suggests that *regional norms*—or regional contagion—may explain why states commit to international norms by acceding to treaties.[11] Although Simmons asserts that rational calculations may motivate states in a region to accept a treaty, she concedes that a normative impetus could be responsible. According to such an ideational logic, states in close geographic proximity may share a common identity, which, when reinforced through close contacts and exchanges, could help to diffuse international norms across the region.[12] Although quantitative work such as Simmons's has linked regional contagion to states' willingness to commit to international human rights norms, no evidence conclusively supports the role of an ideational mechanism. Nonetheless, the argument is provocative, and it is sure to generate further research.

Turning to the domestic level, ideational approaches emphasize the degree to which international norms resonate and are considered legitimate locally. One variant of this argument focuses on the role of *civil society*—including human rights organizations, religious groups, political parties, and student organizations—which engages in symbolic protest and thereby mediates the impact of international pressure. Students of human rights have always favored this approach and its recognition that compliance is as much the result of pressures from "above" as from "below."[13] This set of claims, moreover, is compatible with popular calls for erecting a national "human rights culture." The principal assumption is that international human rights influence will be enhanced when domestic groups within a target state are committed to international norms.

A similar, but less systematically studied, set of arguments draws attention to the *domestic configuration of ideas and identity*. For example, a national leader who is committed to international norms may be able to elicit state compliance even in the face of domestic opposition, as in the successful struggles led by charismatic figures such as Nelson Mandela and Vaclav Havel. According to this perspective, what matters most is that local leaders themselves identify with international norms and mobilize human rights supporters. Although evidence for this approach is mostly anecdotal, often discussed in testimonial or historical writings, the basic claim appears to be widely accepted. More broadly, some scholars have emphasized the extent to which domestic identities and institutional structures mediate the influence of international human rights norms; Jeff Checkel, for example, has investigated these factors in the context of European citizenship and migrant rights.[14]

For all domestic-level ideational arguments, human rights reform depends on local or internal acceptance of international norms. Scholars working in this tradition therefore expect international pressure to be most influential when a "cultural match" or "normative fit" exists.[15] Human rights reform occurs, that is, when international and domestic norms converge.

Research on *transnational networks* bridges international and domestic norms to offer a comprehensive approach, one articulated most extensively by Kathryn Sikkink.[16] This line of reasoning links specifically the international normative context to civil society, while emphasizing the role of socialization. It argues that international pressure is likely to succeed when members of domestic society support international norms and join transnational networks of activists. Transnational networks use instruments of persuasion and moral entrepreneurship to place human rights issues on national agendas, including by lobbying powerful governments. A "boomerang effect" can be evident, as domestic groups bypass an abusive state to forge transnational alliances; these alliances, in turn, may augment international pressure and empower domestic groups.[17] From the perspective of international law, Harold Koh highlights similarly how transnational legal processes can elicit human rights compliance.[18]

The research on transnational socialization is elaborated most fully in the path-breaking volume *The Power of Human Rights*. According to the book's proposed "spiral" model, transnational pressure will lead states to make certain initial concessions, often purely for self-interested reasons. As pressure mounts, and social actors (both international and domestic) attempt to hold a target state accountable, the state may nonetheless undertake more concrete and compliant changes. Eventually, as human rights norms become institutionalized and routinized domestically (or internalized), compliance can become relatively consistent. This model depicts human rights influence as a dynamic process whereby states are socialized—via rational and ideational mechanisms—to accept international norms. Contributors to *The Power of Human Rights* illustrate how human rights socialization operates in diverse case studies, spanning most world regions and the last few decades.

Some studies have extended the basic insights of transnational socialization to other human rights domains. Focusing on the role of discourse, for example, Thomas Risse discusses how "argumentation" can socialize states.[19] He describes how, in the give-and-take of communication, actors commit to normative language and gradually entrap themselves in higher levels of cooperation. Likewise, Daniel Thomas attributes human rights changes in Eastern Europe to the Helsinki norms instituted in 1975.[20] As state leaders in the region were gradually socialized to identify with international society, they complied with international human rights norms out of a sense of appropriateness or obligation. Like other approaches that highlight the role of transnational socialization, the research on discourse and identity traces usefully the causal mechanisms underlying human rights influence.

Ideational-sociological (or constructivist) arguments are all intimately related, with none claiming to compete directly with materialist-rationalist explanations. All in fact acknowledge the importance of material power and self-interested calculations. Their principal aim is simply to problematize state interests, tracing these interests to a set of principled ideas and practices: the international normative context, symbolic protest by civil society, and transnational networks. These approaches all highlight the role of socialization and persuasion and, more generally, of the normative dynamics propelling international human rights influence.

SELF-INTEREST

Materialist-rationalist approaches begin where ideational-sociological accounts leave off: they treat states' interests vis-à-vis human rights norms as given. A key international factor that this set of approaches identifies is the role of institutions and legalization in shaping self-interested behavior. Human rights compliance, according to neo-institutionalists, for example, reflects the strength of *international legal regimes* and their concomitant institutional mechanisms (including transparency, monitoring, and reputational payoffs). Cross-regionally, institutionalists thus expect compliance to be greatest in those regions of the world where human rights regimes are most robust, first Western Europe and then Latin America.[21] International legal scholar Dinah Shelton and her colleagues, for example, have found that these institutionalist dynamics in fact apply to "soft" international norms such as human rights.[22] For those employing this approach, international human rights institutions and regimes essentially equip states to "manage" problems of compliance.[23] The emphasis is on inducing, rather than persuading or coercing, decision makers to comply with international norms.

More policy-oriented discussions center on the benefits of free trade and globalization for human rights. Rather than applying punitive sanctions, advocates of this liberal position assume that greater economic openness will spill over into increasing political reform. Accordingly, trade will provide greater opportunities for societal contact and an exchange of democratic ideas.[24] This position was starkly evident in the United States, eventually winning debates over whether to link China's human rights performance to its most-favored-nation (MFN) status.[25]

Parallel to international institutions and legalization, liberal institutionalists sometimes highlight the role of domestic institutions, such as *regime type* and the *rule of law*. The impact of regime type can vary from issue to issue, but in the human rights arena two prominent causal mechanisms have been identified. The first hypothesis is that compliance is strongest in democratic polities, whereby interest groups have access to the political system and can make it costly for decision makers to break international commitments.[26] Another line of research opened by Andrew Moravcsik's work on republican liberalism suggests that human rights compliance will be greatest in new democracies, whereby decision makers face a climate of uncertainty and can strengthen their domestic positions by binding the state to future compliance.[27] Although Moravcsik focuses on the creation and enforcement of regional human rights regimes, the argument could be applied to compliance itself. Other scholars, including Beth Simmons, emphasize that rule of law may be more important than regime type per se.[28] Accordingly, states with a strong rule of law may stand the most to lose reputationally if they fail to conform to international human rights norms. Simmons's own work on human rights does not emphasize rule of law systems, but a broader body of research indeed posits a potential relationship between this domestic institution and human rights practices.[29] Highly suggestive, moreover, is Simmons's claim that states with a common (versus civil) law tradition may be more reluctant to undertake international human rights commitments by ratifying treaties.[30]

A related perspective draws on both international and domestic institutions to emphasize the process by which international norms become entrenched domestically. Drawing on notions of global interdependence, the focus here is on *institutional embeddedness*.[31] According to this approach, human rights compliance can thrive when international norms are embedded in domestic institutional structures. This enmeshing of international and domestic institutions is crucial for understanding human rights compliance because, among other things, it reduces the costs of building separate domestic institutions or infrastructures to enforce compliance. And by helping to harmonize national laws or create national institutions, international actors can help reduce the likelihood that compliance will be reversed, even in the face of domestic opposition. Although those who have developed this argument have not always focused on human rights questions, the emphasis has been on the transmission of liberal values across states and international institutions.[32] The approach thus squares remarkably well with the advocacy world's emphasis on human rights capacity building, or the process through which international actors gradually secure compliance by creating and strengthening local institutions.[33] Most scholars employing interest-driven explanations of human rights change are therefore attentive to some aspect of institutional embeddedness.

POWER

In addition to self-interest, rationalist approaches trace human rights influence to material power, the power of both those applying pressure and target states. The claim here is that compliance will be greatest when international pressure is applied by a *hegemonic state* and the target state is weak internationally.[34] Thus, much of the literature on human rights foreign policy has focused precisely on the role of the United States in applying human rights pressure. Even Ernst Haas, who typically emphasized ideational factors, conceded that in the case of human rights a *target state's vulnerability* is the most important factor explaining the impact of international pressure.[35] This set of approaches also considers the power of coercive *sanctions*, whether applied through interstate bargaining or issue linkages. The basic argument is that human rights compliance is most likely when states (either bilaterally or multilaterally) make their broader military and/or economic relations contingent on state performance.[36] These power-infused arguments pervade almost all accounts of international human rights influence; what remains controversial is their primacy in explaining state behavior.

Domestically, scholars who emphasize the role of power often treat the state and its agents as the locus of compliance. Students of human rights have stressed, in particular, the nature of the *governing coalition*. The assumption is that international human rights pressure will be most effective when a moderate government faction is willing to use international pressure to further its own domestic goals.[37] Moving from the government in power to *bureaucratic politics* more broadly, policy makers increasingly stress the role of issue-specific administrative units or regulatory agencies. The assumption is that powerful state actors, beyond national leaders, must support and be endowed with sufficient resources to secure compliance. Instituting long-lasting human rights change will therefore require developing strong human rights agencies within the state apparatus. In particular, bureaucrats charged with promoting human rights compliance will be the engines of change, helping to translate political will into policy reform. This perspective has found widespread policy support in recent years, especially within international organizations such as the United Nations that promote the creation of governmental human rights institutions.[38]

A *two-level games approach* is perhaps the most comprehensive explanation of international human rights influence. It focuses squarely on bargaining power, first using transnational networks to explain the application of international pressure and then joining international pressure and a government-coalitions argument to claim that compliance is tied to interstate bargaining.[39] The dominant image is one of national leaders negotiating simultaneously on international and domestic "chessboards." Two-level theorizing traces human rights compliance to domestic politics in the countries applying pressure (namely the preferences of the leader and the nature of the win set, or the agreements that societal actors would be willing to ratify), as well as in the target state (a moderate faction in the government and the existence of human rights nongovernmental organizations with transnational contacts).

Toward Synthesis

This vast body of research has identified multiple and reinforcing links between international human rights pressure and state behavior. Analysts working in this area often draw simultaneously on power, self-interest, and norms, as well as on international and domestic factors, to offer comprehensive accounts of human rights behavior, thus belying the distinct categories shown in Table 2. Indeed, a move toward theoreti-

synthesis now characterizes the research on international human rights influence.

Perhaps one of the best examples of such a comprehensive approach is Susan Burgerman's work on the role of the United Nations in promoting human rights reform in Central America.[40] Burgerman lists five conditions that together account for the degree of human rights compliance: the existence of relevant international norms, the material interests of a major power, transnational network activism, domestic allies in target states, as well as domestic political elites who either view themselves as being vulnerable internationally or care about their international reputations. Her analysis spans most of the factors covered in the literature, exemplifying a trend toward broad and multifaceted explanations of international human rights influence. This trend reflects a wider call in international relations theory for combining rationalist approaches, which focus on power and self-interest, with constructivist perspectives that emphasize the role of norms.[41]

Together, the efforts sketched here have laid the foundations for a research program that was largely uncharted over a decade ago. Scholars in this area, however, must now begin to grapple more directly with additional questions, including why support on behalf of international norms does not always lead to greater human rights reform. Put differently, the research on human rights influence must account for why states sometimes persist in violating international human rights norms.

The Violations Gap

Compliance and violation are often considered two sides of the same coin. Realists, for example, expect human rights violations to be pervasive, because it is not in most states' material interests to attach sufficiently high costs to noncompliance. This explains, Stephen Krasner maintains, why violations persist alongside strong rhetorical commitment to international human rights norms, what he describes as "organized hypocrisy."[42] For neo-institutionalists, states violate international norms when institutions and legal regimes are weak and, consequently, transaction costs run high and reputational benefits remain low. As Chayes and Chayes summarize, human rights violations arise when the conditions supporting compliance are absent or weak: international norms are ambiguous, states lack the resources to comply, or certain economic and social prerequisites are missing.[43] In short, states violate international human rights norms out of either incapacity or deliberate choice, two conditions that international institutions can ameliorate.[44]

Despite their persuasiveness, rationalist approaches can be limited in predicting when states will violate international norms. On the one hand, they argue convincingly that if the costs of noncompliance are sufficiently high and the benefits of compliance are inordinately low, it may well be in decision makers' interests to violate a norm. On the other hand, insofar as these approaches tend to predict that human rights violations will occur only when the conditions facilitating compliance break down or are absent, they risk taking norm violations largely for granted.

Ideational arguments fall into a similar trap. Some ideational arguments do recognize that countervailing norms can lead to norm violations. Norms of self-help or nonintervention, for example, can constrain the impact of international human rights pressure. Yet ideational approaches often face the challenge of what Paul Kowert and Jeff Legro have called a "ubiquity" of norms, or a failure to anticipate which norms will prevail.[45] For ideational accounts, norm violations still hinge on the conditions supporting compliance. States will violate international norms when transnational communication falls apart, civil society is weak, or absent a "cultural match" between international and domestic norms. Compliance remains the default outcome, and determining which norms matter continues to be the Achilles' heel of researchers in the ideational camp.

Some of the difficulty in explaining state violations may arise from a tendency to focus overwhelmingly—albeit understandably—on the *illegality* of state abuses. When violations are examined only in the context of international norms and law, they are treated as deviant behavior. Yet when violations are viewed as more general instances of state behavior (for example, coercion), a broader range of explanations becomes relevant. Indeed, a large body of human rights research already explains why states violate international norms independently of why they comply with them.[46] Incorporating such explanations, alongside those identified by the research on international human rights influence, should lead to even more comprehensive and persuasive accounts of state responses.

According to quantitative human rights studies and comparative politics research, three closely related conditions can structure the decision to violate international human rights norms: national security threats, pro-violation constituencies, and rules of exception (or exclusion). These are not the only factors identified in the literature, but they are among the most important.[47] Each of these factors, moreover, complements existing accounts of international human rights influence by highlighting respectively the role of power, self-interest, and norms. (See Table 2.) Together, they suggest the limits of international human rights influence.

Explaining Human Rights Violations

Whether human rights pressure can coerce, induce, or otherwise persuade states to comply with international norms may depend on what exactly is at stake. The stakes are especially high when the state's basic interests—or the interests of those who support an existing regime—are threatened. Accordingly, one of the principal incentives that can propel states to violate international human rights norms of personal integrity are *threats to national security*, especially when an armed group challenges the state's authority. A large body of quantitative research furnishes strong statistical evidence that one of the leading conditions under which states violate international norms of personal integrity is precisely armed conflict.[48] Historically, states have more often than not considered armed threats justifications for the use of repression.[49] Although armed groups do not always threaten a regime's security objectively, this is beside the point: states guard jealously their role as the legitimate holders of the use of force in their territory. Virtually all governments will treat any group that bears arms and challenges its power as a threat to national security. Indeed, in the hierarchy of sometimes competing political goals, the state apparatus chooses time and again national over personal security. All states, that is, respond to national security threats by violating personal integrity to at least some degree, regardless of any international or domestic human rights pressures.

By extension, a state's violation of international norms can depend on the support of *pro-violation constituencies*, which can reside inside or outside the state apparatus. Supporters of human rights violations can include members of the coercive apparatus and domestic economic elites. These groups may rely on the state to maintain order and stability, or they may benefit directly (e.g., professionally or economically) from violating international norms. These constituencies in fact can be just as influential as their "pro-compliance" counterparts; when their interests are threatened, they lobby for and consent to policies associated with norm violations.[50] National security threats, in particular, can induce pro-violation constituencies to mobilize. By introducing uncertainty, these threats challenge the interests of various pro-violation groups, including the coercive apparatus' very raison d'être and the well-being of the economic elite. In these situations, the survival of a privileged group's interests can itself be at stake; and the costs of *not* violating international norms will likely trump the costs associated with human rights pressure. State elites who rely on these pro-violation groups for their power have strong domestic incentives to break international norms, even in the face of pressures for compliance.

The actual capacity of pro-violation constituencies to influence policy, however, depends on their institutionalized and ongoing access to decision making. In the human rights sphere, the access that pro-violation constituencies enjoy, relative to their pro-compliance counterparts, is evident in the degree of democratic rule. Pro-violation constituencies thrive in less democratic systems, wherein complying with international human rights norms may be deemed riskiest, because compliance would limit what the state is permitted to do in protecting itself and its allies against purported threats. And although even strongly democratic states commit human rights abuses when faced with threats to national security, the presumption is that repression is more widespread and disproportionate in less democratic polities.[51]

In the case of personal integrity rights, democracy can therefore serve as a general if imprecise barometer of pro-violation constituencies. It reflects both the strength of pro-compliance constituencies and, more importantly, the balance of power between pro-compliance and pro-violation constituencies. After all, regime type embodies both substantive and procedural preferences about domestic conflict resolution: whether disputes between contending constituencies tend to be resolved by brute force or peacefully via what Adam Przeworski has described as "a system for processing conflicts without killing one another."[52] For other human rights norms or issues, in contrast, regime type may not be a reliable indicator of the strength of pro-violation constituencies.

Finally, and perhaps most fundamentally, domestic *rules of exception* can define what threatens pro-violation constituencies in the first place. These rules specify the conditions under which a state can trade one set of norms for another, or when an international norm can be violated. Rules of exception can be found in formal constitutions and informal belief systems alike. They are not, however, simply post hoc justifications of policy. Instead, they represent a powerful and historically conditioned "myth" that defines the state's interests in a given area and holds social coalitions intact. The myth is that, under certain circumstances, dominant social groups can maintain their basic interests (including their power, identity, even survival) only by breaking a norm. It does not matter if the well-being of these groups is not threatened objectively, but only that they expect it to be.

Rules of exception become apparent when state leaders break international norms and then proffer justifications. State violators tend to justify their actions in terms of a greater national good, such as "personal liberty must be sacrificed for national security." Similar aphorisms are evident outside the human rights domain: Pollution is necessary for development. Nuclear proliferation is the price of national survival. Trade protection is integral to the well-being of local labor. Monetary intervention assures the health of the national economy. Students of international norms consider such justifications to be evidence of a norm's influence; the fact that violators bother to justify their actions shows that they recognize the norm's legitimacy.[53] This may be true, but such justifications also reveal the trade-offs that states routinely make between competing norms.

In the world of human rights, rules of exception long have allowed for national security to trump personal integrity.[54] National constitutions have permitted regimes of exception, in which basic human rights can be suspended when the security or integrity of the nation-state is threatened, that is, in modern states of emergency. Likewise, national security ideologies have justified the use of repression against those who threaten national economic goals, domestic political order, and territorial integrity. And even before contemporary rules of exception found their way into national constitutions and ideologies, the trade-off between personal and national security was integral to the very formation and consolidation of the modern state.[55] State coercion has always been a basic form of social control, quelling social demands that the state is unable or unwilling to meet. Of course, the state has always had great leeway in interpreting the content of national security, free to recast yesterday's partners as today's enemies. What is important, however, is not that the definition of national security is fluid and can be manipulated, but that dominant social groups perceive others as a threat and deem it necessary and appropriate to violate their rights of personal integrity.

Rules of exception can also take the more specific form of *rules of exclusion* or discrimination. Even within relatively democratic polities, these rules can justify the suspension of basic human rights. As Anthony Marx observes regarding the politics of race making and nation building, "State-imposed exclusion of a specified internal group" can be used to "reinforce the allegiance and unity of a core constituency."[56] Thus, the routine suspension of personal integrity rights of minorities and immigrant groups, even in democratic polities such as those of the United States and Europe, reflects collectively held beliefs about who poses a threat to national identity. Indeed, anywhere that powerful groups see others as less equal than themselves, the stage is set for discriminating against certain members of society and violating the personal integrity rights of a wide range of groups: political opponents; noncitizens, indigenous peoples, or minorities; adherents of certain ideologies and religious groups; persons of a given sexual orientation, gender, or age; those at the economic margins of society; and anyone suspected of terrorism or other illicit activity.[57] Although rules of exception may be difficult to track empirically, human rights scholars have studied certain variants of them, including national security ideology and the relationship between economic ideas and state repression.[58] Despite clear methodological challenges, the role of standards, rules, and ideas that conflict with international human rights norms—but define the targets of and rationale for—state repression should not be overlooked.

Regarding their origins, rules of exception (like other ideas and norms) can be created or articulated at certain historical moments by powerful actors. They may even arise out of self-interest. In the beginning, to use Jack Snyder's language in describing myths about empire: "groups having parochial interests . . . including economic sectors and state bureaucracies . . . us[e] arguments about security . . . to justify their self-serving policies in terms of a broader public interest in national security."[59] Yet even if rules of exception are created purely out of self-interest, they can exert a powerful influence once they take hold and become embedded in domestic structures. Rules of exception remind us "how strategic myths come to capture even those who invent them: because the myths are necessary to justify the power and policies of the ruling coalition, the leaders must maintain the myths or else jeopardize their rule."[60]

If rules of exception do change, it may be for the same reasons that other collective ideas tend to change: unexpected and undesirable events occur *and* a socially viable alternative exists.[61] This provides a framework for understanding why human rights pressure contributes periodically, not only to improved human rights conditions but also to the creation of a full-fledged "rights-protective regime."[62] First, rules of exception may change only when the security and economic incentives that compel states to violate international norms also change. Thus, either any national security threat must disappear, or the state must prove incapable of controlling existing threats. Such shifts in national security can arise under various scenarios. For example, if state repression succeeds in eliminating armed groups, the rationale for continued violations all but disappears. Or, less perversely, an armed conflict can be demilitarized by various means, including the assistance of international actors. Alternatively, international groups may help strengthen armed opponents of a state, crippling the state's capacity to control ongoing threats.

Once the national security context changes, pro-violation constituencies finally may be swayed by the economic costs (and therefore futility) of ongoing violations. These economic costs, which can stem directly from human rights sanctions or be magnified by something like an exogenous economic crisis, may then cause a regime's social coalition to collapse. The stage is now set for pro-compliance constituencies to elicit deeper normative change, perhaps even regime transformation.

Such transformation, however, also requires broad societal acceptance of an alternative set of rules. Human rights norms must be supported by a wide range of groups within civil society, not just committed activists. With these new material and social conditions in place, pro-violation constituencies tend to support—or at least not oppose—dismantling the existing system of norm violations. One of the most basic if overlooked functions that advocates of international norms can play, therefore, is to help define a viable alternative future. Altogether, pro-compliance constituencies set the stage for normative change by defining political options and, through their transnational alliances, raising the costs of noncompliance.

Given these multiple contingencies, state leaders cannot always be convinced, coerced, or cajoled into not violating international norms. Precisely because strategic calculations to violate an international norm are rooted in powerful and institutionalized domestic myths, changing norm violations may be much more difficult than commonly thought. The greater any apparent threats to national security, the stronger the pro-violation constituencies, and the more deeply entrenched the rules of exception, the less likely that any actor can transform readily a state's interest in breaking international norms.

Reducing or eliminating state violations may thus require more than raising the international stakes associated with compliance or building a new domestic climate that is more hospitable to international norms, as the research on international human rights influence has often empha-sized. It will require tearing down a domestically entrenched system of noncompliance, or targeting the sources of norm violation, such as the national security context and the economic interests of domestic elites. And while transnational pressure certainly can influence these factors, the effects of this influence are almost always limited to some extent by the ebb and flow of exogenous forces. This should make *both* pro-compliance and pro-violation constituencies relatively sober about the prospects for change. It should also sensitize students of international human rights influence to the multiple contingencies potentially under-lying such change. In contrast to reductionist models of compliance that overlook the sources of norm violation, attention to cross-cutting dynamics predicts complex policy outcomes: faced with competitive pressures to protect and abuse human rights, states will commit publicly to the very international norms that they continue to violate.

Commitments versus Violations

Measuring state compliance can be no less controversial than explain-ing it. Some international legal scholars have voiced their skepticism most forcefully, disputing whether state compliance can even be quanti-fied. Chayes and Chayes, for example, maintain that "the general level

of compliance with international agreements cannot be empirically veri-
fied."[63] Likewise, Dinah Shelton and her colleagues assume that "corre-
spondence of behavior with legal rules is not the same as compliance."
These international lawyers are concerned that any attempt to measure
compliance quantitatively will overlook the "causal relevance" of international norms."[64]

My assumption is that compliance as an outcome is conceptually distinct from its causes. Establishing a causal link between international
norms and state compliance is a very different exercise from defining
and measuring compliance.[65] Even if compliance stems from factors
other than legal norms, it still constitutes compliance, if for no other
reason than the fact that outsiders will label it as such.

MEASURING COMPLIANCE

There are a few options for measuring systematically violations of physical integrity. These include Freedom House indicators, the Political Terror Scale (PTS), and more recently, CIRI human rights data. Because
Freedom House figures focus more narrowly on "political rights" and
"civil liberties" and the PTS does not disaggregate types of abuse, I use
CIRI data.[66] This newer data set has the advantage of differentiating
among the four major types of physical integrity violations: political imprisonment, torture, extrajudicial executions, and disappearances.[67]
Brief descriptions follow, based on CIRI coding.

> *Political imprisonment* occurs when government officials are responsi-
> ble for restricting a person's freedom of movement illegally (e.g., in
> response to noncriminal activity, political opposition, religious be-
> liefs, or identity).
>
> *Torture* is the deliberate infliction of extreme pain (mental or physi-
> cal) approved by government officials; motives are irrelevant.
>
> *Extrajudicial executions* are "killings by government officials without
> due process," regardless of motives. Capital punishment and com-
> bat deaths are excluded.[68]
>
> *Disappearances* refer to instances in which the whereabouts of a person
> are not known publicly and political motivation is suspected.
> Whether a person is eventually found or not has no bearing on the
> category.

Each of these behaviors is coded between 0 and 2, where 0 refers to
frequent violations (defined as more than 50 incidents), 1 denotes occasional violations (more than 1 and fewer than 50 incidents), and 2 rep-

resents no violations.[69] This data set also includes a Physical Integrity Index (ranging from 0 to 9), created by adding the scores for each individual type of abuse.[70]

In measuring human rights commitments, I use standard rather than events-based data, a growing trend among human rights researchers.[71] Instead of counting individual cases of commitment, which risks overlooking important trends and requires a very high level of trust in the data, I evaluate *whether* states commit publicly to international norms. With the exception of ratification, state commitments are coded dichotomously (1 = present, 0 = absent), according to the following criteria:[72]

> *Ratification* denotes formal acceptance of an international treaty by a state. States can sign a treaty, promising to uphold its core principles, or they can ratify a treaty, legally binding themselves to comply with it. Ratification, however, does not necessitate that a state act in accordance with the treaty's precepts, because states often break treaty rules.[73]
>
> *Leniency* requires that a state take specific steps to correct any existing violations. Human rights leniency can include releasing political prisoners, commuting death sentences, or dropping charges against political prisoners. Because most states violate some human rights norms—regardless of their level of abuse—leniency need not coincide with violations.
>
> *Monitoring* occurs when an international actor visits a country to assess the human rights situation. It constitutes a form of transparency, as monitoring leads to information about a state's practices. Instances when a state merely grants monitors permission to visit the country are not counted as monitoring, because invitations can be retracted.
>
> *Implementation* consists of a state altering its domestic rules and institutions so that they conform more closely to international norms. This can entail eliminating repressive laws and organs or creating specific institutions and procedures to monitor compliance (e.g., regulatory agencies). Implementation is distinct from treaty ratification, as even self-executing treaties are not always implemented automatically and fully in practice.[74]
>
> *Accountability* requires that states punish violators of international norms or compensate any victims of abuse. Even a state that generally complies with international law still has an obligation to be accountable for past or ongoing violations. Accountability is therefore possible regardless of the level of abuse.

Despite their differences, these commitments are all public actions that signal a state's *intent* not to violate international norms.

Skeptics might argue that all state responses are too intertwined conceptually to justify disaggregating them. More specifically, one could claim that states may be more willing to undertake commitments in inverse proportion to their level of violation. That is, states that already violate international human rights norms to a relatively high degree may also have fewer treaties to accept, more political prisoners to release, a greater number of requests for monitoring, a larger need to implement international norms, and more abuses for which to be held accountable. Although human rights violations certainly may be related inversely to human rights commitments, there is no reason to assume a priori that they are. For example, both highly compliant and noncompliant states alike have ratified international human rights instruments. Although over one hundred states have accepted the Convention against Torture, Amnesty International annual reports reveal that torture or ill-treatment is practiced regularly in over one hundred countries. Regarding political imprisonment, as the earlier Chinese example illustrates, states can release certain high-profile political prisoners (leniency) at the same time that they increase mass arrests (violations). How can these contradictory patterns be recorded along a single dimension? Differentiating among state responses permits counting the release of individual prisoners alongside the level of political imprisonment, allowing for the possibility that leniency is not always matched by an overall improvement in human rights conditions.

Likewise, one could argue that foreign monitors will not seek access to highly compliant states. Yet Amnesty International regularly visits Scandinavian countries known for their solid human rights practices as well as more notorious violators. Because all countries can be subject to human rights monitoring, and foreign monitors in fact do visit countries with highly diverse human rights records, it may be incorrect to infer violations from monitoring. The same can be said of other commitments. For example, even highly compliant states can fail to ratify international agreements. The United States is certainly not the world's worst human rights violator, yet it has failed to ratify major human rights treaties. By the same token, highly compliant states may not hold individual perpetrators of abuse accountable, while weak post-genocidal states such as Rwanda can pursue accountability, however imperfectly.

In the end, whether a state responds to human rights pressure consistently is an empirical question. A high level of norm violations does not automatically imply that a state will act with leniency in particular cases of abuse or that it will ratify a major human rights agreement, just as a state that commits to international norms will not necessarily abide by these norms. It may well be that hypocrisy is rampant, and egregious violators make the most human rights commitments; but it is equally plausible that states sometimes follow through on their commitments. Consequently, we need a measurement scheme designed to capture these complex state responses.

"LUMPING" VERSUS "SPLITTING" COMPLIANCE

I provide here a first descriptive test for disaggregating state compliance. This test compares two scenarios, using original data from the 1990s (1992–96) and spanning the entire world.[75] The first scenario involves combining, or "lumping," the two types of compliance. This is the conventional view of compliance as a unidimensional concept. In the second scenario, the two types of compliance are "split," or evaluated independently of one another, treating compliance as a multidimensional variable. For each scenario, I compare the percentage of cases that on a year-to-year basis showed one of two outcomes: improvement or nonimprovement. Nonimprovement refers to either deterioration or no change in compliance.

The findings, summarized in Table 3, reveal some difference between the two scenarios. When the conventional approach is taken, and the two forms of compliance are lumped together, 36 percent of all cases showed an improvement in compliance.[76] In contrast, when the two types of compliance are examined separately, 31 percent of the cases showed an improvement in human rights commitments compared to 27 percent in violations. Put differently, lumping both forms of compliance can overestimate human rights change. Perhaps more telling is the fact that in 30 percent of the cases, states *simultaneously* improved their commitments while showing a deterioration in human rights violations. This hypocrisy is almost entirely overlooked when state responses are viewed in isolation from one another.

TABLE 3. TRENDS IN STATE COMPLIANCE: HUMAN RIGHTS CHANGE IN THE 1990s

| | | "Lumping" Compliance | "Splitting" Compliance | |
			Commitments	Violations
Human rights change	No change or deterioration	64.45% (N = 330)	68.87% (N = 396)	73.23% (N = 435)
	Improvement	35.55% (N = 182)	31.13% (N = 179)	26.77% (N = 159)

How we measure commitments and violations may therefore have notable consequences on how we assess human rights change. In particular, treating commitments and violations as if they were a single dimension of the same construct may exaggerate improvements in violation or underestimate the persistence of these violations. This does not mean that commitments and violations never coincide, but it does caution us against conflating how states respond to human rights pressure.

Chapter 3

Skeptics Under Fire: Human Rights Change in the Southern Cone

Latin America served as one of the first testing grounds for evaluating the impact of international human rights pressure. State-sponsored violence in countries such as Chile and Argentina coincided with the strengthening of Cold War international human rights mechanisms in the 1970s. Even relations between the superpowers included a new human rights component, enshrined in the Helsinki Accords of 1975. In the United States, the first legislation linking human rights conditions to broader economic and military relations was enacted, and the arrival of the Carter administration promised to usher in a new era of human rights issues constituting a foreign policy priority. Human rights mechanisms within both the European Parliament and the Organization of American States (OAS) also gained momentum. And Amnesty International, formed only the previous decade, was quickly acquiring a solid base of support worldwide.[1]

In this global context, the governments of Chile and Argentina drew concerted international attention, sparked in no small part by the egregious nature of their abuses. In the case of Chile, international opprobrium began almost immediately after a military coup overthrew the democratically elected government of Salvador Allende on 11 September 1973. Chile's coup unwittingly inaugurated a new era in which human rights abuses are filmed and simulcast abroad. Television spectators around the world had seared into them vivid images of the burning of *La Moneda* presidential palace, mass detentions in the National Stadium, public book burnings, and executions by firing squad.

In the first six months of Chilean military rule, reliable estimates of deaths ranged from 3,000 to 10,000; and detentions lasting longer than 24 hours included at least 60,000, out of a population of almost 9 million people. Over 31,000 employees had to leave public administration by the end of 1975, and about 1,000 academics and 20,000 students were dismissed from universities.[2] This was all the more shocking for a country considered to be Latin America's longest standing democracy. At the time of the coup it must also have seemed remarkable that Chile was party to several international human rights treaties, a vanguard of its time.[3] The Chilean case, in all its gaping contradictions, served as a catalyst for strengthening international human rights mechanisms.[4]

Across the border and less than three years after Chile's military coup, the Argentine state embarked on its own Process of National Reorganization (*El Proceso*). Propelled by a "national security doctrine" that subordinated personal to national security, the 24 March 1976 coup initiated a concerted and systematic policy of "disappearances." The regime's purported goals were to restore national values, eradicate subversion, and promote economic development, all on the path to a future, if illusory, representative democracy.[5] Congress was dissolved, political parties were banned, and all federal judges were replaced. Political detainees were blocked from seeking exile, and crimes relating to "public order" were penalized severely. In the first weeks of military rule, several thousand suspected "subversives" were arrested; political assassinations averaged five per day and death squads murdered over 100 people. Prison conditions deteriorated rapidly, while torture, arrests, disappearances, and deaths in custody all increased phenomenally. In the course of the "dirty war" (1976–83), tens of thousands of people were tortured in over 300 secret detention centers throughout Argentina, and more than 15,000 people disappeared, many of them young workers. Human rights violations were integral to state policy, coordinated by the ruling junta and carried out by an elaborate security network.

Argentina's coup also fueled widespread international opposition, which rallied for the first time against the use of disappearances as a policy of repression. In Europe, the Argentine situation marked the first time that the European Parliament held a hearing on an external political matter. And within the United States, both Argentina and Chile arguably elicited more human rights concern than any other countries in the 1970s.[6]

Despite massive human rights abuses and unprecedented international attention, the impact of human rights pressure against both countries remains unclear. Some analysts emphasize Chile's status as an international pariah and its resistance to international pressure, characterizing it as a modern-day rogue state. Others argue that disappearances would not have ceased in the absence of international human rights pressure.[7] Similar disagreements exist over whether international pressure improved human rights conditions in Argentina. For cynics, any decrease in disappearances was purely coincidental, the result of factors that would have occurred without external pressure. International pressure could not have been effective, they contend, because it was contradictory. International actors may have pressured Argentina publicly, but privately they either consented tacitly or left most sources of foreign assistance intact.[8] Others, however, do trace most changes in human rights practices to international pressure. It was a combination of moral and material pressure that ultimately led the junta to alter its behavior.[9] According to Roberta Cohen, former director of the Washington Office of Latin America, "Almost every major improvement in the human rights situation in Argentina can be traced to some form of international pressure."[10]

Yet the empirical record of the 1970s is far messier than either reading suggests: the two countries simultaneously resisted international pressure and improved some human rights practices. My aim in this chapter and the next is to address this tension head on, pitting skeptics and optimists of international pressure against one another. In this chapter, I examine the skeptics' claims, testing their null hypothesis that international pressure did not lead to significant changes in state behavior. In so doing, I document three phases of international pressure, each representing rising international costs. I then trace human rights compliance in terms of changes in both human rights violations and commitments. My objective is to determine how state compliance covaried with growing international pressure. To further assess this influence, I trace changes in the decision-making process, searching for evidence that international human rights pressure in fact altered decision makers' calculations.

The chapter's principal finding is that international and domestic human rights pressures were indeed influential. Transnational pressure was met by a reduction in human rights violations and an increase in human rights commitments, changes that would have been unlikely in the absence of pressure. Even commitments, especially those involving the release of political prisoners, were significant in improving individual human rights conditions. Additionally, international pressure empowered domestic groups to challenge the state even when they were confronted with highly repressive conditions. A close look at the decision-making process further reveals that leaders in both countries were quite concerned about the costs of international human rights pressure. Any skeptic who dismisses the impact of these pressures is at least partly mistaken.

A Chronicle of Abuse

Military coups in Chile and Argentina brought with them an onslaught of human rights abuse and suffering. Egregious human rights violations included arbitrary executions, forced disappearances, and systematic torture; but they also created a pervasive sense of terror and fear among people in these countries. Despite strong similarities in these neighboring regimes' abuses, human rights violations in the two countries differed in terms of their pace and scope.

Repression under Pinochet's Chile was characterized by two initial trends: institutionalization via decree laws and a high concentration of violence in a very short time. In 1973 alone, the regime issued almost 250 decrees that served to institutionalize repression; approximately another 100 decrees remained secret. These institutional moves translated into overwhelming and unrelenting state violence, exemplified vividly by a few-day killing spree known as the "caravan of death." Roving helicopters traversed the countryside, with security forces slaughtering suspected regime opponents and others standing in their wake. This intensive and concentrated pattern of abuse set Chile apart from the more protracted nature of detentions and disappearances that would take place in Argentina.[11]

Repression, however, soon became highly centralized in Chile, marked by the junta's October 1973 announcement to end summary executions.[12] Concurrently, the junta created the DINA (Directorate of National Intelligence) Commission, followed by DINA itself in mid-1974. DINA became almost immediately a highly autonomous agency that engaged in widespread repression, including foreign operations. State responsibility for DINA's abuses, moreover, was indisputable. This was a government intelligence service that was staffed by members of the armed forces and was under the junta's direct control. While DINA was the state's principal coercive instrument, many other state intelligence services also operated in Chile; and in 1975, the joint command began coordinating the activities of these various intelligence services.[13] DINA's creation nonetheless was essential, as it served to replace the early practice of indiscriminate disappearances and vigilantism with a policy of forced and selective disappearances and repression. As a military officer later conceded, the Chilean armed services had committed early mistakes and resorted to improvisation but later had become "professional torturers."[14] Pinochet sealed this repressive trend when he announced in February 1974 that the state of siege and curfew would continue, political activity would be banned for at least five years, and the military would rule indefinitely.[15]

Nor was any respite to be found in the legal system. Despite having issued an historic statement at the end of Allende's regime, one accusing the government of disregarding the rule of law, the Supreme Court soon compromised its independence. It recognized the junta, purged judges who had shown proclivity toward Allende's government, and turned over jurisdictional power to the military courts. Military courts had not operated in Chile for almost a century, but they swiftly administered authoritarian justice, branding all allegations of torture as political and inadmissible arguments.[16] In this legal context, some incommunicado detentions exceeded 300 days, and the writ of habeas corpus remained inoperative and contradictory. While almost 7,000 writs were filed on behalf of individuals arrested between the coup and the end of 1974, the courts accepted only 10 of these. When the nongovernmental Comité de la Paz presented 905 cases to Santiago's appellate court in 1974, for example, 60 percent were rejected within a year. By December 1974, the junta issued a decree constitutionalizing all laws propagated since the coup.[17] As the minister of justice summarized in 1975, justice in Chile is simply "a matter of having or not having faith in the Junta."[18]

During the first year of military rule in Argentina, human rights violations also were exceedingly high and included systematic torture and disappearances. Over seventy detention centers were opened in 1976 alone, and almost half of all disappearances during the dirty war occurred then. Anyone perceived to oppose the regime—trade unionists, students, defense lawyers, intellectuals, journalists, psychiatrists—was targeted for state repression. A number of incidents that year drew international attention and exemplify the scope of this repression. On 16 September, now known as the "night of the pencils," ten teenagers were kidnapped in La Plata after signing a petition in favor of school subsidies; all were tortured by electrocution and only three survived. Two Uruguayan politicians disappeared in May 1976 and were later found dead. Five members of a religious order were killed in a Buenos Aires church, and an Irish priest was kidnapped and tortured in October. Parliamentary representatives Hipólito Solari Yrigoyen and Mario A. Amaya were abducted in August 1976; Solari Yrigoyen was allowed to leave Argentina in May 1977 (following a Venezuelan request during oil negotiations), while Amaya died from injuries.[19]

Human rights abuses in Argentina, moreover, were supported by an elaborate institutional structure that the junta created soon after the coup and that fortified the legal bases of state repression. The regime thus made it legal for war councils to try subversives *in camera* and for firing squads to kill an individual within 48 hours of sentencing. Employees could be dismissed without compensation or warning on grounds of national security, although most of those fired were merely union activists.[20] The Supreme Court continued to support the junta even when lower courts upheld human rights norms. In November 1976, for instance, the Supreme Court overruled a federal court decision that granted Argentines the right to apply for exile.[21] In terms of legal protection, the judicial system was wholly ineffective, failing to provide human rights victims and their families with any relief. The state repressed those under its rule viciously, while victims had no recourse to formal justice.

International Human Rights Pressure

International reaction to these military coups was swift and intense, and focused sharply on human rights demands. Human rights pressure against these two countries progressed roughly through three phases: the emergence of a transnational network, the use of diplomatic and multilateral threats, and the enforcement of sanctions by the regional hegemon. Each of these periods, as Table 4 describes, occurred at different times in the two countries. Each period also corresponded to parallel and reinforcing rises in domestic human rights pressure and transnational activism. Documenting these myriad pressures, including concrete human rights demands, is essential for assessing their impact. And while specific to these Southern Cone countries in the 1970s, the pressures described here continue to exemplify what many human rights violators can expect today from a concerted transnational human rights campaign.

AN EMERGING TRANSNATIONAL NETWORK

Almost immediately after the 1973 coup in Chile, foreign governments began linking their bilateral relations to human rights compliance, and regional organizations chastised the regime for its abuses. Most Western European governments cut off aid to Chile, suspended relations, or at least lowered their diplomatic representations. All socialist countries, with the exception of China and Romania, terminated aid and cut diplomatic ties with Pinochet's regime.[22] The United States also pressured Chile, albeit in highly contradictory ways. While congressional opposition to Chile mounted in the United States, especially after the death of two U.S. citizens (Frank Teruggi and Charles Horman), loans from private U.S. banks actually rose.[23] Regionally, the Inter-American Commission on Human Rights (IACHR) determined in mid-1974 that a pattern of gross human rights violations existed in Chile; the Commission

TABLE 4. INTERNATIONAL HUMAN RIGHTS PRESSURE AGAINST CHILE
AND ARGENTINA, 1970s

		Chile	Argentina
Period I	Emerging transnational network	1973–mid-1974	1976
Period II	Diplomatic and multilateral threats	Late 1974–75	1977
Period III	Hegemonic enforcement of sanctions	1976–80	1978–80

released later that year a 175-page report, based on 600 complaints, which accused the Chilean government of violating at least 10 basic human rights.[24]

Pressure from international organizations also was immediate and intense, mobilized around a broad international solidarity movement. Groups such as the United Nations Educational, Scientific, and Cultural Organization (UNESCO), the International Labor Organization (ILO), the Non-Aligned Movement (NAM), and the World Inter-parliamentary Union condemned human rights abuses in Chile and in some cases even excluded the country from their ranks. Partisan groups such as Socialists International and the World Union of Christian Democracy joined the normative assault against the regime, just as an International Investigatory Commission on the Crimes of the Chilean Military Junta formed in early 1974.[25]

Almost three years after the Chilean coup, a 1976 coup in Argentina elicited a very similar international response. Especially after European citizens began disappearing, European governments threatened their bilateral relations with Argentina and canceled several military training exercises. The United States, for its part, held a congressional hearing on human rights in Argentina and conducted regular diplomatic inquiries. Beyond that, however, interbureaucratic wrangling within the State Department and Cold War thinking within the administration impeded any stronger bilateral confrontation.[26]

Multilaterally, groups such as the U.N. Sub-Commission on Human Rights and the European Parliament issued condemnatory resolutions against Argentina. The U.N. High Commissioner for Refugees (UNHCR) placed the country at the top of its agenda, allotting almost three-quarters of its funds for 1977 to Argentina.[27] International nongovernmental organizations such as the International Commission of Jurists (ICJ), Amnesty International, and the New York–based Lawyers Committee for Human Rights also applied steady pressure on Argentina's junta.[28]

And from the first days of authoritarian rule, international actors established close relations with members of the domestic opposition in both countries. In Chile, foreign organizations fomented ties with the ecumenical Committee for Peace in Chile (COPACHI), created after the coup by Santiago's Catholic archbishop to provide emergency humanitarian relief. The World Council of Churches served as the organization's first contact and provided it with funds and international publicity.[29] The National Committee for Refugees (CONAR), another Chilean ecumenical group, also had ties to the United Nations and Protestant churches. In Argentina, relatives of the disappeared began almost immediately after the coup to file hundreds of habeas corpus writs on behalf of missing family members. In the last week of May 1976 alone, they submitted almost 200 petitions to the federal court of Buenos Aires. Repression at home was having a "boomerang effect," as local victims persuaded foreign governments to apply more intense pressure. For instance, after the regime abducted two members of one of Argentina's few human rights organizations (CADHU), the organization moved abroad where it began lobbying wholeheartedly for even stronger international pressure.[30]

Diplomatic and Multilateral Threats

It was not long before diplomatic and multilateral threats intensified against both countries. By late 1974, international pressure had risen both bilaterally and multilaterally against Chile. Following a congressional Democratic victory in the United States, both houses of Congress voted in December 1974 to suspend all military aid (including noncommercial sales) to Chile and to place a $25 million ceiling on economic aid. The Ford administration then recommended in late 1975 that Congress suspend military aid to Chile under the Military Assistance Program (MAP). Senator Kennedy further introduced an amendment that would deny all military sales, transfers, or donations to Chile. U.S. foreign assistance to Chile was contradictory, and a slew of funds remained intact—the Food for Peace program, for which Chile was one of the largest recipients in Latin America; housing guarantees; OPIC investment insurance programs; and most aid that was in the "pipeline"—but U.S. pressure now included concrete threats.[31]

Pressure from Western European countries likewise mounted against Chile. Most notably, France canceled a meeting in early 1975 of the Paris Club, where Chile's debt was to be renegotiated, after a half dozen European countries refused to attend. The British used the occasion to draw an explicit link to human rights: "Our attitude to any further requests for rescheduling—and we hope of our fellow creditors—will take into account Chilean policy on human rights."[32] After Sheila Cassidy, a British doctor, was detained and tortured in Chile, Britain took an even firmer stance and recalled its ambassador.

Multilaterally, pressure on Chile grew from both international organizations and multilateral financial institutions (MFIs). Within the United Nations, the General Assembly issued its first resolution condemning human rights violations in Chile in November 1974, and a special U.N. Ad Hoc Working Group on Chile was created three months later. Although similar U.N. groups existed for Israel and South Africa, the Chilean case represented the first time that a "consistent pattern of gross human rights violations" was examined in the absence of an international conflict.[33] A U.N. General Assembly resolution upped the ante

TABLE 5. U.N. GENERAL ASSEMBLY RESOLUTIONS AGAINST CHILE: VOTING
BY PRINCIPAL TRADING PARTNERS, 1974–78

	1974	1975	1976	1977	1978
West Germany	F	F	A	F	F
Japan	F	F	F	F	F
United States	A	F	A	F	F
Brazil	O	O	O	O	O
Argentina	O	O	O	O	O
United Kingdom	F	F	F	F	F
Italy	F	F	F	F	F
France	F	F	A	F	F
Netherlands	F	F	F	F	F
Belgium	A	F	F	A	A
Ecuador/Venezuela	A	—	—	F	F
Spain	A	O	A	A	F

Source: International Monetary Fund, *Direction of Trade Statistics* (Washington, D.C.: IMF, multiple years); and *Yearbook of the United Nations* (New York: United Nations, multiple years), vols. 28–32.

Note: The resolutions refer chronologically to UNGA Resolution 3219 (XXIX), Res. 3448 (XXX), Res. 31/24, Res. 32/118, and Res. 33/175. F = Favor; O = Oppose; A = Abstain.

in 1975 and accused Chile of fomenting "the institutionalized practice of torture."[34] These United Nations resolutions enjoyed wide support, including from most Western European countries; even the United States supported the 1975 U.N. resolution (see Table 5). In the economic sphere, the Chilean case provided the World Bank with its only non-unanimous decision in 1974 and one of the few in its history: 41 percent of bank members either voted against Chile or abstained on the basis of human rights criteria.[35]

By early 1977, Argentina also had become the target of both bilateral and multilateral threats. The United States linked bilateral military relations to Argentina's human rights record, although it merely emphasized the regime's failure to control extremists' abuses. More concretely, the United States announced in February 1977 a 50 percent reduction in foreign military sales (FMS) earmarked for Argentina in 1978, and it initiated plans to phase out future military training programs.[36] And in what would prove to be a significant diplomatic maneuver, Assistant Secretary of State for Human Rights and Humanitarian Affairs Patricia Derian conducted the first of three visits to Argentina in March 1977.[37]

As the year progressed, the United States began making good on its threats, voting against five loans for Argentina that would potentially affect $304 million, the largest amount of loans threatened during the entire Carter administration. Still, U.S. votes were mostly symbolic, because in the end all loans were approved. In fact, multilateral loans increased after the 1976 coup, reflecting U.S. and World Bank approval of the junta's economic stabilization program.[38]

Despite these inconsistencies, U.S. pressure now emanated from the highest levels. Secretary Vance visited Buenos Aires in 1977 and presented junta members with a list of 7,500 people known to have disappeared.[39] Presumably, human rights demands were also raised in other high-level visits in 1977, including a meeting between the U.S. treasury secretary and Argentina's economic minister, as well as between General Jorge Videla and President Carter in September when the Panama Canal treaties were signed. Still more concretely, a proposal introduced by Senators Edward Kennedy and Franck Church to cut all military aid to Argentina passed in mid-1977.[40]

Just as diplomatic and multilateral threats were launched against these Latin American regimes, international assistance to human rights groups within these countries proved pivotal. As much as 98 percent of the funds used by church-related humanitarian programs in Chile originated abroad. Foreign sources funded Chilean institutes, which served as party headquarters in "academic disguise."[41] Domestic groups in turn fortified international activism. Most notably, relatives of the disappeared organized and began forging strong transnational relationships. In mid-1975, for example, the Christian Churches Foundation for Social Welfare (FASIC) was created in Chile. This ecumenical group, which assisted political prisoners and their families, developed ties with international refugee agencies.[42]

Similar dynamics were evident in Argentina. International actors strengthened human rights organizations, especially legal and family-based ones, by providing them with foreign contacts and financial resources. Notable among these groups was *Las Madres de Plaza de Mayo*, a group of mothers of the disappeared who protested symbolically by holding regular Thursday vigils in Buenos Aires' central plaza. A like-minded group of grandmothers (*Las Abuelas de Plaza de Mayo*) also received financial and technical assistance from foreign groups in its efforts to establish genetic links with missing grandchildren. These family-based human rights groups were bolstered by the arrival in 1977 of Tex Harris to the political section of the U.S. embassy in Buenos Aires. Harris, among other things, kept these groups informed of visiting Americans whom they could lobby.[43] Legal groups also gained momentum during this period. In April 1977, for instance, Argentine lawyers entered a habeas corpus petition on behalf of over 1,500 *desaparecidos*. The case, *Pérez de Smith, et al.*, went to the Supreme Court three times and became an important symbol of using legal means to wage human rights opposition.[44] Increased activism by civil rights groups ener-

TABLE 6. U.S. MILITARY SALES AGREEMENTS AND
DELIVERIES TO CHILE, 1975–78

	Agreements	Deliveries
1975	37,900	12,256
1976	8,794	38,154
1977	235	56,024
1978	—	10,993

Source: Statistical Abstract of Latin America, 24 (Los Angeles:
UCLA Latin American Center Publications, 1984), 205.
Based on U.S. Department of Defense data.

Note: Figures are in thousands of U.S. dollars.

gized international actors, permitting them to launch an even more vigorous human rights campaign.[45]

ENFORCEMENT OF SANCTIONS

International pressure climaxed when the United States, as the regional
hegemon, enforced human rights sanctions. Following a visit by U.S.
Treasury Secretary William Simon to Chile in mid-1976, which marked
the highest-level official visit since the coup, the U.S. Congress finally
voted to suspend all arms sales and limit economic aid to Chile to $27.5
million.[46] (For the reduction in military sales, but rise in deliveries, see
Table 6.)

On the diplomatic front, this was a period of noteworthy departures.
Secretary of State Kissinger, previously a tacit supporter of the Chilean
regime, now began pressuring the junta. He announced in February
1976, for example, that he would not visit Chile on his upcoming tour to
Latin America; in the region, he called on Latin American governments
to pressure Chile. And in a June speech before OAS foreign ministers,
the U.S. secretary of state linked human rights practices explicitly to
bilateral relations. Even in a private meeting with Pinochet, Kissinger
purportedly raised the question of human rights.[47] The shift may have
reflected in part the U.S. presidential campaign, whose attention to human rights issues itself served to pressure the regime. In an October
1976 televised debate, for instance, presidential candidate Jimmy Carter
accused Chile of violating human rights and vowed to oppose the regime
if elected.[48]

Once in office, the new Carter administration continued to apply
diplomatic pressure alongside ongoing sanctions. Secretary of State
Cyrus Vance, in a June 1977 meeting with Chile's foreign minister, went

as far as to demand that the regime lift the state of siege, dissolve DINA, and reinstitute the rule of law.[49] That same month, the United States postponed its final decision on a loan to Chile, pending clear human rights improvements. These pressures were followed by a series of high-level and official U.S. visits to Chile, culminating in a September meeting of President Carter and General Pinochet in Washington, D.C., for the signing of the Panama Canal Treaty.[50]

U.S. pressure continued to mount against Chile for the remainder of the decade. Much of this pressure concerned the extradition of Michael Townley, Pedro Espinoza, and Manuel Contreras. These men were wanted for the 1976 assassination of socialist leader and former foreign minister Orlando Letelier, as well as his assistant Ronnie Moffitt, who was killed by a car bomb in Washington, D.C. On the one hand, the United States rewarded the extradition of Michael Townley in 1978 by granting Chile $38 million in commercial export credits. On the other hand, Chile's refusal to extradite the other two men led the United States to recall temporarily its ambassador from Chile and to implement a series of economic and diplomatic sanctions in 1979 and 1980. This case would continue to color U.S.-Chilean relations for well over a decade.[51]

The Carter administration did not relent when it came to Argentina. In October 1978, the United States suspended all military sales and assistance to Argentina. The U.S. Export-Import Bank (Eximbank) also rejected export credits. Admittedly, however, international human rights pressure continued to be contradictory. Although Eximbank's rejection served to pressure the junta, it was partially offset by the willingness of other governments to supply Argentina with similar export credits. On the day after Eximbank funding was withdrawn, both Japan and Great Britain offered to replace U.S. funds.[52] In the United States, the incident served to heighten public and congressional concern over the domestic economic costs, namely lost jobs, of applying human rights pressure.[53]

Thus, the United States began extending a few diplomatic carrots. U.S. Undersecretary of State for Political Affairs David Newsom went to Buenos Aires in early 1978 with a proposal: if Argentina were to accept a visit from the IACHR and restore the right of exile, the United States would relax its position. In particular, the United States would approve export licenses for items purchased by Argentina before the U.S. congressional arms ban had gone into effect. In exchange, the junta was to provide relatives of the disappeared with information and to cease the use of torture and disappearances. That May, the U.S. ambassador to Argentina further requested that 10,000 political prisoners be released.[54]

By late summer of 1978, the United States continued its sanctions policy but incorporated "quiet diplomacy" into its strategy, now bargaining with the junta behind closed doors. On Argentina's initiative, U.S. Vice President Mondale met Videla in Rome. In exchange for the junta issuing an invitation to the IACHR, the United States would approve export licenses and Eximbank funding, as well as send Assistant Secretary of State Viron Vaky to Argentina as proof of improved bilateral relations. On 26 September, after the junta issued an invitation to the IACHR, the United States kept its promise and reversed the Eximbank decision.

As other U.S. sanctions remained in place, contradictions in U.S. pressure revealed long-standing interbureaucratic rivalries. For instance, in late 1978, the U.S. Overseas Private Investment Corporation (OPIC) stopped accepting applications for investment in countries with human rights violations, including Argentina and Chile. A few months later, the United States informed Argentina that it might oppose multilateral bank loans in 1979 if human rights abuses persisted. U.S. pressure was still evident in 1980, when the State Department's annual report described human rights practices in Argentina as "the worst in the hemisphere." But just as U.S. pressure continued on course, the U.S. defense establishment attempted to draw closer to Argentina.[55] Pentagon officials, for example, visited Argentina in December 1979 to discuss military assistance for the first time since 1973.[56] The United States had moved to enforce human rights sanctions, but contradictions still abounded.

Beyond the United States, international human rights pressure from other quarters continued to intensify against both countries. European Community (EC) members stopped all economic and nonhumanitarian aid to Chile, threatening further economic sanctions. The EC moved its Latin American headquarters from Santiago to Caracas and called for a full investigation into disappearances.[57] Closer to home, the Inter-American Regional Organization of Workers (ORIT) joined the bandwagon of multilateral pressure against Chile by initiating a trade boycott, supported by the heads of national unions in the United States. Additionally, in July 1978, the U.N. Working Group on Chile called on the junta to account for all disappearances, permit political exiles to return to Chile, and release over 200 political prisoners; and the U.N. General Assembly established a financial fund to assist victims of torture in Chile.[58] U.N. pressure intensified with the appointment in 1979 of a special rapporteur for Chile, charged with preparing human rights reports. These reports covered the years 1979–82, coinciding with annual General Assembly resolutions in which an overwhelming majority of countries singled out Chile for its human rights abuses.

Multilateral actors continued to target Argentina as well. The United Nations applied steady pressure against Argentina, albeit somewhat less publicly than against Chile. Above all, in 1979 the U.N. Sub-Commission placed Argentina under the jurisdiction of the 1503 procedure, a confidential blacklist procedure that NAM had succeeded in blocking until then and that the regime itself had worked hard to avoid.[59] In Europe, the European Parliament (EP) made a possible comprehensive cooperation agreement contingent on human rights reform.[60] Following Amnesty International's recommendation, moreover, the EP took advantage of the upcoming World Cup soccer match in summer 1978 to hold a hearing on human rights issues in Argentina. The hearing that May marked the organization's first debate on an extraregional matter; and in July the Parliament passed a resolution condemning the junta.[61] The IACHR itself issued in April 1980 a critical 374-page report, based on over 5,500 allegations of abuse in Argentina. The report pressed the junta to account for the fate of the disappeared, among other wrongdoings.[62]

Domestically, human rights organizations proliferated more than ever in both countries.[63] Local human rights groups made greater use of legal measures and protests, especially after corpses of the disappeared washed ashore or were discovered in unmarked mass graves. In January 1976, after Chile's *Vicaría de la Solidaridad* replaced COPACHI, the Catholic Church began opposing the regime more openly, including by organizing a symposium on human rights that INGO representatives attended. Church authorities began filing petitions on the disappeared with the Supreme Court, presented legal claims on behalf of people who had been tortured, and offered legal assistance to those returning from exile.[64]

New groups also began mobilizing on behalf of human rights. Chilean women who had met in morgues, hospitals, and outside detention sites searching for family members began to convene regular workshops in 1976. Known as *arpilleristas* for the pieces of cloth they sewed into quilts—portraying stories of disappearance and loss—these women toured foreign capitals and helped to mobilize international support.[65] In parallel fashion, relatives of the disappeared who staged a hunger strike in mid-1977 at the Santiago offices of the Economic Commission for Latin America toured European countries and the United States, publicizing the plight of the disappeared. The Latin American organization SERPAJ, which to this day calls for nonviolence in defending and promoting human rights, saw its origins in Chile in November 1977.[66] And in late 1978, Jaime Castillo Velasco—who had been minister of justice in the early 1960s—founded the nongovernmental Chilean Human Rights Commission. The commission, which aimed to improve contacts between the human rights community and the broader political opposition, had strong international ties, including formal affiliation with INGOs such as the ICJ and the International League for Human Rights.[67]

Domestic human rights groups in Argentina also became more active precisely when human rights sanctions were enforced. *Las Madres* met with heads of state in the United States and Europe, and sent delegates to international organizations and to testify before the U.S. Congress. The group continued to receive significant foreign funding, and its standing was enhanced by its nomination for the Nobel Peace Prize in 1980. The publication a year earlier of Jacobo Timerman's book chronicling his captivity and release, *Prisoner Without a Name, Cell Without a Number*, further helped to mobilize international public opinion.[68] With human rights sanctions in place against the two Southern Cone regimes, international and domestic advocates reinforced each other while calling unequivocally for an end to human rights violence.

Reduced Violations

Skeptics of human rights pressure must contend with the fact that in both Chile and Argentina rising transnational pressures were followed by a decline in human rights violations and a rise in human rights commitments. State repression dropped precipitously after U.S. sanctions were enforced and transnational human rights pressure intensified. Human rights pressure, moreover, seemed to have a cumulative impact, as relatively smaller increases in pressure led to proportionately greater rises in compliance.

In Chile, human rights violations changed dramatically in late 1976. First, the number of political prisoners declined significantly. And as Table

TABLE 7. DISAPPEARANCES IN CHILE, 1973–76
(NUMBER REPORTED)

Year	Disappearances		
	Santiago	Provinces	Total
1973	101	149	250
1974	194	27	221
1975	57	18	75
1976	104	5	109
1977	5	7	12
1978	1	0	1

Source: Inter-American Commission on Human Rights, *Report on the Situation of Human Rights in Chile* (Washington, D.C.: IACHR, 1985), 73, 78, and 113. Based on annual and monthly reports of the *Vicaría de la Solidaridad.*

7 shows, by early 1977 no new reports of disappearance surfaced, and the government announced it was closing two large detention centers. The heavy use of exile, which had been a central instrument of regime consolidation, concluded as well. In its place ensued a more ambiguous period of "repressive stabilization."[69]

The Chilean judiciary also began devoting greater attention to human rights issues. Lower-ranking judges and appellate courts turned to human rights questions, in some cases helping to ease human rights restrictions. Santiago's appellate court, for example, ordered the junta in early 1978 to allow a dozen leaders of the Christian Democrats recently exiled to move freely within the province where they were being held.[70] Likewise, the courts began appointing independent judges to investigate disappearances, especially after corpses of the disappeared were discovered and public pressure mounted. Human rights activism by Chile's judiciary therefore rose at the same time as human rights violations declined.

When transnational human rights pressure peaked against Argentina in 1978, the pattern of abuse in that country also changed, both quantitatively and qualitatively. Most noticeably, the number of disappearances fell sharply (see Table 8). Disappearances dropped by 69 percent, from 3,098 recorded cases in 1977 to 969 in 1978. Between 1978 and 1979, disappearances dropped even more dramatically by 81 percent, followed by a 54 percent decrease between 1979 and 1980. Likewise, the number of clandestine detention centers fell by almost four-fifths be-

TABLE 8. DISAPPEARANCES AND DETENTION SITES IN ARGENTINA, 1971–83

	Disappearances		Clandestine Detention Sites (#)	
Year	Number	Change (%)	Opening	Closing
1971–73	29	—	0	0
1974–75	405	+ 1297	7	0
1976	4,105	+ 914	74	27
1977	3,098	− 25	4	13
1978	969	− 69	2	38
1979	181	− 81	0	5
1980	83	− 54	0	4
1981–83	30	− 64	0	1 (1983)

Sources: Figures on disappearances are based on data provided in Margaret E. Keck and Kathryn Sikkink, *Activists Beyond Borders: Advocacy Networks in International* Politics (Ithaca, N.Y.: Cornell University Press, 1998), 108. Figures for clandestine detention centers are based on Federico Mittelbach, *Informe sobre los desparecedores* (Buenos Aires: Edicione de la Urraca, 1986). These authors rely, respectively, on CONADEP (National Commission on Disappeared People) and CELS (*Centro de Estudios Legales y Sociales*).

tween 1977 and 1978. In cases of arbitrary arrest and detention, government officials now tended to recognize detainees within days of abduction, and periods of detention were relatively short. Signs of limited judiciary independence also became apparent. In a widely publicized decision in July 1978, for example, Argentina's Supreme Court decided that journalist Jacobo Timerman's house arrest was not warranted by the state of siege. More broadly, the Supreme Court recognized in 1978 that the government was restricting habeas corpus. The Court took another important step when it accepted an appeal from the relative of a missing person in 1979 and ordered an appellate court to investigate the case, reversing its earlier practice of declaring disappearances outside its competence.[71] The judiciary, slowly but significantly, was paying heed to international human rights norms.

Human Rights Commitments

A similar dynamic undergirded other state responses: as human rights pressure rose, so did both governments' public commitment to international norms. These commitments took various forms, including allowing human rights monitors to visit these countries; practicing occasional leniency; and in the case of Chile, changing domestic institutional structures, or implementing international human rights norms. In fact, these regimes' willingness to undertake human rights commitments was evident even in state rhetoric.

THE RHETORIC OF COMMITMENT

Words matter, and on a fundamental level, states respond to human rights pressure with rhetoric. The Southern Cone regimes were no exception to this. Beginning with the March 1974 Declaration of Principles, Chile's junta portrayed human rights as natural rights that lay at the foundation of Chilean democracy.[72] Pinochet himself presented an "evolutionary" concept of human rights. Drawing on organic conceptions of the state, the Chilean leader depicted human rights norms as universal and inviolable but hierarchical.[73] And in Chilean responses to international organization(IO) reports, the government reiterated its alleged commitments. It emphasized the judiciary's independence; the importance of human rights accountability; and Chile's essential respect for and safeguard of human rights, especially nonderogable ones.[74] The government even attempted to play a leadership role in regional human rights forums. In March 1976, it introduced a memo—"Means to Promote Respect for Human Rights and to Facilitate Cooperation by Member States for that Purpose"—to facilitate discussion within the IACHR.[75]

Beginning in mid-1975, moreover, Chile's Interior Ministry admitted to holding over 700 political prisoners. A few months later the government further conceded that approximately 42,000 people had been arrested legally since the coup.[76]

The junta also assured foreign actors that it would comply with international norms. Responding in private to early U.S. pressure, junta members pledged that they would "uphold all Chile's obligations in the field of human rights."[77] Assurances became more concrete in later periods. In 1976, for example, Pinochet not only promised U.S. Treasury Secretary Simon that human rights would be improved, but he also agreed more specifically to accelerate the release of political prisoners, not tolerate repression, and meet with U.N. representatives to discuss the conditions of a visit. In June 1977, Pinochet similarly promised the U.N. secretary general to account for the fate of relatives of twenty-six hunger strikers.[78]

The rhetoric of commitment was equally firm in Argentina. In a speech one week after the coup, Videla emphasized the regime's legitimacy. The general observed, "For us, respect for human rights comes not only from law and international declarations, but results from our profound Christian conviction on the fundamental dignity of man. We assumed power precisely to protect man's natural rights."[79] Videla remarked again in July, "All Argentines will recognize that what is truly at stake is freedom and respect for human rights."[80] Like Chile, the junta worked to assure international actors of its compliance with international human rights norms. For example, after disappearances rose, government officials promised an "exhaustive investigation" and assured that refugees would not be repatriated against their will.[81]

Beginning in 1977, Argentine state elites also began releasing figures on political detainees. The regime admitted that, under the discretion of the executive, it was holding over 3,000 people in preventive detention. By April 1978, it published a list of over 200 detainees who had been reported as disappeared. A similar list was provided in August and another one of over 150 people in December.[82]

Argentina's regime then moved to emphasize the legality (not mere legitimacy) of its actions. As part of an international campaign directed by the U.S. public relations firm Burston Marstellar, a 1978 government advertisement in the *Wall Street Journal* read, "Government actions under the state of emergency are always under the surveillance of the judicial system."[83] In its replies to the U.N. Sub-Commission, the Argentine government now emphasized the judiciary's strength and independence. Likewise, the "Political Bases" statement of December 1979 highlighted the constitutional sources of the *Proceso* and the government's responsibility in guaranteeing full respect for civil and political liberties. The junta similarly began to portray in humanitarian terms laws that were being criticized for exonerating the armed forces as attempts to relieve the burden of families whose members were missing.[84]

And in each country, the regime took the significant step of justifying its human rights violations when presented with incontrovertible evidence of noncompliance—bodies of the disappeared washing ashore or being discovered in unmarked sites.[85] Perhaps most dramatically, in a mid-1977 meeting with President Carter, General Pinochet alluded to the insignificance of any disappearances compared to the well-being of Chile's overall population: "What is more important," Pinochet asked, "ten million people or 10,000 individuals?"[86] In mid-1978, junta member General Fernando Matthei also conceded indirectly to the disappeared: "Allende threatened us with the specter of one million deaths from civil war. Now we worry because perhaps 600 people disappeared."[87] In Argentina, similar government justifications began in mid-1977, following new U.S. demands that national security no longer be used as an excuse to violate human rights. More specifically, the change occurred between Patricia Derian's first visit to Argentina in March 1977, when she confronted government officials with concrete numbers of disappeared, and her second visit that same month. In the brief interim, the regime's rhetoric shifted although Argentine domestic politics had not changed.

Justificatory rhetoric therefore amounted to an implicit admission of culpability, signaling some degree of human rights influence. In the two Southern Cone countries, the timing of these justifications varied depending on when evidence was discovered and when foreign actors issued specific demands. Argentina began justifying its human rights practices only after the United States threatened sanctions, whereas Chile did not do so until after sanctions were already implemented. For both regimes, however, the shift to justifying state practices occurred in 1977, coinciding with new and vigorous demands by the Carter administration.

ACCESS TO MONITORS

Even at the height of repression, both regimes allowed international human rights monitors into the country. Chile's government permitted the IACHR's executive secretary to visit as early as October 1973. It also gave access to delegations from Amnesty International, the ICJ, and the ILO; and a five-member team from the IACHR was allowed to visit the country in July and August 1974.[88] The government, however, did not allow U.N. monitors into Chile until 1978, when it caved in to one of the principal international demands and approved a visit by the U.N. Ad Hoc Working Group on Chile. State officials portrayed Chile as the first country having the courage to accept a U.N. human rights inspection team, and they emphasized the role of the visit in setting a valuable precedent for other countries. According to an official spokesperson, the regime had "nothing to hide."[89] The turnaround appears to have been the work of U.S. bargaining. The U.S. representative to the United Nations Commission on Human Rights traveled to Chile and met with Pinochet twice, purportedly to negotiate the U.N. visit. More specifically, the United States advocated disbanding the U.N. group in the aftermath of the visit, a wish that came true when the group's mandate was terminated in 1979.[90]

Argentina's junta also allowed human rights monitors to visit the country. Early INGO visits included the Paris-based International Federation of Human Rights, the Bar Association of New York City, and the Lawyers Committee for International Human Rights. The government even dared in 1976 to invite Amnesty International for an on-site visit, although a similar visit to neighboring Chile a few years earlier had backfired. The concession did not seem to pay off for Argentina either after Amnesty International issued a critical report. The junta responded by curtailing further international monitoring until 1978. Then, two weeks before a stipulated deadline and despite repeated earlier refusals, the junta finally agreed to invite the IACHR. This was coincidentally around the same time that Chile accepted the U.N. visit.[91] In both cases, international actors welcomed these invitations as positive signs of cooperation and improvement.

EXAMPLES OF LENIENCY

In addition to permitting monitors to visit their countries, the two regimes responded to human rights pressure by acting leniently in specific instances, especially by releasing political prisoners. Initially, Chile's junta restricted national departures to foreigners, especially refugees from other dictatorships. By 1974, however, at least 15,000 Chilean refugees had gone to Argentina and 1,500 to Peru. Overall, in the first two years of military rule, about 20,000 Chileans had left the country for political reasons.[92] The regime entered into a series of agreements with international organizations to arrange the release of certain groups, although initially few political figures were released. An agreement with the UNHCR, for example, permitted most of the remaining detainees in the National Stadium to go abroad. The government also signed agreements with the Inter-Governmental Committee on European Migration and the ICRC.[93] Gradually, the junta began allowing people detained for crimes against state security to depart Chile in September 1974. This trend intensified in January 1975, when the junta released 200 political prisoners. For the first time, group releases included high-profile detainees who were the subject of international pressure, including the head of UNCTAD's third session and the former president's sister, Socialist Deputy Laura Allende. Likewise, UNCTAD leader and former Foreign Minister Clodomiro Almeyda was released following international pressure, including a U.N. resolution. By year's end, the Interior Ministry had announced the immediate release of at least another 50 political prisoners.[94]

The rate at which political prisoners were released mirrored the intensification of human rights pressure. Thus, as the prospect of sanctions grew in early 1976, Chile's regime authorized safe passage for the majority of people seeking political asylum in foreign embassies, including leaders of the armed opposition. And hours after the U.S. treasury secretary's visit to Chile was announced on 4 May 1976, several of Allende's Popular Unity leaders were released from prison. Between May and November 1976 alone, several hundred political prisoners were released, including Chilean Communist Party leader Luis Corvalán, who had been the subject of much international pressure and whose release was part of a prisoner exchange with the Soviet Union. Indeed, most prisoners detained under the state of siege were released in 1976.[95]

Argentina followed suit in releasing political prisoners, especially detainees who were the subject of international pressure. In one of the earliest cases of this, scientists from the Argentine Energy Commission were released following protest by the international scientific community. And in October 1977, a dual Argentine-Austrian citizen who had been detained and tortured for over a year, Veronica Handl-Alvarez, was released unexpectedly after the Austrian government issued her a visa.[96]

Group releases in Argentina became still more common in late 1978. Thus, in a Christmas amnesty, over one hundred prisoners were set free. Six trade union leaders were later freed unexpectedly in 1979; and former President Héctor Cámpora, who had taken refuge in the Mexican embassy, was allowed to leave Argentina. Even more publicized was the release in September 1979 of Timerman, who had been the subject of high-level diplomatic pressure. And Adolfo Pérez Esquivel of SERPAJ, jailed incommunicado for fifteen months, was released into restricted liberty after he was nominated for the Nobel Peace Prize in 1980.[95] By all accounts, these releases confirmed the power of human rights pressure.

IMPLEMENTING INTERNATIONAL NORMS

In stark contrast to Argentina, Chile also responded to human rights pressure by implementing international norms or changing some of its domestic institutional structures to accommodate international norms. These institutional changes accelerated after international pressure intensified in 1976. Before then, the regime had created only the National

Executive Secretariat for Detainees in 1973, which the junta portrayed as a humanitarian organization that could provide the same services to families of detainees as local NGOs. Argentina also had created a similar registry under the Interior Ministry in 1976, purportedly to process inquiries from relatives of those who were missing.[98]

The first real signs of institutional change in Chile were evident in April 1975, when the regime issued a new national security code. The new law required, among other things, that the security services notify family members of a detention within forty-eight hours and bring a detainee before the appropriate authorities within five days; the law also defined new crimes such as kidnapping. And it ruled that people pending trial or serving sentence—*procesados* and *condenados*—could petition to have their sentences commuted to forced exile. In communications with the United Nations, Chilean officials described the new national security code as an example of human rights progress.[99]

After 1976 the regime implemented international human rights norms by issuing new laws, opening the door to longer-term reform. This was also the year that Chile, unlike Argentina, ratified the International Covenant on Civil and Political Rights. Beginning in January, a decree on the treatment of detainees was portrayed by the government as a significant legal improvement in the human rights arena, one warranting that the diplomatic corps be invited to the signing ceremony. Likewise, a set of constitutional acts relating to personal integrity was enacted in 1976 and presented as evidence of the regime's human rights commitments. One act (No. 3) offered a catalog of legal rights, including the right to appeal and to file preventive writs of habeas corpus. In addition to these legal changes, Pinochet announced in a well-known speech in Chacarillas in July 1977 further institutional reform, including holding general elections before 1986. According to Pinochet, this would be part of a gradual development toward an "authoritarian democracy" in which human rights protection would co-exist with the rule of law. Pinochet went as far as to refer to a period of recovery, during which the military would rule with civilian cooperation, and even a transition period that would begin in 1981.[100]

For the first time, moreover, there was an apparent move in Chile to deinstitutionalize state repression. In August 1977, on the day following the arrival of U.S. Assistant Secretary of State for Inter-American Affairs Terence Todman, the government announced DINA's dissolution. The government emphasized that the new CNI (*Centro Nacional de Informaciónes*), the body created in DINA's place, was a separate agency under the direct control of the armed forces rather than the junta. Chile's observer at the United Nations Human Rights Commission even noted that the CNI is "a new entity, different from the Directorate of National Intelligence; it lacks the powers of detention possessed by DINA."[101] Outside observers welcomed the move as evidence of human rights reform.

Other regulatory reforms soon followed, culminating in a new constitution in 1980. The government took a significant step in March 1978, when it lifted the state of siege, which had been in place since the coup. In another positive move, persons previously sentenced by military trials were permitted to have their sentences commuted in exchange for exile. That same month Pinochet issued a general amnesty to anyone who had committed a crime since the coup, a foresighted move whose legacy would reach into the next century. Moreover, in 1978 Pinochet announced preparations for a new constitution, ended curfew, and revoked media censorship. The long-awaited constitution in 1980 itself appeared to be a turning point toward democracy and human rights reform: it drew on Chile's juridical traditions, including human rights norms; established an eight-year transition period; and, remarkably, set a date for ending military rule.[102]

Calculations of State Interest

Any assessment of the impact of international human rights pressure must also take decision makers' calculations into account. Otherwise, the possibility remains that changes in state compliance coincided with but were not caused by human rights pressure. A close look at the decision-making process in both Southern Cone countries reveals that human rights pressures, even when weak and contradictory, were in fact influential. Not only did these pressures covary with improvements in state compliance, but much evidence suggests that human rights pressure actually altered the calculations of Chilean and Argentine decision makers. Political leaders in both countries reacted to the potential costs associated with human rights pressures, changing their behavior to avoid international recrimination.

DECISION MAKING IN CHILE

As early as 1974, Chile's government appeared to feel the weight of human rights pressure and responded defensively. It initiated a propaganda campaign to counter international human rights pressure. This included taking out half-page ads in the *Washington Post* and the *New York Times*, specifically to oppose an ICJ report on Chile. Also early on, Pinochet argued that being appointed "supreme head of the nation" would help to secure domestic and international legitimacy, implying that such legitimacy was in question.[103] Even more telling was Pinochet's later acknowledgment that holding prisoners in the National Stadium and conducting public executions had been his greatest mistakes, given the public criticism they had generated.[104]

Following U.S. threats to suspend military aid to Chile, the junta took even more defensive steps. First, it hired a New York public relations firm, which, among other things, proposed placing paid advertisements in foreign newspapers. Pinochet's speech in response to the 1975 U.N. vote, for example, appeared as a full advertisement in the *London Times*.[105] Likewise, the government's leeriness of transnational human rights alliances may have been manifest in a 1975 decree requiring domestic private organizations to disclose all international currency transactions.[106] In a more far-reaching strategy, the regime restructured foreign policy making. After the U.N. vote in late 1975, the junta announced that the Foreign Service would be reorganized to redress the failure of Chile's foreign policy. About ten ambassadors were replaced and a greater effort was made to balance the number of civilian and military ambassadors, although almost half of all diplomatic personnel had already been dismissed since the coup. In an interview in 1975, Pinochet bluntly accused foreign service officers of not defending the country properly against an international human rights campaign.[107]

The junta's concern with international pressure led it more specifically to monitor U.S. public opinion closely, as well as to diversify the country's relations and actively enlist diplomatic support. In mid-1977 Chile attempted, albeit unsuccessfully, to create a united front among its Southern Cone neighbors to oppose international human rights pressure. Pinochet himself established contacts with foreign diplomats in Chile, while the foreign minister went on a tour of Arab countries to solicit votes at the United Nations.[108] An examination of U.N. votes by countries with which Chile initiated diplomatic relations between 1973 and 1980 shows that, of twenty-seven countries, five changed their votes from negative ones to abstentions; seven others continued to vote against Chile, while the remainder continued to abstain.[109] That Pinochet took notice of human rights pressure is clear in his memoirs, where he records that the *New York Times* and the *Washington Post* referred sixty-six and fifty-eight times, respectively, to human rights practices in Chile in 1976.[110] In mid-1977, the treasury minister also toured European countries to obtain loans that could help reservice Chile's foreign debt; and the foreign investment statute was revised, offering concessions that might offset an unexpectedly low level of investments.[111] Contrary to its statements, wherein the Chilean government implicitly denied the impact of human rights pressure, its broader actions suggested otherwise.

International human rights influence became most apparent in 1978. According to Pinochet, international pressure increased substantially against Chile that year, much of it involving human rights issues. This included, Pinochet lists in his memoirs, the continued campaign by the Soviet Union; U.S. pressure, especially regarding the Letelier case; Bolivia's suspension of diplomatic relations; Argentina's rejection of arbitration in the Beagle Islands crisis; the ORIT-led boycott; the symposium on human rights held in November at the Santiago cathedral organized by the Vicaría; condemnation by the Central Committee of the Socialists International in Algeria; the Communist Party's clandestine call for unification of local forces; and the increasing strength of leftist armed groups.[112] Another junta member described bilateral diplomatic relations that year with the United States as "very bad," although relations with the U.S. military were deemed "very good" and those with economic circles "excellent."[113] Finally, international human rights pressure appears to have shaped the decision to incorporate international economic criteria more fully into foreign policy. An International Economic Relations office was created within the Foreign Ministry in 1978, the first major reform of the Foreign Ministry since 1962, largely to improve Chile's international image.[114]

Human rights pressure seems to have imposed costs even when the Chilean regime failed to comply. For example, although the refusal to permit the U.N. group into Chile appears at first glance to be a recalcitrant state response, it needs to be viewed in its proper context. In the aftermath of the IACHR's visit and its highly critical report on Chile, it must have seemed to Chilean government officials that they could no longer control the impact of visits by international actors and that the costs of such a visit could be too great. Instead of treating this refusal as straightforward resistance to human rights pressure, the refusal may reveal regime leaders' perceptions of the potential costliness of such pressures. Taken together, these developments suggest that human rights pressure had a powerful impact on state decision making in Chile.

Argentina's International Image

International human rights pressure threatened national leaders in Argentina almost immediately after the coup. In discussing international pressure in mid-1976, for example, the interior minister referred to thousands of letters that were arriving daily to government offices.[115] More directly, the Foreign Ministry described early international pressure as follows: "It began with tactful diplomatic inquiries. Then it rapidly grew in scope and intensity to an aggressive, open campaign against our country and its government."[116]

The junta's concern for international human rights pressure also was evident in a concerted public relations campaign. Soon after the coup, Argentina signed a contract with the U.S. public relations firm Burston

Marstellar to improve its image abroad and attract investments from multinational corporations. A central aspect of the campaign was to portray the junta's commitment to international human rights norms. For the sum of $1.2 million, a 35-page report—"Improving the International Image of Argentina"—was prepared for the Argentine government on how to enhance its image in North America and Europe.[117]

Government officials considered even relatively weak forms of international pressure potentially costly. For example, in order to counteract the growing influence of exiles on foreign governments, a "pilot center" was established at the Paris embassy to coordinate a disinformation campaign. Regarding pressure from international agencies, one official noted in an internal Foreign Ministry memo in mid-1977, "Even if the international organizations cannot themselves impose concrete or binding sanctions . . . they can exert a moral pressure which can have an indirect effect on bilateral relations with other countries."[118] More generally, Argentina attached a relatively high priority to responding to pressure from international organizations. Rather than following the common practice of having agency representatives compile reports, replies to the OAS and the United Nations were prepared by U.N. Ambassador Gabriel Martínez himself and other key ambassadors.[119]

Concerned about *public* pressure from international bodies, which could destabilize bilateral relations, the government shifted its strategy within the United Nations. Argentine policy went from avoiding the "institutionalization" of Argentina's case by means of the 1503 procedure to preventing a public debate and the creation of an expert group within the organization, developments that could raise the specter of bilateral government pressure. After the Sub-Commission voted for the first time to send Argentina's name to the Commission on Human Rights (CHR) in March 1979, Martínez advised the junta to cooperate with the United Nations in order "to ensure the confidential passage of the communications." According to Martínez, this would have the following effects: "First, the debate on Argentina will be closed. Second, it will preclude any other action to reopen the issue in a public debate." "Once more," he noted, "our observer delegation was able to avoid the institutionalization of the 'Argentine case' at the level of the Commission and Subcommission."[120] The Foreign Ministry also appeared concerned about "possible negative effects" within the CHR in 1980. Thus, the Foreign Ministry recommended to Argentina's government in early 1980 that it not reply to Swedish protest over a disappearance until after the CHR session. Commenting on the IACHR report, Foreign Minister Washington Pastor remarked tellingly, "The international repercussions could be considerable," in particular, "the attempt to generate worldwide publicity, as well as its determination to ascribe responsibility to the armed forces."[121] Likewise, decisions by international organizations not to single out Argentina were hailed as diplomatic victories. The Foreign Ministry described the OAS's decision to exclude Argentina from a general resolution as "one of the most resounding successes of Argentina's diplomacy," one that brought "a definitive end to the human rights chapter."[122]

Both foreign and military documents reveal a mounting concern with international human rights pressure after 1978. The promilitary publication, *Carta Política*, observed in August that "the principal problem facing the Argentine state has now become an international siege."[123] And in the aftermath of the Eximbank denial, the aim of Argentine policy was, according to one government official, to avoid "an escalating confrontation which will harm our relations in any substantial way. We must not exalt this question, or inflame public opinion, and must strive to keep our remaining areas of contact with the United States intact."[124]

If international pressure altered calculations of interest, it was also because it threatened the regime's economic policy goals. The *Proceso*'s economic program consisted of using state intervention to attract foreign capital, namely by opening the economy and reforming the financial system. National economic policy thus required that the country be deemed creditworthy in order to acquire low-interest loans. The continued development of domestic manufacturing projects, for example, depended on foreign investment.[125]

Given the junta's economic objectives, the fact that international pressure itself was largely symbolic and often contradictory may not have mattered. In fact, with the exception of military sales agreements, most major forms of U.S. governmental assistance to Argentina actually increased during the dirty war (see Table 9). Executives from leading banks and corporations in the United States and Europe continued to meet with Argentine government officials. The Eximbank decision itself entailed potential rather than actual costs for Argentina; according to government cables of the period, the junta could have financed the project anyway.[126] Rather, it was the potential costs to Argentina's broader international relations, not just the immediate costs of human rights pressure, which shaped the calculus of state leaders.

Conclusions

The evidence presented in this chapter suggests that international human rights pressure was indeed influential against both Chile and Argentina in the 1970s. Above all, human rights violations declined in both countries after international pressure climaxed in the mid- to late 1970s. And as international pressure intensified over time, both govern-

TABLE 9. U.S. GOVERNMENTAL ASSISTANCE TO ARGENTINA, 1976–80

	Military Sales and Transfers (Thousands U.S. $)		
Year	Military Sales Agreements	Military Sales Deliveries	Arms Transfers
1976	18,962	8,299	12,028
1977	19,516	6,815	13,129
1978	5,569	9,439	23,625
1979	—	6,859	36,408
1980	—	14,595	22,378

	U.S. Loans and Investment in Argentina (Millions U.S. $)		
Year Investment	Grants and Loans	Eximbank Loans	Direct
1976	—	36,098	1,366
1977	—	19,636	1,490
1978	27.4	21,000	1,658
1979	32.8	19,893	1,850
1980	81.0	11,767	2,494

Source: Statistical Abstract of Latin America, 24 (Los Angeles: UCLA Latin American Center

ments committed increasingly to international human rights norms in their rhetoric and actions. The evidence also shows that decision makers in the two countries altered their calculations in direct response to human rights pressure. Although one could argue that domestic human rights pressure alone could have produced these effects, this misses the full picture: international actors shaped critically the ability of societal groups—labor unions, political parties, church-related groups, and human rights organizations—to pressure the regime in the first place.

Not only did increases in international pressure lead to reduced violations and greater human rights commitments, but state responses matched international human rights demands closely. In Chile, for example, the decision to allow political prisoners to depart the country in September 1974 was made at a time when the issue of detainees had come to constitute the principal demand by foreign governments. Likewise, when group releases began in January 1975, it was only in the aftermath of the November U.N. resolutions calling for them. Other changes in commitment followed a rise in international pressure: prisoner releases were associated with U.S. Treasury Secretary Simon's visit, the Chacarillas speech came soon after U.S. denial of a loan and the hunger strike by relatives of the disappeared, and DINA's dissolution was announced on Todman's arrival. Despite its manifest contradictions, moreover, international human rights pressure imposed potential costs on these regimes. The Argentine case demonstrates how regime leaders worked furiously to avoid public forms of pressure, which could threaten the country's international relations.

International pressure clearly led to improved human rights conditions in the Southern Cone of the 1970s. This is evident both over time and cross-nationally. Similar pressures, despite being applied at different times against the two countries, were followed by comparable state responses. Specific changes in state compliance, moreover, tended to mirror particular international demands. A dense web of human rights pressure, applied by a range of international actors, ultimately served to empower domestic activists, alter the calculations of state elites, enhance state commitments, and reduce overall violations. If these are the touchstones of policy effectiveness, then in these Latin American countries, human rights pressure was at least partly successful.

Chapter 4

Bounded Optimism: The Limits of Human Rights Influence

A more skeptical story of human rights change can almost always be told. I tell such a story in this chapter, with the aim of pinpointing the exact nature of international human rights influence. What did international human rights pressure achieve, and how did it fail? While human rights improvements may be partly the product of international and domestic pressure, such an account can be incomplete and even misleading. Several issues, detailed in the first part of this chapter and then explained from an alternative viewpoint, cast doubt on the extent to which human rights pressure alone led to reduced violations in the Southern Cone of the 1970s and 1980s. This is not simply a case of seeing the cup as half empty rather than half full. This version of the story needs to be told. From a human rights perspective, it uncovers the neglected suffering of those living under hypocritical regimes. Theoretically, it reveals more completely the myriad conditions under which international human rights policies can be influential.

Persistent Puzzles

Despite clear human rights improvements in both Chile and Argentina, certain aspects of both states' compliance remain puzzling. First, why did both states change some of their human rights practices more than others? In both countries, only some human rights violations, notably disappearances, declined substantially. Other human rights violations that had comparable international costs associated with them and similar normative standing (e.g., prohibitions against torture and rights to legal protection) persisted or increased. Even when human rights conditions improved, both regimes also attempted to make ongoing violations more difficult to detect. Nowhere is this exemplified more jarringly than in Chile, where the regime turned to memory-altering drugs to induce partial amnesia in torture victims.[1]

A second puzzling change in compliance involves issues of timing. Even if the impact of international pressure were cumulative, one would have expected at least some violations to drop off when the United States threatened sanctions. In Chile, however, the total number of disappearances *increased* in 1976 by one-fourth what it had been in 1975, while doubling in Santiago.[2] Nor is it clear why Argentina dared to engage in a high level of state repression precisely when costly international pressure was mounting against its Chilean neighbor.[3] It is also unclear why Chile reintensified its violations in 1980, a period when it was subject to consistent human rights pressure and was undertaking substantial commitments. Why did changes in human rights violations persist in one country but not the other despite comparable and ongoing pressures?

Third, why did the two regimes vary in the degree to which they undertook human rights commitments despite their vast similarities? Put differently, why did Argentina appear to resist human rights pressure to a greater degree than did Chile? The Chilean government—led by a hard-liner—changed many of its national laws and institutions, incorporating international human rights norms at least nominally into its domestic structures. Argentina's regime, on the other hand, did not implement international norms despite comparably rising human rights pressures. A close look at these regimes' violations, commitments, and even rhetoric suggests that there is more to the story than meets the eye.

DEFIANT ABUSES

Any chronicle of human rights change must look beyond the number of human rights abuses to examine closely how the *institutions of repression* themselves change. Human rights improvements can be understood only in this broader institutional context of violations. Students of state coercion, as varied as Charles Tilly and Michel Foucault, have long recognized that repression is an institutionalized practice more than a discrete or random set of events.[4] Legal institutions, for example, can serve to justify and hide human rights violations, silencing human rights victims and blocking their access to the state. Even if governments improve certain human rights practices, a full and accurate assessment of human rights change requires a deeper examination of the state apparatus. Has it been legally empowered to commit new and systematic abuses, or perhaps trained to obscure and obstruct traces of abuse? Do human rights victims and their supporters have access to effective mechanisms of protection? When broader criteria such as these are employed, the effects of human rights pressure may appear more modest.

In Chile, the institutionalization of state repression continued unabated, as did many human rights abuses, even as international and domestic pressure rose. Chile reduced—but did not eliminate—the use of disappearances in late 1976 and 1977, a period when hundreds of short-term arbitrary detentions and the regular use of torture continued. And just as the use of disappearances declined, the regime actually opened new and infamous detention centers where torture was practiced (e.g., Monte Maravilla). The terror campaign even moved abroad, with an armed attack against the Christian Democratic leader Bernardo Leighton and his wife in Rome in late 1975, as well as the widely publicized murder of Orlando Letelier in the United States.[5] These events signaled the formation of Operation Condor, a clandestine regional network of intelligence services responsible for thousands of cases of cross-border repression that was coordinated out of Chile.[6] And shortly before the OAS General Assembly meeting in 1976 in Santiago, DINA agents allegedly murdered twenty-nine members of the Chilean Communist Party's Central Committee. This was followed in mid-1976 by a fresh wave of political arrests, and in 1978 these arrests *tripled* what they had been a year earlier.[7] Procedurally, the security services continued to arrest people without issuing warrants or showing proper identification. Nor were families of detainees informed within forty-eight hours of an arrest, as a new law required. The junta even launched a systematic campaign against the Vicaría and other domestic human rights groups with transnational ties. It was indeed a period of reduced repression, but this change was severely limited in scope.[8]

Even after the human rights climate improved, the use of torture actually rose in Chile in 1979 and 1980, and people once again were exiled internally. By 1981, CNI was responsible for new cases of disappearance. More broadly, coercion was reinstitutionalized at the turn of the decade, as a series of decree laws extended the executive's power. Decree Law 2621 of 1979, for example, included antiterrorist provisions, and Decree Law 3451 of 1980 extended the period of detention under states of emergency to twenty days.[9] Civil liberties in Chile were eroding just as the regime undertook extensive human rights commitments. And while international pressure had curtailed Chile's capacity to acquire weapons for national defense, ironically sanctions had a negligible impact on the ability of the police and security forces to purchase arms for repression.[10]

The Chilean judiciary's growing attention to human rights issues also can be exaggerated. For example, when criminal court judge Tomas Dahm broke ranks in 1976 and attempted to visit a secret detention center, not only did the Supreme Court fail to act but also all three of the detainees in question were "disappeared." And following a Supreme Court statement in October 1976 that it could not intervene in or revise executive decisions, most special independent judges declared themselves incompetent when faced with evidence of state involvement; the majority returned human rights cases to military courts. Throughout the 1970s, Chile's judiciary remained formalistic, accepting the official version of events, while the government blocked any efforts at judiciary independence.[11]

Similar restrictions were evident in Argentina. At no time during military rule, even after the use of disappearances declined, did Argentina's junta take concrete steps to dismantle the repressive system. In fact, in 1977, as the regime was committing publicly to international norms, over 3,000 disappearances took place and four new clandestine detention centers were opened[12] (see Table 8). Foreigners continued to disappear, including a Swedish teenager who was mistaken for a Montonero supporter, three U.S. citizens, and two French nuns. In both late 1976 and early 1977, the regime introduced amendments that increased the power of the security apparatus and legalized the status quo of repression. Decree 21,456, for instance, increased the severity of all penalties relating to subversion. Likewise, filing applications to go into exile became a much more onerous process. A U.S. government declassified memorandum highlights the disturbing persistence of torture:

In May 1978, the US Embassy reported that "physical torture continues to be used regularly during the interrogation of suspected terrorists and so-called 'criminal subversives' who do not fully cooperate." It reports that if there has been a net reduction in reports of torture, this is not because torture has been foresworn but "derives from fewer operations" because the number of terrorists and subversives has diminished.[13]

The document also notes that "arrests and disappearances currently continue." And as evidence of the military's involvement in human rights abuses mounted, the government did not investigate these claims nor seek information as to the whereabouts or fate of alleged victims.[14] New legal restrictions also were introduced, despite some judicial activism on behalf of human rights protection. Remarkably, Argentina's junta did not even close the most notorious detention center, ESMA, until the transition to democracy was imminent in 1983. According to the director of an infamous "task force" in Argentina, Jorge Contreras, detention centers were closed after 1978 because the number of targets had fallen: there was no longer the "need to maintain space for large numbers of people."[15]

Indeed, human rights abuses in Argentina became increasingly selective, often targeting human rights activists. As late as 1979, the secretary of the Commission of Families of the Disappeared was abducted, just as a prominent member of *Las Madres* was kidnapped in August 1980. In September 1979, the government issued the Presumption of Death Law (Law 22,068), which allowed anyone reported missing during the previous five years to be declared dead. The regime portrayed it as a concession to relatives of the disappeared, who would be entitled to pensions and other compensation. In practice, the junta attempted actively to block investigation into its role in the disappearances; after all, presumption of death could be established through a judicial ruling, even against the family's wishes, and, once established, relatives could claim life insurance but no longer initiate any legal action.[16] No effective legal protection existed against past or ongoing human rights violations. The state of siege was not suspended and all remaining political detainees were not released unconditionally until 29 October 1983, just one day short of the democratic elections.[17]

Human rights violations certainly declined in both countries, though the improvements were at best partial. The number of abuses dropped, especially egregious ones, but the repressive apparatus was not dismantled, just as many human rights violations persisted and rights to legal protection were flouted. Qualitatively, human rights violations in both countries simply became more selective and difficult to detect. Although human rights pressures were followed by marked improvements in both countries, these improvements should not be exaggerated in the face of ongoing and systematic abuse against individual human beings.

HYPOCRITICAL COMMITMENTS

Changes in human rights commitments also were much more circumscribed than they might appear at first glance. These commitments were often launched strategically to mold public opinion. For example, Chile accepted certain human rights monitors whom it thought it could control, while denying visits to foreign parliamentarians. In September 1976, a visit by two Canadian deputies was rejected en route; that December, the junta also denied access to the World Inter-Parliamentary Union. More broadly, on-site visits by foreign human rights monitors continued to be supervised, officials provided evasive answers, and visitors were not allowed to speak with high-profile prisoners.[18] Public commitments to the contrary, the regime cooperated only halfheartedly with international monitors.

The same was true in Argentina. Despite the regime's apparent openness to human rights monitors, the junta placed numerous restrictions on all visits, transferring prisoners and blocking inspection teams from certain areas. Permitting human rights monitors into the country appeared to be a two-pronged strategy of appeasing international actors while obscuring state responsibility for past abuses. This pattern was evident prior to the IACHR's 1979 visit, when security agents raided the Buenos Aires offices of three leading human rights organizations and confiscated 3,000 signed testimonies. For the visit, the government partially reconstructed official detention centers that the IACHR was scheduled to visit and removed incriminating evidence; prisoners themselves were moved out of Buenos Aires. The direct impact of on-site monitoring, moreover, appears to have been minimal. As a result of even the IACHR's long-awaited visit, only one student was released.[19]

Other human rights commitments were no less hypocritical. While both regimes were increasingly forthcoming in revealing information about political detainees, they understated the number of detainees and excluded information on disappearances. Even the release of political prisoners, which was rightfully applauded, had its defects. In both countries, many of the prisoners released were subsequently placed under house arrest or restricted liberty, whereas others were actually redetained.[20]

And despite what appeared to be extensive regulatory overhaul in Chile, the regime did not alter the structural bases of norm violation nor dismantle the repressive apparatus. If anything, institutional reform made the structure of repression less apparent but no less real. Chilean state officials portrayed their ratification of international human rights treaties, for example, as evidence of their commitment to human rights norms. Yet in practice, they failed to incorporate the treaty's obligations into domestic law. This would have required publishing the ICCPR in the Official Gazette (*Diario Oficial*), something that had never been done.[21] Chile's ratification of this important international treaty thus carried no domestic legal weight. Similarly, although Chile's Constitutional Act No. 3 of 1976 seemed to implement international human rights norms impressively, Act No. 4 effectively canceled any human rights protection by providing for emergency periods that restricted, if not suspended, personal freedoms.[22]

These regimes therefore continued to embrace international norms in largely superficial ways, although outside observers often welcomed any seemingly positive change. Although Chile's dismantling of DINA was widely viewed as a step in the right direction, its successor (CNI) essentially continued DINA personnel, premises, and records.[23] Even as institutional reform accelerated in 1978, a state of emergency remained in effect and all political parties continued to be outlawed. The state of siege itself was reimposed in Chile's El Loa province in September 1978, when workers protested peacefully to demand higher wages. About seventy workers were arrested and sent to remote areas of the country.[24] That April, the junta presciently declared an amnesty for all crimes committed since the coup, an amnesty that would effectively block state accountability into the next century. Even the broadly acclaimed 1980 constitution, itself accepted by a nondemocratic plebiscite, served to expand states of exception, extend the constitutional role of the armed forces, and prolong the longevity of Pinochet's authoritarian regime.[25]

THE RHETORIC OF REJECTION

The use of human rights rhetoric can be interpreted in different ways. First, human rights rhetoric can be viewed as a positive sign. Even if insincere, the assumption is that norm-infused discourse can elicit new communicative dynamics, which in turn can help engender future policy change.[26] Alternatively, when governments reject human rights norms and pressure, observers often downplay the significance of this rhetoric, attributing it to recalcitrant hard-liners, or they interpret it as evidence of ineffective human rights pressure. A close look at the discourse in the Southern Cone, however, suggests another possibility. Rejecting international norms can be a form of strategic communication, a deliberate means of influencing international actors. While the rhetoric of human rights rejection does not necessarily negate international influence nor refute optimists' claims, it does shed important light on state tactics.

Contrary to dominant accounts, the Chilean regime rejected international human rights pressure consistently throughout the 1970s, at the very same time that it continued to deploy the language of human rights. Significantly, moreover, contradictory rhetoric emanated from the same members of the regime, rather than being divided neatly between hard- and soft-liners. This was evident from the first days of military rule. Chilean government officials initially described international pressure as illegitimate and interventionist. Foreign Minister Huerta, for example, stated before the U.N. General Assembly in October 1973 that "no state, and no international organization, has the right to meddle in or judge what has taken place in my homeland."[27] The junta further noted that "attempts by foreign governments to intercede on behalf of Chileans imprisoned . . . will be rejected."[28] International pressure was generally portrayed as an orchestrated campaign, or communist conspiracy, intent on influencing public opinion. Accordingly, three days after the coup, the front page of the government-controlled newspaper *El Mercurio* covered "Chile's False Image Abroad."[29]

The regime launched its own aggressive counteroffensive campaign, which it dubbed "Operation Truth." Paralleling the defensive public relations campaign, which adopted human rights rhetoric, the goal was to deny violations, reject foreign pressure, and launch counteraccusations against international actors. Government officials soon began denying human rights violations unequivocally. Foreign Minister Ismael Huerta declared at the United Nations in 1974 that torture was not practiced in

Chile.[30] And the president of the Supreme Court, in a statement opening a new judicial year in 1975, similarly denied the existence of any egregious human rights violations in Chile: "With regard to torture and other atrocities, I can state that here we have neither firing squads nor iron curtains."[31]

As human rights demands intensified, the junta moved to reject international pressure on technical and concrete grounds as well. In response to the IACHR's First Report on Chile in 1975, the Chilean government highlighted the report's mistakes and omissions, and argued that the organization lacked evidence to treat Chile as a general "case."[32] Similarly, Chile's representative to the UNCHR objected to the U.N. Working Group's interference in its internal affairs and double standards, accusing Chile's critics of even worse human rights violations.[33] Rejection took the added form of "reverse issue linkages," wherein the Chilean government warned foreign officials that bilateral relations would be harmed if human rights pressure continued. Thus, the foreign minister threatened to suspend copper shipments to England, block flight concessions to an Italian airline, and renege on debt repayments to Britain.[34]

The language of rejection only appeared to grow stronger as human rights pressure rose. In a speech in early 1976, Pinochet declared that Chile was a sovereign nation that would never concede to foreign pressure. At the OAS meeting in Santiago later that year, as on other occasions, the Chilean government stated that it had a right to conduct its internal affairs as it saw fit. Pinochet responded to the 1976 U.N. resolution by contending that international accusations were unjust, lacked "moral authority," and constituted an aggressive act aimed at isolating Chile economically. Likewise, in response to a telegram from the UNCHR in 1976 calling for detainees to be released, Chile explicitly used the argument of noninterference, while Chile's ambassador to the OAS declared as late as 1976 that human rights pressure interfered with the country's right to conduct its internal affairs. The junta also counterattacked the U.S. civil rights record, characterizing international human rights pressure as biased and hypocritical. In an 11 February 1978 editorial, El Mercurio addressed these issues under the title of "Human Rights and National Interests," noting the absence of human rights pressure against countries such as Iran and South Korea.[35]

The Chilean government even went as far as to reject all U.S. economic assistance that was tied to human rights compliance. After human rights sanctions went into effect, the junta stated in October 1976 that it did not want to participate in a bilateral assistance program in which it was subject to "political exploitation."[36] Again in June 1977, Pinochet rejected similar aid fully, noting Chile's moral commitments:

"We are not beggars. We are a sovereign, independent country. If they are going to assist us, let it not be under a system of propaganda or attacks. We respect human rights." While extra-officially the government may have communicated to the State Department that it was interested in receiving U.S. funds, publicly the Chilean junta's rhetoric remained confrontational.[37] It portrayed the ORIT-led boycott in 1978, for example, as an economic aggression that would serve only to enhance the country's internal cohesion.[38] Even as Chile's leaders reduced some human rights violations and articulated the country's commitment to human rights, they bothered to reject international human rights pressure publicly.

Throughout its own dirty war, Argentina's government also rejected international human rights pressure vehemently. Government officials both described external pressure as part of an international Marxist conspiracy and appealed to the principle of nonintervention. The regime rejected international human rights pressure by linking Argentina's bilateral relations to U.N. human rights pressure, including the U.N. Working Group on Disappearances. Within the Working Group, Argentina's ambassador threatened to cancel a $2 billion contract with Holland and to close Argentina's agricultural mission in The Hague. Martinez also linked human rights pressure to Argentina's negotiations over the Malvinas/Falklands, its arms purchases from France, and its grain supply to Senegal.[39] This type of reverse issue linkage occurred on so many occasions that the U.N. Sub-Commission issued a statement in 1976, the first of its kind, affirming that its members would not be intimidated.[40]

Argentina joined Chile in denying the existence of systematic human rights abuses. In response to Amnesty International's 1976 visit, for instance, an Interior Ministry official denied the use of torture. A government official told Amnesty International monitors, "If anyone violates human rights in Argentina, it is undoubtedly the terrorists."[41] And in response to Amnesty International's subsequent 1977 report, the junta accused the organization of targeting Argentina selectively and rejected Amnesty International's report because it lacked "truth and objectivity." The report led to a severing of Argentina's relations with Amnesty International and to a general attack on the credibility of human rights NGOs, a campaign launched successfully within the United Nations.[42] In a December 1977 interview, Videla likewise stated, "I categorically deny that there exist in Argentina any concentration camps or prisoners being held in military establishments beyond the time absolutely necessary."[43] Even much later, similar responses were evident. "In the Argentine Republic," the government replied to the United Nations as late as 1980, "there are no secret places for detaining people, nor do the prison establishments contain any detained who are not listed on the records."[44]

Argentina's junta labeled most pressure by the United States an interference in its internal affairs and rejected all FMS credits and economic assistance that were tied to human rights performance, despite the fact that it was not even a recipient of such economic assistance.[45] In response to the announced reduction in U.S. military aid in February 1977, the Foreign Ministry followed Chile's lead and charged that the United States was not taking into account Argentina's security. In various government memoranda, the decision was described as "arbitrary," "immoral and unilateral," as well as a violation of the 1964 U.S.-Argentine agreement: "The reduction showed interference in the internal affairs of our country and a lack of knowledge about the Argentine situation."[46]

And rather than gradually desisting from rejecting international human rights pressure, rejection constituted a consistent response throughout the dirty war. Even following the highly touted IACHR visit, the junta described the organization as biased, and threatened to resign from the OAS if it issued a condemnatory resolution. When the IACHR's report was published in 1980, the junta refused to release it.[47]

These rejections appear to have been mostly a means of influencing international actors. Argentina's government thus rejected U.S. human rights pressure while drawing parallels between itself and the Soviets. After a growing, if undramatic, political rapprochement between the two countries in 1979, Argentina began claiming that the two countries were subject to similar international interference in their human rights practices. In a joint communiqué in August 1980, the two governments stated, "We oppose the creation of supranational organizations especially on human rights within the United Nations. The creation of these organizations would entail interference in the internal affairs of other states."[48] A visit by U.S. General Andrew Goodpaster to Buenos Aires confirmed the apparent effectiveness of playing the Soviet card to influence U.S. human rights policy.[49] The visit was viewed in Argentina as a victory: "Our non-adhesion to the grain embargo . . . has provided the most effective means to force a change in U.S. human rights policy towards Argentina."[50]

Although the rhetoric of rejection may not furnish strong evidence against optimists' claims, it should not be dismissed as simple backlash. It signals, on the one hand, the stubborn power of pro-violation groups and domestic rules of exception. This translates into concrete cases of abuse, and it makes subsequent human rights reform more difficult than it may appear in hindsight. This rhetoric also suggests that states communicate strategically, deploying commitments and rejections simultaneously to counteract accusations of noncompliance. If this is the case with language, we should be even more wary of the persistence of systematic human rights abuses and the hypocrisy of some state commitments. Disentangling the origins of these complex state responses requires venturing beyond human rights pressures, to explore a prior question: what pushed these states to violate human rights in the first place?

Domestic Threats and Norm Violations

An underappreciated part of the story of human rights change is the role played by armed threats. Long before an international human rights regime formed in the mid-twentieth century, states have used such threats to justify state repression. Certainly, armed groups do not always threaten a regime objectively. They are more often than not weaker than the state apparatus, relatively disorganized, and rather easy to kill or send into exile. Yet these armed threats are also one of the most frequent pretexts for using state repression. Once this rationale disappears, it becomes difficult for political leaders to sustain the same level of coercion.

Armed Groups in Chile

Chilean governments long have used threats to national security to justify violating personal security. In a foreboding way, Chile was the first country in Latin America both to achieve constitutional consolidation and to invoke a state of siege. Drawing mostly on Spanish and Belgian legal models, national security norms were first codified in Chile's constitution of 1833, which provided the executive with vast emergency powers to suspend basic civil and political rights.[51]

This legacy persisted into the 1970s, when it was reinforced by the introduction of neoliberal economic ideas that depended on a stable social climate and a quiescent labor force. Armed groups and other regime opponents upset neoliberal requirements for social docility and national stability. In this context of polarization, the stated purpose of repression in Pinochet's Chile was to prevent the rise of a Marxist armed threat. In reality, armed groups in Chile did not threaten the state objectively; they were insufficiently armed, relatively small in number, and quite fragmented.

Yet two sets of institutionalized ideas deemed repression an appropriate form of social control. First, the already mentioned neoliberal economic agenda called for export-oriented growth, free trade, and drastically reduced social spending. This economic plan required that domestic stability be maintained at all costs. Previous attempts to liberalize the economy had failed, according to University of Chicago–trained

Chilean economists, precisely because past economic policies had caved in to the vagaries of social demands.[52] Second, the Cold War provided a compelling national security doctrine (NSD), which labeled leftists as enemies of the state. And to be labeled an enemy implied that one's personal security could be sacrificed for the greater good of the body politic. Just as the United States trained local security officers in techniques of repression, NSD provided a global, moral rationale for when and how to coerce dissidents.[53] This national security doctrine fused with prevailing economic ideology, as the former provided the latter with the requisite stability to thrive. Decision makers and powerful domestic groups stood to gain from the arrangement, promising them security and economic well-being. These powerful actors quickly bought into and perpetuated these twin myths: economic liberalization necessitated repression and armed groups threatened national security.

Armed violence in Chile had actually surfaced a few years before the coup, intensifying after Salvador Allende's leftist *Unidad Popular* government unexpectedly won national elections in 1970. Guerrilla groups such as the MIR (*Movimiento de la Izquierda Revolucionaria*) adopted ideas about armed struggle in the socially radicalized context of the 1960s. They launched their ideological offensive in labor strikes, land seizures, and factory takeovers. While visible, they were hardly a match for a coercive apparatus that had been given sweeping powers by Allende himself and was bolstered by right-wing paramilitary groups.[54] Although government officials justified all deaths in the 1970s as necessary by-products of a struggle against so-called subversives, in the end only 6 percent of those who died in conflict belonged to the state security apparatus, compared to 40 percent from leftist groups.[55] Had the threat posed by these groups been more substantial, these casualty figures certainly would have been quite different.

For Chile's military and its social allies, however, the existence of subversives created wartime conditions, which in turn required nothing short of authoritarian rule. Initial decrees were described as *bandos*, or ordinances, a term denoting internal war.[56] The state of war would require the complete elimination of the subversive threat. In the widely quoted words of Air Force General and junta member Gustavo Leigh, the armed forces needed to "extirpate the cancer of Marxism."[57] Consequently, the government attempted to justify its human rights behavior by offering proof of this internal threat. To excuse the extralegal execution of dissidents, for example, military officers invoked the argument that dissidents were escaping (the "law of flight"). The language of war was extended to describe human rights advocates, who were labeled enemies and traitors with links to international Marxism. More specifically, a display of guerrilla arsenals was taken around the country in late 1973 to reinforce the image of a concrete and dangerous domestic threat.[58] Even U.S. government officials at the time emphasized the role that armed groups played in shaping Chilean leaders calculations. In a memorandum to the U.S. secretary of state, an American official in Chile noted in 1973: "How the military leaders proceed in this area from now on will be influenced to some degree by outside opinion, and particularly by ours, but *the major consideration will continue to be their assessment of the security situation.*"[59]

Then, in 1976, the situation changed dramatically. The leadership of the principal armed groups had left the country, many members of the rank and file had been "disappeared" or gone underground, and no armed confrontations involving leftist groups were visible.[60] The regime's extreme repressiveness itself had served to eliminate the armed threat; and in the absence of such threats and at the peak of economic recovery, the regime's rationale for maintaining a high level of repression was all but gone. Then and only then, did human rights pressure coincide with a decline in violations.

As armed confrontation ended, Chilean officials now justified ongoing coercion in terms of a diffuse propaganda war being waged by leftist groups. The opposition, according to the government, was deliberately attempting to provoke repression and harm the government's image. As Table 10 shows, government justifications for the state of siege shifted subtly, from a "state of war" or "internal defense" to "internal defense" and "disturbance," depending on the visibility of armed groups.

The pendulum swung back in 1979 and 1980, when human rights violations rose again despite international and domestic pressures. Beginning in 1979, renewed violence, especially by FPMR (Manuel Rodríguez Patriotic Front) and MIR, reemerged. The FPMR was part of a group within the Communist Party that, after being subjected to repression,

TABLE 10. ATTRIBUTIONS OF THREAT: STATES OF LEGAL EXCEPTION
IN CHILE, 1970s

September 1973–September 1974	State of emergency and state of siege due to *state of war*
September 1974–September 1975	State of emergency and state of siege due to *internal defense*
September 1975–September 1977	State of emergency and state of siege due to *internal security*
September 1977–March 1978	State of emergency and state of siege due to *internal disturbance*
March 1978–March 1981	State of emergency

Source: Adapted from Comisión Andina de Juristas, *Perú y Chile: Poder judicial y derechos humanos* (Lima, Peru: Comisión Andina de Juristas, 1988), 229–30.

shifted its strategy to the use of armed force. The MIR, for its part, launched "Operation Return" after 1980, carrying out public bank robberies and bombings. Most notably, the MIR assassinated Lt. Colonel Roger Vergara, head of army intelligence. Purportedly in retaliation for this incident, the government created the anti-subversive command, a commando unit directed against domestic terrorism, while the CNI-inspired Avengers (COVEMA) also committed human rights violations. In general, the CNI led a renewed policy of repression and counterinsurgency.[61]

Yet the 1979 and 1980 rise in violations coincided with an increase in transnational human rights pressure. Within the United Nations a special rapporteur was appointed to monitor Chile in 1979. General Assembly resolutions during this period passed with overwhelming majorities. And the Carter administration, reacting to insufficient cooperation on the Letelier case, imposed new sanctions against Chile, including suspending Eximbank loans and joint naval exercises. Despite this international pressure, when faced with a resurgence of armed conflict, the Chilean regime did not hesitate to respond with concerted violence.

In the final analysis, the virtual elimination of an armed threat in 1976 compelled the regime to reduce the overall level of violations so as to maintain its social coalition intact. And as long as the basic foundations of the regime continued to be authoritarian, the decline in human rights violations could only be partial. To escape accusations of repression, tactics were altered and ongoing abuses were made more selective and difficult to detect. Only violations that were no longer necessary for domestic purposes, that were likely to appease external actors, or that promised to deflect international accusations of noncompliance were altered. This explains why disappearances declined most markedly, while other violations persisted. Ironically, human rights pressures may have induced the regime to eliminate armed groups quickly and effectively. When armed groups reemerged at the turn of the decade, however, the regime showed its true colors and moved to break international norms.

Human rights pressures against Chile were therefore effective in delegitimizing the use of repression and in raising the costs of noncompliance, outcomes that led to some human rights improvements. But they alone cannot explain why only some violations changed only some of the time. Paradoxically, human rights improvements obscured two disturbing trends: the persistence of serious abuses and, more perversely still, the fact that human rights pressures were most effective only once the regime had crushed its armed opponents. The first trend reflects the ongoing strength of pro-violation constituencies and regime ideologies. The second points to the primacy of national security threats. Together, they bridge the gap dividing skeptics and optimists of human rights pressure.

NATIONAL SECURITY IN ARGENTINA

The idea that internal security justified the use of repression was equally long-standing in Argentina, dating to the period of state formation and constitutional consolidation. These ideas were imported from the European context to Argentina, where they joined local socioeconomic disparities to produce officially sanctioned coercion. The result was that rules (or "states") of exception were institutionalized beginning with the first decree of personal security in 1811. According to that decree, personal security required that citizens enjoy basic rights, such as those of due process, as well as freedoms from torture and forced exile. But the same decree also allowed for these rights to be suspended "in the remote and extraordinary case of threats to public tranquility or security of the fatherland."[62] These exceptions proved to be the legal foundations for subsequent state repression in Argentina. Particularly during periods when the state did not want to or could not distribute fiscal rewards, it turned to the coercive apparatus for social control.[63] And in the aftermath of World War II and in the context of Cold War politics, U.S. foreign assistance programs reinforced the practice of containing internal social threats through state coercion.[64]

Support for the use of repression intensified as domestic unrest mounted in the years leading up to the dirty war, especially in the aftermath of General Juan Carlos Onganía's national security regime in 1966. Following the 1969 "*cordobazo*," when the military regime violently suppressed student and labor protests in the city of Córdoba, urban guerrilla groups and right-wing death squads emerged onto Argentina's domestic scene.[65] During subsequent civilian rule in the early 1970s, right-wing death squads such as Triple A (*Alianza Anticomunista Argentina*) carried out hundreds of forced disappearances. On the left of the political spectrum, the *Montoneros* and the *Ejército Revolucionario del Pueblo* (ERP) also engaged in acts of violence.[66] To meet this high level of social polarization, both General Alejandro Lanusse's brief military government in 1971 and Juan Perón's rule increased state coercion.[67]

State repression reached its apogee during Isabel Perón's government (1974–76), when at least twenty antiterrorist laws were passed to control domestic opposition and assure the success of orthodox economic policies.[68] Accordingly, Argentina's first secret detention center was opened in 1974, followed by six more in 1975, all before the outbreak of the actual dirty war. When the economy deteriorated shortly thereafter due to hyperinflation and a serious balance-of-payments deficit, the armed forces pointed to the state of the economy and the need to fight a domestic war against subversion to justify their intervention on 24 March 1976. By then the use of state repression enjoyed widespread domestic support, both on the part of the armed forces and foreign-trained economic technocrats as well as from broad segments of Argentine society.[69]

The military and its allies pointed to armed groups and other "subversives" as a threat that justified both a coup and an inordinately high level of repression. Indeed, Argentine rulers and economic technocrats fostered the idea that economic growth required using coercion to control the demands of a large labor force. The governor of Tucumán province confirmed the economic objectives of state repression when he described the purpose of coercion in 1976 as follows: "The Army's role is to give economic policy 'space' and time to succeed."[70] Thus, armed opposition groups threatened the regime's economic project more than its physical security, but in the context of the prevalent economic ideology and an invigorated military, armed groups provided ample reason for the state to engage in repression.[71]

It does not matter that armed groups never actually threatened the regime's viability and survival. The military, after all, far outnumbered any radicalized groups. Even a regime hard-liner conceded as early as mid-1976, "Subversion is generally in retreat and on the way to collapse."[72] ERP leader Mario Roberto Santucho had died in July 1976 and the group as a whole suffered heavy casualties; *Montoneros* founder Mario Firmenich also left for Italy in 1977.[73] Government documents conceded that "Montoneros forces have been weakened to a degree unsuspected by public opinion. At the same time, their basic infrastructure intelligence has almost been annihilated. . . . The fact that most important leaders have escaped abroad is an evidence of their precarious condition." And regarding the ERP, the same document claimed that this organization, "practically destroyed in the military field, has not been able to recover since the death of its major leader, Roberto SANTUCHO, alias Robby, and his staff."[74] Also in mid-1977, Videla issued a secret order calling for the campaign against subversion to continue although 90 percent of subversive organizations had been destroyed.[75] As in Chile, state repression essentially had eliminated armed opponents, either killing them or driving them into exile.

As it became apparent that the regime had eliminated armed opponents, repressive policies diminished. The first decline in human rights violations—a drop in the number of disappearances—was evident in 1977, with the actual defeat of armed groups (see Table 8). Continuing a policy of repression nonetheless allowed the state to control political opposition and advance private economic interests. In the absence of a concrete threat, this required that the regime prolong the *myth* of an armed assault. Soft-liner General Viola, for example, assured a meeting of business executives that although 7,000 to 8,000 subversive criminals had been detained, about 1,200 still remained in Buenos Aires.[76] The message was clear: heavy repression must persist. The junta's active perpetuation of national security ideology was thus critical; it helps to explain why the largest decline in human rights violations did not occur until 1978, after armed groups had already been dismantled.[77]

Once it was apparent that the junta had eliminated all armed insurgents, it was forced to adjust its policies accordingly. The military had lost its principal rationale for waging a campaign of terror. Facing transnational human rights pressure, the regime could no longer justify the same level of state repression against an invisible enemy. With the pretext for repression gone, human rights conditions were free to improve.

Even after its armed opponents had been removed, however, the junta justified its hold on power and its ongoing abuses by redefining threats to national security. The regime acknowledged that although armed threats had declined, it now faced an ideological enemy. The threat of "subversive acts" was repackaged into the danger of a "subversive mentality."[78] As General Suárez Masón noted, "It would be absurd to assume that we've won the war against subversion because we have eliminated its armed threat."[79] An Argentine general later concurred, "We have to control the educational, industrial, and neighborhood environment, which is where the remainder of terrorist delinquency has hidden."[80] Videla similarly described a terrorist in 1978 as "not just someone with a gun or a bomb but also someone who spreads ideas that are contrary to Western and Christian civilization."[81] And in anticipation of the IACHR's report, the junta issued its own report emphasizing the threat posed by subversives: *Evolution of Terrorism in Argentina.*[82] One scholar describes this shift as one from a "counterrevolutionary logic" of repression to a "foundational logic," wherein state repression became "an inherent structural characteristic of the regime."[83] Indeed, the armed forces continued formally their antisubversive alert as late as mid-1979, bolstering an ongoing pattern of abuse (e.g., via Army Directive No. 604/79 of May). And official orders purportedly called for treating *Montoneros* no differently than before: "torture and summary execution being their lot."[84] The only key difference was that other groups could now avail themselves of the legal system.

Human rights violations in Argentina therefore changed in very specific ways. The regime reduced the number and targets of abuse, but it did so mostly to avoid further international condemnation. For example, it reduced the practice of disappearances but it continued to engage in torture. Essentially, human rights violations declined in tandem with their domestic usefulness. International and domestic pressures certainly raised the costs of state repression. Yet in the context of authoritarian political institutions, and an entrenched national security ideology fused with neoliberal economic ideas, armed groups made the domestic costs of foregoing repression unacceptably high. When the threat posed by these groups was abolished, transnational human rights influence could fill the void.

International Pressure and Policy Debates

The picture painted so far of human rights influence is at best contradictory, with improvements occurring alongside ongoing abuse and hypocrisy. Conventional wisdom often attributes such contradictions in human rights policy to regime divisiveness. Persistent human rights violations and recalcitrant state responses are traced back to hard-liners, whereas positive changes in compliance are deemed to be the work of moderates. Certainly, regimes are often split over how to respond to international human rights pressure, and evidence from the Southern Cone supports this. However, a related set of dynamics may also be at play. While international human rights pressure led to policy debates in both countries, these debates revolved mostly around how far the state should go in *committing* to (not violating) international norms. Intraregime debates essentially hinged on a central question: "How much should we appease international actors?" These regimes did not debate the desirability of ongoing violations. On the contrary, in the context of authoritarian rule, a strong consensus existed that any opposition to the regime could be met with repression.

This is clearly seen in Chile, where despite policy disputes all government factions agreed on one issue: a monetarist economic model was desirable, and this required both strong international economic relations and the use of repression to control labor's demands.[85] Even a U.N. commission report confirmed that the "suppression of or serious restriction on civil and political rights are, inter alia, *necessary* to impose and enforce the economic and social policy of the government."[86] This interdependence between state repression and the economic development model was apparent in DINA's mission statement, which called for both protecting national security and promoting national development.[87]

Where the various factions disagreed was on the relative weight they should accord foreign investment versus state repression. On the one hand, for soft-liners, the need to attract foreign investment was paramount to most foreign policy decisions. While they supported the use of repression, soft-liners also were concerned with appeasing international actors via public commitments. On the other hand, for the

Chilean military, "repression always remained more important . . . than the need to overcome persistent international condemnation."[88]

International human rights pressure—alongside the onset of an economic crisis, the regime's consolidation, and the Catholic Church's critical stance toward the regime—served over time to widen the gap between soft- and hard-liners. On the civilian side, calls were issued for a more pragmatic foreign policy beginning in 1974. Pro-government sources such as *El Mercurio* and *Qué Pasa* joined in taking a critical stance toward Chile's international isolation.[89] The nationalist hard-line faction nonetheless disagreed over the extent to which repression posed a serious international problem worthy of concrete changes, such as the release of political prisoners or revision of legal codes.[90] Furthermore, the extent to which international pressure entered into the decisions of individual state agents engaged in repression remains unclear. Standard accounts often assert that, when faced with international pressure, individual abusers will think twice before violating human rights norms. Yet when Doctor Sheila Cassidy was held in detention in Chile's Villa Grimaldi camp in October 1975, she claims that the men who kidnapped her warned, "Our image abroad is so bad that we don't care."[91]

As international pressure intensified, one thing is clear: debate within the government mounted over how to respond to this pressure. The view that human rights practices were responsible for Chile's international isolation became increasingly pervasive.[92] In addition to debating the general parameters of how the state should respond to international pressure, policy disputes focused specifically on human rights commitments. A key source of internal strife in mid-1978, for example, was Chile's cooperation with the United States on the Letelier case. Soft-liners pressed for conceding to U.S. demands, while hard-liners portrayed U.S. pressure as an attack on Chilean sovereignty.[93] Policy debates in Chile, therefore, were exacerbated by human rights pressure, itself evidence of international influence; but these debates centered on how far the regime should commit publicly to international norms. Whether repression should be a tool of state policy was not contested.

Policy debates in Argentina proceeded along similar lines. Immediately after the coup, the junta was relatively united in responding to human rights pressure. All state actors involved in relevant decision making—economic technocrats, Foreign Ministry officials, and the security apparatus—shared a dual interest in employing widespread repression while portraying a moderate international image. The junta's quest to achieve economic development by means of state repression was reinforced by the armed forces' powerful role in Argentina's economy and society.[94]

Divisions over whether to commit publicly to international human rights norms, however, began surfacing in 1977. Starting with Amnesty International's report that March, regime hard-liners opposed changing state behavior for the sake of international actors. For hard-liners who viewed military rule in absolute terms, any change in internal practices threatened their professional, corporate interests. Soft-liners' primary interest in transitional and shared civilian rule was compatible with a strategy of appearing moderate internationally, while using repression to assure economic success. Videla, himself a soft-liner, stated as early as 1975, "As many people as necessary will die in Argentina to restore order."[95] Regime splits, moreover, were exploited internally. For example, navy leader Admiral Eduardo Emilio Massera, who ran the infamous ESMA detention center and largely controlled foreign policy, blamed the other armed services for human rights abuses, in an attempt to gain backing by international actors and promote a personalist agenda.[96]

The question of publishing lists of political prisoners and releasing detainees also proved to be a strong point of contention within the regime. For example, when the Supreme Court ordered Timerman's release, Videla threatened to resign if the Court's decision were defied, while other moderates approved immediate exile. Hard-liners, however, allegedly attempted to block his departure physically and, perhaps partly in protest, provoked an attempted mutiny.[97] Both soft- and hard-liners shared similar interests in using repression to further economic development, while differing on the strategies they should use in responding to international pressure.

In shaping policy debates, human rights pressure served above all to redefine the international problems and options that decision makers faced. Perhaps the most dramatic evidence of this was given by an Argentine Foreign Ministry official, who summarized policy choices in mid-1980:

a) [Political] detainees must be tried, freed, or given the right to leave the country; b) measures must be taken to explain the fate of the disappeared persons; c) there must be no new actions which constitute a violation of human rights; d) constitutional government must be restored. Taken in the context of the first three proposals, it is this last measure which will permit a return to a full and normal international relations for Argentina.[98]

International human rights pressure clearly was crucial in defining the options before state elites, although it cannot always explain the timing or degree of policy change. As long as ruling factions in both countries agreed that repression was an appropriate means of controlling social demands and ultimately promoting economic growth, policy debates would continue to focus on human rights commitments.

COHESIVE DECISION MAKING IN CHILE

If international pressure led to policy debates, the impact of these debates depended on the particular structure of decision making. In the case of Chile, a cohesive decision-making structure permitted Pinochet to control policy disputes effectively and respond to human rights pressure despite the opposition of some regime members. Unlike elsewhere in the Southern Cone, Chile had a four-man junta, including a representative of the police. More importantly, executive power was vested centrally on Pinochet, in contrast to Argentina where the junta (i.e., representatives of the three armed services) held this power jointly. Some political economists have argued that these different decision-making structures shaped the capacity of Latin American regimes to implement economic policies.[99] In a similar vein, these structures may affect states' capacities to respond to international human rights pressure in controversial ways. A cohesive decision-making structure allowed Pinochet to employ nonconsensual means to control conflict within the regime, including changing the very rules of the game; this, in turn, may explain why Chile's junta implemented international norms to such a high degree. In contrast, rulers operating within more fragmented systems of decision making, as in Argentina, may have to resort more often to intraregime bargaining and consensus building, undermining their capacity to respond to human rights pressure. Accordingly, state commitments themselves can reflect a state's organizational capacity to deflect international pressure.

Pinochet responded to early critics by forging a consensus: the executive had to be unified if the regime were to succeed in the face of international human rights pressure. With the purported aim of eliminating organizational redundancies, Pinochet undertook a series of measures that enhanced his own power while increasingly isolating military hardliners. Beginning in April 1974, Pinochet altered the military leadership, introducing the first in a series of retirements and promotions.[100] A couple of months later, the Statute of the Junta was passed, against strong resistance from other junta members. The statute effectively transferred legislative power to the junta and vested executive power in the president. In so doing, Pinochet succeeded in being designated both junta president and army chief of staff. Alongside the new statute, Pinochet took critical steps to consolidate its rule. Above all, he replaced his cabinet with sympathizers, a move that served to solidify Pinochet's standing.[101]

In shifting power away from military hard-liners, Pinochet both strengthened the role of a group of U.S.-trained liberal economists in policy advising and maintained a firm grip on the repressive apparatus.

Even an economic shock policy was implemented without the participation and over the objections of the relevant minister from the armed forces.[102] Privately, in a confidential September 1975 order, the president granted DINA exclusive authority to arrest people for political crimes and to investigate infiltration into the armed services. Publicly, however, Pinochet sought to reinforce his image as a neutral and legitimate ruler. His title of "supreme head of the nation" was changed to the more democratic sounding "president of the republic."[103]

Significantly, Pinochet used international human rights pressure as an excuse to consolidate his own power. This situation is somewhat different from one frequently discussed by students of human rights, wherein soft-liners appeal to international norms to strengthen their domestic positions. Pinochet, as a hard-liner, used international pressure precisely as a way of differentiating Chileans from the outside world.[104] International pressure was an explicit call for national identity and unity, a means of confronting the unjust accusations of international actors who were conspiring with national subversives. Thus, following a U.N. resolution against Chile, the government rallied a special military ceremony at the Escuela Militar.[105] National unity, however ostensible, could then be held up as proof of the regime's legitimacy.

As human rights pressure increased, Pinochet responded to rising policy debates nonconsensually. He continued to orchestrate retirements and promotions within the military, and he created broader institutional counterweights. In late 1975, for example, he established the Joint Command, a group designed to coordinate the various intelligence agencies; it was intended as a counterbalance to DINA. Concern (especially within the army and air force) had been growing over DINA's highly concentrated and growing power.[106] Pinochet further reinforced the power of the economic team in foreign policy. He appointed Hernán Cubillos, a civilian from the business sector, as foreign minister, and former treasury minister Jorge Cauas as ambassador to the United States. It is noteworthy that Cubillos himself had been nominated foreign minister in 1974, but had been rejected in favor of a member of the military.[107]

Moderates acquired increasing organizational power within the regime because of Pinochet, but once they had this power they were able to influence policy. Civilian advisers and military moderates, who controlled almost three-fourths of the state's coercive apparatus, supported introducing regulations that would enhance the regime's legitimacy before an international audience.[108] This was especially evident in the decision to hold a national plebiscite in 1978. Following the U.N. resolution in 1977, moderates such as Justice Minister Mónica Madariaga and legal adviser Jaime Guzmán (the architect of the 1973 Declaration

of Principles) became concerned that popular indifference to the resolution signaled a lack of support for the regime. Thus, they proposed
the plebiscite, which was portrayed as pro-Pinochet and a rejection of
international pressure. The text of the plebiscite read: "In the face of international aggression against our nation, I support President Pinochet's
defense of Chilean dignity and reaffirm the legitimacy of this sovereign
government to lead us in the process of institutionalization." "Yes" was
denoted by a Chilean flag and "no" by a black square. Seventy-five percent of Chileans purportedly supported the junta.[109] Held over the objec-
tion of junta members, the plebiscite led to even greater personalization
of the regime, or what Manuel Garretón refers to as the "personalization
of leadership" alongside "juridical institutionalization."[110]

Moderates then called on the regime to respond to human rights
pressure with concrete commitments. They persuaded Pinochet to allow
the U.N. Working Group to visit Chile, a visit that Pinochet initially
feared would result in a devastating report.[111] Government moderates
further urged that the state of siege be lifted as proof that the civil war
had concluded. They advised Pinochet to make the Chacarillas speech
and to sign the infamous 1978 amnesty.[112] The primary justification for
all of these decisions was that they would improve the country's image
abroad and therefore its bilateral relations.

Pinochet subsequently forged a strong consensus among most social
and economic sectors that the regime should work to counter international pressure.[113] Consequently, the Chilean leader pursued more fully
a civilian-pragmatic approach in both foreign and domestic policy. The
foreign minister announced an opening and dialogue with all countries,
including socialist ones. Within the United Nations, and in a significant
departure from past policy, Chile's representative did not launch anti-
communist tirades or attack countries critical of Chile.[114] On the domestic front, political changes were made with an eye to the international
audience. Thus, the decision to designate 1985 as a key date in a six-year
transition was taken by the *Asesoría Política*, an organ that was controlled
partly by Foreign Ministry officials. Moderate technocrats also promoted a series of labor reforms, seeking to contain the opposition by
altering the structural bases of society.[115] Even as internal tensions ran
high, the government always sought to demonstrate that it enjoyed popular and military support. For example, the regime organized a meeting
in Santiago to reject the 1978 ORIT-led boycott against Chile, which was
attended by government-backed labor leaders and Pinochet himself; the
meeting produced a document titled "Commitment to Chile."[116]

To assure the success of these policies and his own personal survival,
Pinochet continued to control regime divisions. This entailed, among
other things, balancing civilian and military power. At the same time

that a civilian was appointed to head the Foreign Ministry, Pinochet created a cabinet-level position of vice-minister as a counterweight and
staffed it with a member of the army, in an effort to shift foreign policy
away from the navy.[117] Members of the regime who opposed the new policy direction were dismissed. Even junta member Gustavo Leigh was
removed from office for resisting the pace and nature of institutional
change.[118] These dramatic changes also may have reflected the Chilean
regime's mounting isolation both at home and abroad. The resignation
of Chile's ambassador to the United States, for example, was widely interpreted as a sign of the regime's internal weakness or increasing vulnerability to pressure from domestic labor and human rights groups.[119]

Yet in the absence of a cohesive decision-making structure, the
Chilean regime may not have been able to go as far to appease international human rights critics. Disagreement within the regime was simply
too high. Rather, the coherent structure of decision making allowed
Pinochet to alter gradually the power balance between regime hard-
liners and soft-liners. Although Pinochet's own personal idiosyncrasies
may have made him particularly adept at controlling such conflicts, it
was the institutional context that permitted him to shift the very rules
of the game. Chile's decision-making structure explains why the regime
was able to implement international human rights norms in the face of
strong intraregime debates. Pinochet could rely on nonconsensual
methods, including the use of retirements and promotions or the creation of institutional counterbalances, to subordinate hard-liners. This
in turn permitted the Chilean regime to respond to human rights pressure with precisely the types of domestic changes that were the gist of
policy debates.

Fragmentation in Argentina

In sharp contrast to Chile, human rights decision making in Argentina
was fragmented from the onset of military rule. Government responsibility was spread across the three armed services, and the police were
not under the administrative control of the armed forces. Responsibility
was further divided within each service among *grupos de tarea*, or what essentially amounted to counterinsurgency task forces. The country itself
was divided into five "zones," 35 "subzones," and 210 "'areas," each controlled by local commanders.[120] With the partial exception of some elite
intelligence units that acquired increasing independence from their
service (e.g., the navy's GT 3/32 at ESMA), the system of repression remained highly hierarchical even if subject to competing jurisdictions.[121]

As policy debates over international pressure mounted, the government's inability to control hard-liners within the security forces surfaced.

This was especially true with regard to the disappearance of individual foreigners and the release of detainees who were the object of foreign governmental pressure. In order to preempt compliant gestures by soft-liners, hard-liners engaged in particular instances of repression, including the widely publicized murder of two French nuns. The increasing autonomy of hard-liners also was manifest as intelligence organizations took their activities abroad. Between 1977 and 1979, for example, officials from the GT 3/32 were sent throughout Latin America to kidnap or kill *Montoneros* in exile. Likewise, Elena Holmberg, the Argentine diplomat who led the disinformation center in Paris and whom hard-liners did not consider to be sufficiently aggressive, was recalled to Buenos Aires in October 1978, kidnapped, and murdered.[122] Hard-liners acted autonomously in these cases because they viewed international pressure as a threat to their professional interests. In fact, some have speculated that navy intelligence killed the French nuns precisely to prevent Admiral Massera (who had publicly blamed the army for their disappearance) from releasing them, a move that would make the military appear weak. In asserting their interests, furthermore, hard-liners benefited from extensive coordination among the security forces of the Southern Cone, including the now-notorious Operation Condor.[123]

For soft-liners, who were willing to appease international actors, these inconsistencies proved costly. When human rights victims targeted by international actors were killed, as in the case of foreign citizens, soft-liners found themselves in a difficult position, denying the existence of a clandestine repressive apparatus but unable to provide information about the fate of foreign victims. As a Foreign Ministry official remarked in July 1977, the disappearance of foreigners "seriously disturbed" Argentina's bilateral relations.[124] Regime moderates were severely constrained in their capacity to provide evidence to international actors of their human rights commitments. They resorted to blaming lower-ranking members of the armed and security forces.[125] Only in a few cases were soft-liners able to extract concessions from their counterparts through bargaining. For example, Videla reportedly conceded a generalship to hard-line Colonel Ramón Camps, head of the Buenos Aires police force, in exchange for the release of Professor Armando Bravo. Bravo was a well-known figure in the labor movement and co-president of a human rights organization; his disappearance had been "officialized" when President Carter mentioned his name to Videla.[126]

As international actors began calling on the junta to be accountable, soft-liners tried to convince their opponents within the regime to adopt an image of moderation in order to be "protected from international pressure to make an accounting for the past."[127] Hard-liners' intransigence on the question of accountability was expressed by Army Deputy Chief of Staff General José Antonio Vaquero in October 1980: "In terms of the actions against terrorism, no one is permitted now nor will be permitted in the future to conduct any investigation whatsoever."[128] Yet hard-liners did concede on one issue that had proven especially divisive. They agreed to permit the IACHR to visit Argentina, thus satisfying one of the key U.S. demands. Soft-liners, in turn, who were now in charge of the Foreign Ministry, assured that the regime could control the IACHR visit and use it to its advantage.[129] Argentina's moderates therefore relied, when possible, on intraregime bargaining to control policy disputes over compliance, in contrast to the patrimonial politics, forced retirements, and rule altering that were common in Chile. Still, these moderates were interested only in appeasing international actors, not dismantling the system of repression.

All of these changes occurred against the backdrop of growing institutional divisions. In May 1978, the positions of commander in chief and president were separated organizationally, thereby splitting the military as institution (comprised of the junta) from the military as government (embodied in the presidency).[130] Although the move was portrayed publicly as an end to a period of exception, and the beginning of popular participation and convergent civil and military interests, in practice the new arrangement served to compartmentalize the armed forces further.[131] Hard-liners for their part targeted human rights activists and pressed for additional restrictions on legal protection, including the Presumption of Death Law that sought to foreclose future accountability for disappearances.[132]

In general, then, the structure of decision making in Argentina explains moderates' limited capacities to control policy debates and respond to international human rights pressure with a higher level of commitment, including why they failed to implement international norms. While moderates approved the use of state repression, a fact that the subsequent human rights trials of the military junta demonstrated, they also wanted to appease international actors with concrete gestures and public commitments. This was an uphill battle with hard-liners, who more often than not got their way.

Existing accounts are correct to note that moderates used international human rights pressure to reinforce their positions domestically and promoted human rights change. Yet what may be most interesting for understanding issues of compliance is why Argentine moderates did not undertake even more human rights commitments or attempt to implement international human rights norms, if doing so would have strengthened their domestic standing even further.

THE ROCKY ROAD TO DEMOCRACY

The conventional wisdom is that human rights pressure contributes to democratization in the long term. Human rights pressures, after all, have preceded most contemporary democratic transitions. By responding positively to human rights pressure, nondemocratic regimes may unwittingly undermine their legitimacy and create space for democratic reform. The devil, of course, is in the details. And in examining the long-term effects of human rights pressure, one key puzzle that arises is why a rights-protective, democratic regime is created *when* it is. Chile and Argentina illustrate this particular challenge. These countries democratized at different times: Argentina in the early 1980s, after only a few years of military rule, and Chile well after being in power for over a decade. Human rights pressures alone cannot explain this shift, because Chile was subject to the same pressures but democratized later. Explaining this difference in timing, or the duration of authoritarian rule, is nonetheless essential for understanding the conditions under which human rights pressures can be influential. The findings here suggest that such pressures set the stage for subsequent democratization in the Southern Cone, itself contingent on the national security context and economic environment. Personal and national security remain inextricably linked.

ENDING THE DIRTY WAR IN ARGENTINA

In the early 1980s, dominant social groups in Argentina withdrew their support from the state, specifically its policy of repression. This shift reflected new security and economic interests. On the one hand, with the state having ferociously eliminated all armed groups, the country no longer faced an internal security threat. On the other hand, the economic interests of elites were now threatened, especially in the context of an economic crisis and ongoing human rights sanctions. Confronted with these new realities, as well as enduring transnational pressure, systematic repression was no longer deemed necessary nor desirable.

Argentina's dominant groups did not favor the use of repression in 1980 and 1981, but neither did they support a full regime change at this time. Instead, they initially called for an institutional solution that would appease human rights pressure. The armed forces found this solution in the "Malvinas option," or the invasion of the British-controlled Falkland Islands. This solution, intended partly as a diversionary tactic away from human rights problems, backfired when a military debacle served as a sudden catalyst for democratization.[133] Indeed, the military's defeat in Malvinas had an enormous and immediate impact on Argentina's elite. It deflated the armed forces' iron hold over national security.

After all segments of society joined to demand their removal from power, Argentina's armed forces declared an amnesty for themselves in September 1982 (Law of National Pacification) and began to negotiate their way out of power. Raul Alfonsín, a member of the human rights movement whose campaign featured a strong human rights platform, was elected president a month later. The dirty war thus gave way to a rights-protective regime in 1983.

Without domestic pro-compliance constituencies, who bravely promoted human rights during the country's darkest days, regime change may not have taken the direction that it did. Human rights protection was integral to Argentina's democratic transition precisely because pro-compliance constituencies had forged strong transnational alliances and coalesced with a broad array of social groups domestically. Even the military's fall from grace cannot alone account for why constituencies that previously had supported the military regime now favored democratization and the protection of human rights. Indeed, groups that had supported repression and authoritarianism pushed for democratization only when security threats changed and an economic crisis magnified the defects of the regime's economic policies as well as the costs of even weak and contradictory human rights sanctions. But the fact that the regime turned to human rights norms per se was squarely the work of pro-compliance constituencies.

International human rights pressures contributed to democratization by raising the costs of human rights violations and strengthening domestic pro-compliance constituencies. These constituencies, in turn, performed a fundamentally transformative role by helping to define a viable alternative political future. Without changes in the national security context, however, it is unlikely that transnational human rights pressure alone would have produced radical democratic reform in a country of over 15,000 *desaparecidos*.

Regime Change in Chile

Although Chile also underwent an economic crisis in the early 1980s, it managed to avoid regime change until later in the decade. As detailed earlier in this chapter, Chile was different from Argentina in one important regard. Armed groups had resurfaced in 1980, engaging in sporadic but public attacks against the regime. As long as Pinochet could point to these groups as constituting an internal security threat, dominant actors in Chilean society continued to support the state's use of repression even when faced with an economic crisis.

In fact, repression intensified severely in 1983 and 1984, just as a series of massively unprecedented protests broke out throughout the country.

People were kidnapped and detained for crimes against state security; torture against political detainees was practiced systematically; due process was severely restricted, if not altogether absent, while prisoners were often held incommunicado; and the armed forces conducted massive searches and raids in Santiago. At the same time that already democratic Argentina was grappling with the human rights trials of former military leaders, the Chilean regime reopened in November 1985 the concentration camps of Pisagua and Conchi, housing about 700 people in them. Between 1981 and 1987, almost 400 people were killed, over 100,000 people were arbitrarily arrested, and more than 5,000 people were subject to torture or other cruel treatment. The human rights tragedy of the 1970s was not yet over.[134]

Despite the heavy repression, Pinochet moved in 1988 to declare a plebiscite that would launch Chile's transition to democracy. It was a period of international and domestic human rights pressure, as well as economic growth. After unexpectedly losing the plebiscite, although winning over 40 percent of the popular vote, Pinochet agreed to withdraw from power and permit democratization. Many powerful members of society did not withdraw their support from Pinochet, but for reasons discussed here, they did agree to support regime change and moved toward greater human rights protection. Indeed, in December 1989, Patricio Aylwin won a sweeping victory in presidential elections and entered office in March 1990. Commemorating the past, he gave his inaugural speech in the same National Stadium where the military regime's first victims had been publicly detained and executed before world audiences.

This democratic transition occurred on the coattails of human rights pressure, which had been mounting against Chile in the mid-1980s. Following a cycle of social protest and vicious repression in 1983 and 1984, transnational human rights pressure targeted the regime. Significantly, even the Reagan administration, which had essentially given the Pinochet regime a green light for most of the 1980s, applied pressure. U.S. policy began shifting in 1985, when the United States abstained for the first time on a $430 million loan by the Inter-American Development Bank. And in 1986, the United States took the unprecedented step of sponsoring a resolution against Chile in the CHR. In 1987, the Reagan administration further intensified its pressure, abstaining for the first time on a U.N. General Assembly vote against Chile and on three World Bank loans. The policy reversal may have reflected a combination of factors, including personnel changes within the State Department, the rise of a strong opposition in Chile, fears of a return to leftist rule in the context of heightened Cold War politics, and even a new global wave of democracy.[135]

Pinochet initially responded to this renewed pressure as he had done so in the past, by undertaking human rights commitments. He lifted the state of siege in mid-1985 but retained the state of emergency. The regime also claimed to uphold its international human rights obligations; it released certain political prisoners; and it allowed some exiles to return, all the while blaming terrorists and "subversives" for its broader actions.[136] In mid-1985, the regime went as far as to enter into a broad-based national accord, calling for but not instituting a full transition to democracy and human rights protection.

International pressure during the 1980s was critical in eliciting human rights commitments from the regime, in a way that domestic groups alone could not necessarily accomplish. After all, while domestic opposition to the regime proved crucial in mobilizing international pressure, Pinochet's regime responded to these pressures with repression. Fourteen national protests were held between 1983 and 1985. These national nonviolent protests, initially called by the Confederation of Copper Workers and supported by a "Democratic Alliance" of parties, challenged the regime openly. The regime responded with concerted arrests, injuries, and assassinations. Observers have described one such incident, for example, as a direct reaction to domestic human rights pressure: state officials sanctioned slitting the throats of three well-known community activists—José Manuel Parada, Santiago Nattino, and Manuel Guerrero—and then brutally dumped their bodies on the side of a highway.[137]

It is difficult to imagine that Pinochet and his supporters would have respected, let alone called for, the plebiscite if armed groups had been active in Chile. Armed groups had reappeared in Chile in 1980, with the pace of their activities picking up in 1983.[138] Four years later, however, armed groups showed signs of divisiveness. The MIR was split over the use of armed conflict; in 1987, one splinter group (MIR Renewal) even joined the United Left in parliamentary elections. Likewise, the Manuel Rodríguez Patriotic Front (FPMR), formed in 1983 by the Communist Party, attempted but failed to carry out an elaborate set of operations in 1986, including assassinating the president. More importantly, in 1987 the FPMR was dealt a heavy blow when CNI killed almost twenty of its members in "Operation Albania." Later that year, the Communist Party essentially confirmed its armed defeat by renouncing its insurrectionary strategy.[139] Armed opponents were no longer a viable excuse for sustained repression and authoritarian rule. Indeed, it is no coincidence that the plebiscite was proposed in 1988, a time when armed groups were all but absent from the domestic scene and international pressure was intense. Although small armed rebels would reemerge in Chile in later decades, new democratic institutions would also check the scale and magnitude of state repression.

To the extent that human rights pressures shaped democratization in Chile, this success may have depended on three conditions: armed groups had been defeated or explicitly renounced the use of force; international pressure intensified to the point where it threatened the economic interests of Chilean elites, even during a period of economic growth; and a broad spectrum of domestic actors mobilized in support of human rights and democracy. The international costs of violating human rights had therefore risen at the same time as the domestic utility of violating these norms had declined. With a strong pro-compliance constituency waiting in the wings, dominant groups in Chile hedged their bets on a rights-protective democracy.

Conclusions

The success of international and domestic human rights pressures is highly contingent, a cautionary tale of compliance or bounded optimism. Human rights pressures redefined policy options and recast policy debates, making ongoing violations illegitimate and costly. However, the timing and degree of policy changes were severely constrained by the existence of armed threats and the interests of pro-violation constituencies. This explains why so many violations persisted or reemerged even in the face of consistent human rights pressure. It also explains why the number of violations was greater in Argentina, where armed groups had figured more prominently. Certainly, armed groups on their own did not lead inexorably to state repression; but in the context of powerful domestic actors who stood to gain from these violations, and domestically institutionalized ideas about the appropriateness of such actions, armed groups provided the regime with a national security rationale for violating international norms despite human rights pressure.

State commitments also reflected these cross-cutting pressures. While growing pressure was followed by rising human rights commitments, these commitments did not represent a fundamental change in state interests. For example, legal revisions in Chile served to incorporate international human rights norms into domestic structures, only to be overridden by parallel domestic laws that legitimated violations. Likewise, when DINA was dismantled, it was merely replaced by CNI. The net result was that violations became more difficult to detect but no less real. None other than Colonel Juan Manuel Contreras, the head of DINA, was sent on a secret mission to CIA headquarters in August 1975, with the purpose of explaining "recent measures taken by the Chilean government to improve its *image* on the civil rights issue."[140] Human rights commitments were a form of self-presentation and influence more than anything else.

The same is true of Argentina's responses, which were attempts to sway international actors. For example, although observers have often depicted Argentina's decision to invite Amnesty International as evidence of changing interests, a closer look at the background to the visit suggests otherwise. The actual visit was marred by government interference in the group's work, a disinformation campaign launched in the local media, and retaliation against people who met with the delegation. The possible benefits of using Amnesty International's visit to control international pressure may have weighed more heavily for the Argentine junta than the failure of Amnesty International's visit to Chile a few years earlier. According to a Foreign Ministry official, the aim of the visit was to get the world "to understand our situation." As another official later admitted, "If the government thought it useful, or controllable, it had a misjudged or incomplete picture of the mood outside the country."[141] Argentina's national leaders were creating an image of compliance without actually complying. The state's responses were internally consistent but complex and, ultimately, self-serving.

In the end, human rights pressures had a differential impact on state violations and commitments, as evidenced in policy debates. International pressure exacerbated regime splits, but mostly over the question of commitment. That the state had to sacrifice personal for national security itself was not disputed. Subsequent commitments, moreover, reflected leaders' organizational capacity to control regime disputes and appease international actors; the presence of moderates was essential, but their impact still depended on the structure of decision making. Chile's cohesive structure helps to explain why a hard-liner implemented international norms extensively, compared to the fragmented structure in Argentina that tied the hands of moderate regime leaders. The military's historically stronger role in Argentina certainly may have been important in shaping hard-liners' interests or conceptions of what they stood to lose by committing to international norms. The military's corporate interests, however, do not clarify sufficiently how regime leaders negotiated internal disputes over time.

Alternatively, one might argue that Argentina was able to resist human rights pressure to a greater degree than Chile because it was less dependent internationally. In particular, Argentina's relations with the Soviet Union may have given it more options.[142] This overlooks several points, however. First, while Argentina retained its relations with the Eastern bloc, its trade with the Soviet Union did not increase significantly until after 1979. Second, Argentina's international financial autonomy was not high, a sector that was critical for the Argentine economy.[143] Third, much evidence indicates, as this study shows, that Argentine decision makers were in fact concerned about international human rights pressure and that resistance itself was partly a means of influencing international actors.

Nor is it likely that state responses were the product of mimicry. The Argentine dirty war started in 1976, when the worst violations in Chile were coming to an end. The Argentine junta, moreover, repeatedly refrained from associating itself with the Chilean regime despite concerted efforts by the latter. If anything, documentary evidence shows that Argentina wanted to avoid the international pressure to which Chile had been subjected. This was the basis of several moves by Argentina: the decision to engage in clandestine repression, efforts to avoid a political rapprochement with Chile in spite of the latter's efforts, and its strategy of blocking its human rights situation from being institutionalized within the United Nations.

Chile's historically strong legalistic tradition is no more adequate in explaining that state's responses to human rights pressure. Arguably, such attachment to the rule of law and Pinochet's own constitutionalism could explain why the regime implemented international norms. Yet it is also true that Argentina's government was itself attentive to legalism, evident for example, in its rhetorical responses to human rights pressure. Nor is it fair to say that Argentina lacked any legalistic foundations. Legalism may account for Chile's extensive institutional changes, but it cannot explain the complete absence of these changes in Argentina, a regime that was equally concerned with appeasing international actors.

The limits of human rights pressure are also evident in the transition to democracy. Human rights pressures were significant in defining an alternative political future and making ongoing noncompliance costly. However, in both Chile and Argentina, regime change did not occur until armed opposition groups no longer threatened the regime visibly. Personal security remained hostage to the national security context; and ironically, human rights reform ultimately hinged on the success of prior state *repression.*

The story told here complements the dominant model of human rights change. Kathryn Sikkink, in particular, has described Argentina's responses to international human rights pressure during the dirty war as moving along a continuum, from denial and rejection of international legitimacy to lip service and "cosmetic cooperation" to eventual change in domestic repressive practices. Sikkink nonetheless admits that "[a]lthough these stages progressed in a roughly chronological manner, there was continual overlap and backtracking."[144] My argument is that the overlap and backtracking of these state responses was the rule rather than the exception.

Despite the gap between human rights commitments and violations, commitments were influential in at least two important ways. First, human rights commitments directly improved personal security, as evident in the release of political detainees. The role of even hypocritical human rights commitments in improving the quality of individual lives should not be overlooked. Second, human rights commitments may have been related indirectly to actual reform, insofar as they "fed back" to affect future international pressure. This indirect effect was more complicated. On the one hand, international pressure led to monitoring, which facilitated subsequent international pressure, and to strengthening the domestic political opposition, which also made further international pressure possible and was significant for later democratization. On the other hand, high levels of human rights commitment had a more uneven impact on international pressure. While a few international actors used these responses to illustrate the gap between the regime's public image and its practices, foreign governments often took human rights commitments at face value.

Treating state responses to international human rights pressure as if they reflected changes in state interest may have been partially detrimental in the end. The evidence suggests that if foreign governments had interpreted changes in compliance as attempts at manipulation, and had used this knowledge as the basis of further pressure, the effects of international pressure may have been greater. Instead, international actors such as the United States applied ongoing (if somewhat contradictory) pressures but failed to question the limits of state responses, reinforcing the view that such responses were effective appeasement strategies. Even changes in rhetoric mattered. Observers at the time repeatedly mistook these regimes' words as evidence of their changing interests, and states that applied human rights pressure placed some stock in stated commitments to international norms. In a 1976 debate in the European Parliament, for example, parliamentarians noted that Argentina's "General Videla has since the takeover repeatedly stated in public his respect for individual freedoms and human rights."[145]

The impact of human rights pressures is ultimately limited by the incentives and ideas that push states to violate international norms, including any apparent threats to national security. Had international actors understood this pathology more fully, they may have been able to overcome it. More consistent international pressure would have led at a minimum to greater public commitments, sometimes entailing concrete human rights improvements. And by defining a viable alternative and raising the costs of repression, international pressure may also have helped to accelerate the dynamics of democratization. Ironically, however, the Chilean and Argentine regimes' responses had the effect they were intended to have on international audiences, while human rights pressure against these authoritarian states was less effective than it might have been.

Chapter 5

State Responses in Global Perspective

Two decades after military coups erupted in Chile and Argentina, international human rights norms had undergone phenomenal transformation, leading some observers to declare a change in "world time."[1] More human rights treaties existed, a critical mass of states had ratified these treaties, and transnational networks of activists mobilized on behalf of human rights victims everywhere. Despite deep pockets of resistance in this post–Cold War world, international human rights norms appeared to be acquiring global legitimacy. World attention turned increasingly to human rights abuses associated with ethnic strife and civil war, while "humanitarian intervention" became a common fixture in the toolkit of international actors. These trends were tied closely to a worldwide wave of democratization, the end of the Cold War, and broader processes of globalization and technological change. When one considers that in the 1990s two war crimes tribunals and a treaty instituting an international criminal court emerged, the decade appears as a watershed for human rights progress.

Indeed, the 1990s should offer a relatively easy test for assessing the impact of international human rights pressure. I use quantitative techniques to see how well the book's argument holds up over time and across a large number of cases. Are human rights pressures differentially associated with state commitments versus violations in the post-Cold War period? The data include 172 countries over a five-year period in the 1990s (1992–96).[2] A series of mini case studies then sketches why human rights pressures led to human rights reform in Eastern Europe and South Africa but not yet in China, Israel, or Cuba. Returning briefly to the Southern Cone, the chapter concludes with a discussion of the limits of democratization in shaping human rights compliance.

Pressures from Above and Below

It can be difficult to isolate the impact of different types of human rights pressure. For example, is unilateral pressure more effective than multilateral pressure? Does the impact of international and domestic human rights pressures differ? Statistical methods permit us to disaggregate these differential effects, even if subtle political demands cannot always be quantified readily. My goal is to complement the case studies, probing more fully the relationship between specific human rights pressures and diverse state responses.

All states are subject to some degree of international human rights pressure, or demands that they comply with international norms. Although only some states face actual sanctions, all states confront normative pressures for human rights compliance. These pressures can vary in intensity, and they can derive from both state and nonstate actors. Consequently, I examine here the effects of several types of human rights pressure: sanctions applied by the United States, multilateral sanctions, interstate contagion (regional and global), pressure from international NGOs, as well as pressure from domestic human rights groups.

In theory, sanctions are potentially the most costly forms of international human rights pressure.[3] They reflect seriousness on the part of the sender, because sanctions raise the costs of noncompliance for both the sender and the target state. Not surprisingly, policy debates about human rights pressure often revolve precisely around the question of whether sanctions, versus other types of pressure, should be imposed.

Sanctions refer here to economic sanctions in which one of the sender's principal stated foreign policy goals is human rights reform. More generally, an economic sanction entails "the deliberate, government-inspired withdrawal, or threat of withdrawal, of customary trade or financial relations," including in military transactions.[4] After the Cold War, these sanctions were construed in the broadest terms possible. Indeed, the global prominence of human rights issues in the 1990s inserted human rights expectations into most sanctions packages. In some cases, human rights reform was the overt and overwhelming purpose of the sanctions (e.g., Guatemala and Nigeria); in other instances, human rights demands were implicit in sanctions targeting democratization (e.g., Cambodia and Sierra Leone) or civil war (e.g., the former Yugoslavia and Liberia). Table 11 summarizes the human rights goals of economic sanctions applied or in effect against more than fifty countries in the 1990s, a period dubbed the "sanctions decade."[5] It does not matter that international actors may have had motives other than human rights advancement in applying these sanctions. Human rights protection was a public rationale for the application or continued application of sanctions in virtually all of these cases, presumably giving target states a reason to adjust their human rights practices accordingly.

I focus on three major issues regarding the impact of sanctions. First, I consider the role of *unilateral* sanctions, namely those applied by the

TABLE 11. ECONOMIC SANCTIONS WITH HUMAN RIGHTS GOALS, 1990s

Target Country	Principal Sender	Years	Human Rights Goal
Afghanistan (Taliban)	United States, United Nations	1999–	Broad conditions
Albania	Greece	1994–95	Jailed ethnic leaders
Algeria	European Union	1992–94	Democracy
Angola (UNITA)	United States, United Nations	1993–	Civil war
Burundi	East African Members of Organization of African Unity	1996–99	Democracy
Cambodia (Khmer Rouge)	United Nations, United States, Germany	1992–	Democracy
Cameroon	United States	1992–98	General human rights
Chile	United States	1975–	General human rights
China	United States	1989–	General human rights
Colombia	United States	1996–98	General human rights
Cuba	United States	1960–present	Broad conditions
El Salvador	United States	1990–93	General human rights
Equatorial Guinea	European Union, Spain	1992–	General human rights
Estonia	Russia	1992–99	Minority rights
Ethiopia	United States	1977–92	General human rights
Fiji	India, Australia, New Zealand	1987–98	Democracy
Gambia	United States, European Union, Japan	1994–98	Democracy
Guatemala	United States	1977–	General human rights
Guatemala	United States, European Union	1993	Democracy
Haiti	United States	1987–90	General human rights
Haiti	United States, United Nations	1991–94	Democracy
Indonesia	United States, United Kingdom, Netherlands	1991–	General human rights
Iran	United States	1984–	Broad conditions
Iraq	United States	1980–	Broad conditions
Iraq	United States, United Nations	1990–	Broad conditions
Kazakhstan	Russia	1993–96	Ethnic minority
Kenya	Western donors	1990–93	General human rights
Latvia	Russia	1992–98	Minority rights
Lebanon	United States	1987–97	Broad conditions
Liberia	United States, United Nations	1992–98	Civil war

(continued)

TABLE 11. (*Continued*)

Target Country	Principal Sender	Years	Human Rights Goal
Libya	United States	1978–	Broad conditions
Malawi	United States, United Kingdom	1992–93	General human rights
Nicaragua	United States	1992–95	Broad conditions
Niger	France, United States	1996–97	Democracy
Nigeria	United States, European Union	1993–98	General human rights
North Korea	United States, United Nations	1950– 1993–1994	Broad conditions
Pakistan	United States	1979–	Broad sanctions
Paraguay	United States, Mercosur	1996	Preventing coup
Peru	United States	1991–95	General human rights
Romania	United States	1983–93	General human rights
Rwanda	United Nations, United States	1994–95	Reduce civil violence
Sierra Leone	United Nations, Economic Community of West African States	1997–99	Democracy
Somalia	United States, United Kingdom	1988–	General human rights
South Africa	United Nations	1962–94	Apartheid regime
South Africa	United States	1985–91	Apartheid regime
Sudan	United States	1989–	General human rights
Sudan	United States	1993–	Religious persecution
Suriname	Netherlands	1982–91	General human rights
Syria	United States	1986–	Broad conditions
Thailand	United States	1991–92	Restore regime
Togo	United States, France, Germany	1992–94	General human rights
Turkey	Greece and European Union	1986–	General human rights
Turkey	European Union	1995	General human rights
Turkmenistan	Russia	1991–93	Minority rights
USSR	United States, European Community	1991	Democracy
Vietnam	United States	1954–98	Broad conditions
USSR	United States	1975–94	Right to emigration
Yugoslavia (Serbia/ Montenegro)	United Nations	1991–	Civil war
Zaire	United States, Belgium, France	1990–97	Democracy
Zambia	Western countries	1996–98	General human rights

Source: Adapted from "Chronological Summary of Economic Sanctions for Foreign Policy Goals, 1914–99" (Washington, D.C.: Institute for International Economics, n.d.). Available at http://www.iie.com/research/topics/sanctions/sanctions-timeline.cfm.

United States. Since the United States is the hegemonic actor in the post–Cold War international human rights regime, any pressure it applies could prove critical.[6] Second, even if unilateral pressure is important, *multilateral* human rights pressure also might be essential. Multilateral pressure consists here of more than one government imposing sanctions or sanctions applied by an international (or regional) organization.[7] For both U.S. and multilateral pressure, I examine all countries in the world between 1992 and 1996, recording whether pressure applied by a particular actor was present (a value of 1) or absent (0) in a given year. I also lag by one year both unilateral and multilateral sanctions to ensure that they preceded, and thus could exert a causal influence over, state behavior.[8] Third to introduce a more dynamic element to the analysis, I record the total number of years for which sanctions were imposed on a country, or the duration of the sanctions. If the costliness of sanctions matters, their influence should cumulate over time.[9]

States can also persuade their counterparts to accept international human rights norms through nonmaterial means, including their own example. For instance, Beth Simmons has argued that a state's willingness to commit to human rights norms is shaped profoundly by the extent to which countries in a particular region are committed to these norms.[10] Presumably, states in close proximity to one another will be more likely to mimic each other's behavior, especially when a critical mass of states in the region acts comparably. According to this scenario, state compliance is the result primarily of contagion, as international norms diffuse across a region or even globally. Although contagion has been used mostly to explain states' commitment to international human rights norms, nothing suggests that it cannot be applied to explain violations as well, because both "good" and "bad" norms could diffuse. I evaluate here the impact of both regional and global contagion.[11]

Beyond states, international nonstate actors and transnational networks are perhaps the principal carriers of international norms. As detailed in previous chapters, these actors forge alliances with one another and apply normative pressure on states; they define appropriate standards of behavior and persuade states to comply. For target states confronting intense external scrutiny, the publicity campaigns generated by international nonstate actors can make compliance more appealing. States facing more social pressure from international human rights NGOs should therefore be more willing to comply. I measure INGO pressure in terms of the number of nongovernmental groups that target a given country from abroad.[12]

In addition to international sources of pressure, *domestic human rights groups* can be powerful agents of change. As representatives of civil society, domestic groups can organize resistance against a noncompliant state and provide a crucial link to broader transnational movements (see Chapter 2). In general, domestic human rights pressure should lead to improved human rights conditions. I measure domestic pressure in terms of the number of human rights groups (logged) within a country. This variable was coded based on data from the *Human Rights Internet Reporter: Masterlist*, a source underutilized by human rights researchers.[13] The number of domestic human rights groups ranged from zero in countries such as Armenia and Qatar to 210 in the Philippines and 685 in the United States. On average, most countries had approximately 29 human rights organizations.

Sources of Human Rights Behavior

How are human rights pressures in fact related to particular state responses? To what degree does human rights behavior reflect other factors, including prior violations, armed conflict, and democratic governance? Interstate contagion, economic development, or trade openness? And how are all of these factors related to human rights commitments versus violations? I address these questions using probit analysis with robust standard errors.[14] Including robust standard errors protects against overestimating the likelihood of statistical significance, a problem arising when cross-sectional time series data are used.[15] Measurement issues for all variables used in this analysis are summarized in the Appendix.

In examining human rights commitments and violations, I evaluate the role of several factors: international and domestic human rights pressures, armed conflict and regime type, as well as various control variables. Regarding human rights pressures, as detailed, I evaluate separately the following factors: U.S. human rights sanctions, multilateral sanctions, the duration of both types of sanctions, regional and global interstate contagion, INGO pressure, and pressure exerted by domestic human rights groups. Additionally, I consider the impact of *armed conflict* and *regime type*, two potentially significant factors that are central to this book's broader argument. Armed conflict refers here to the use of armed force between a group and a national government. I measure armed conflict as a dummy variable, depending on whether the conflict resulted in at least twenty-five deaths.[16] I do not differentiate more fully among varying levels of conflict intensity, because the CIRI data used to measure human rights violations already takes numbers of deaths into account. Armed conflict was present in about one-fifth of all the cases.[17]

As Chapter 2 discusses, regime type can also be an important determinant of human rights behavior. Not only do pro-violation constituencies have less institutionalized access to decision making in democracies, but the normative appropriateness of using repression is much lower than it is in more autocratic systems. I measure regime type using standard Polity IV data, and its twenty-one-point index estimating the relative degree of democracy and autocracy. The assumption is that more democratic regimes will be more prone to comply with international human rights norms, showing both higher levels of commitment and lower levels of violation.

To control for other potentially relevant factors, I include the role of *trade openness, economic development, emerging democracies,* and *prior human rights conditions.* A country that is more open to foreign trade (i.e., one that is more economically interdependent with other countries) should have a greater incentive to respond positively to human rights pressure. Leaders of less open countries, in contrast, should be more impervious to the costs associated with human rights pressure and therefore less likely to comply with international norms.[18] Economic development is another factor that may affect human rights practices, although its effects could be mixed. On the one hand, research on state repression suggests that less economically developed countries will experience more domestic instability, arising from unmet social needs, and will therefore be more likely to violate rights of physical integrity. On the other hand, a realist argument that focuses on national economic power predicts that weaker states will be less able to resist human rights pressures and thus more likely to comply with international norms.[19]

Recent research also suggests that newer democracies may be more likely to commit to international human rights norms. According to this republican liberal argument, national leaders commit to a human rights regime as a way of reducing the domestic uncertainty that characterizes and threatens emerging democracies.[20] Thus far, the democratic lock-in proposition has been tested to explain the formation of Europe's human rights regime and why states ratify major human rights treaties. Relying on Polity IV data, I extend this reasoning to examine whether different state responses are affected by the emerging nature of a democracy.[21]

Finally, the recursive effects of human rights behavior may be substantial in explaining a state's responses to pressure.[22] Past violations could exert a lingering influence, so that noncompliant states are more likely to continue violating international norms, a finding that already enjoys strong quantitative support. Likewise, prior commitments should elicit greater future commitments, as social groups take their cue from state commitments to mobilize and apply further pressure. Put differently, committing to international norms can open discursive space and entrap state actors—through a path-dependent logic—into undertaking even more commitments. To control for these possibilities, I include in the analysis both a state's score on the Physical Integrity Index lagged by one year (to measure past violations) and the total number of major human rights treaties that a country had ratified by 1992 (to measure prior commitments).[23]

Findings and Implications

The findings are numerous (Tables 12 and 13), suggesting how and why states respond to human rights pressures in varied ways.[24] For example, they confirm that human rights pressures are most closely associated

TABLE 12. SOURCES OF HUMAN RIGHTS COMMITMENT, 1990S: PROBIT ANALYSIS

Variable	Ratification	Monitoring	Leniency	Implementation	Accountability
U.S. sanctions (T-1)	.07 (.36)	−.08 (.12)	−.16 (.12)	.32 (.11)***	.23 (.12)**
Duration of U.S. sanctions	−.01 (.02)	.00 (.01)	.02 (.01)***	−.01 (.01)	−.01 (.01)
Multilateral sanctions (T-1)	−.20 (.47)	−.09 (.36)	.27 (.13)**	−.21 (.08)	−.24 (.10)
Duration of multilateral sanctions	.02 (.03)	.31 (.16)**	−.01 (.01)	.04 (.02)***	.02 (.01)*
Economic development	−.02 (.04)	.02 (.01)	−.01 (.01)	.01 (.01)	−.01 (.01)
Trade openness	.01 (.03)	−.04 (.01)	.03 (.01)***	.02 (.01)**	−.03 (.01)
Emerging democracies	−.26 (.28)	.19 (.10)**	.01 (.12)	.14 (.11)*	.21 (.10)**
Armed conflict[a]	.00 (.25)	.26 (.07)***	.09 (.08)	.16 (.07)**	.00 (.07)
INGOs	.02 (.02)*	.00 (.01)	.01 (.01)*	−.01 (.00)	.00 (.00)
Regional contagion	1.98 (.41)***	1.09 (.25)***	.79 (.24)***	1.17 (.24)***	1.06 (.18)***
Global contagion	.29 (.92)	.57 (.50)	.73 (.34)**	.02 (.49)	.46 (.81)
Democracy	.02 (.02)*	−.01 (.01)*	−.02 (.01)***	−.00 (.00)	.00 (.01)
NGOs (log)	.00 (.06)	.07 (.02)***	.03 (.02)	.03 (.02)*	.06 (.02)***
Prior commitments	−.23 (.04)	.02 (.02)*	.01 (.02)	.01 (.01)	−.01 (.01)
Past violations	−.03 (.05)	.01 (.01)	.02 (.02)	.03 (.01)**	.00 (.01)
N	551	499	494	494	494
Pseudo R²	.17	.21	.23	.11	.17
Prob > chi²	0. > 0000	0. > 0000	0. > 0000	0. > 0000	0. > 0000
Log Likelihood	−190.20	−269.47	−264.92	−278.71	−282.65

Note: Robust standard errors are in parentheses. The ratification model is run using ordered probit analysis. All other commitments are analyzed using standard probit analysis and reporting slope coefficients.
[a] A two-tailed test of significance is used for this variable.
* Significant at .1. ** Significant at .05. *** Significant at .01.

TABLE 13. SOURCES OF HUMAN RIGHTS VIOLATIONS, 1990s: PROBIT ANALYSIS

Variable	Physical Integrity Index	Disappearances	Political Killings	Political Imprisonment	Torture	Change in PII
U.S. sanctions (T-1)	-.05 (.20)	-.23 (.26)	-.18 (.26)	-.01 (.28)	.28 (.25)	.00 (.09)
Duration of U.S. sanctions	.02 (.01)	.02 (.01)	.03 (.02)	-.00 (.01)	.00 (.01)	-.00 (.01)
Multilateral sanctions (T-1)	.27 (.26)	.66 (.45)	-.02 (.33)	.72 (.35)	-.31 (.30)	.05 (.12)
Duration of multilateral sanctions	-.03 (.02)*	-.11 (.09)*	-.02 (.03)	-.06 (.04)*	.06 (.06)	-.00 (.01)
Economic development[a]	-.06 (.03)**	-.02 (.04)	-.04 (.03)	-.02 (.03)	-.01 (.03)	.00 (.01)
Trade openness	-.05 (.02)***	-.07 (.03)**	-.06 (.03)**	-.04 (.03)*	-.04 (.02)*	.01 (.01)
Emerging democracies	.05 (.19)	.02 (.27)	.11 (.27)	.46 (.21)**	-.23 (.18)	.06 (.09)
Armed conflict	.63 (.15)***	.68 (.17)***	.71 (.18)***	.34 (.18)***	.20 (.18)	-.09 (.05)**
INGOs	.01 (.01)	.01 (.01)	.01 (.01)	-.01 (.01)	.00 (.01)	-.00 (.00)
Regional contagion	.24 (.06)***	1.84 (.57)***	1.50 (.24)***	.86 (.21)***	.82 (.22)***	-.00 (.03)
Global contagion	.82 (.70)	-1.04 (2.03)	.45 (1.12)	2.08 (1.15)*	1.75 (1.55)	-.43 (.27)
Democracy	-.03 (.01)***	.00 (.01)	.01 (.01)	-.08 (.01)***	-.00 (.01)	.01 (.00)**
NGOs (log)	.10 (.04)**	.00 (.06)	.07 (.05)	.24 (.05)	.02 (.04)	-.03 (.02)**
Prior commitments	-.01 (.03)	.07 (.04)**	-.03 (.03)	-.05 (.03)*	-.00 (.03)	.00 (.01)
Past violations	.37 (.03)***	.27 (.04)***	.27 (.04)***	.22 (.03)***	.28 (.04)***	.09 (.01)***
N	549	550	550	549	550	452
Pseudo R²	.24	.30	.32	.33	.24	.16
Prob>chi²	0.>0000	0.>0000	0.>0000	0.>0000	0.>0000	0.>0000
Log Likelihood	-875.15	-262.01	-386.44	-387.77	-444.51	-203.47

Note: Robust standard errors are in parentheses. Change in PII refers to whether an improvement in the Physical Integrity Index occurs from one year to the next; this model is run using standard probit analysis and reporting slope coefficients. All other violations are analyzed using ordered probit analysis.

[a] A two-tailed test of significance is used for this variable.

* Significant at .1. ** Significant at .05. *** Significant at .01.

with improvements in state commitment, not in violations. And, as revealed in the case studies, improvements in human rights violations tend to depend on the absence of armed conflict, just as democratic governance and lower violations go hand in hand. Although the analysis tested for interaction effects, these are not included in the summary tables because they proved insignificant.[25]

Descriptively, some key observations are in order. Although personal integrity violations were frequent in the 1990s, most states bothered to undertake some human rights commitments. The most common type of abuse was torture (present in 81 percent of the cases), followed by political imprisonment (58 percent), extrajudicial killings (51 percent), and disappearances (25 percent).[26] On the side of commitments, states responded with at least one type of human rights commitment almost 90 percent of the time. Yet in the vast majority of even these cases (65 percent), countries still responded with only one or two forms of commitment in a given year. The most common type of commitment was leniency, whereby states corrected particular instances of abuse, followed by human rights monitoring. These broad trends beg the question of why state responses varied as they did.

INTERNATIONAL FACTORS

The most striking international-level finding concerns the significance of regional contagion, which was related to *all* state responses. Even in cases in which the role of material calculations could not be discounted—leniency and implementation—state behavior appeared to be regionally driven.[27] Furthermore, regional contagion increased the likelihood of human rights violations, suggesting that states also mimic internationally illegitimate actions that are deemed regionally appropriate. These findings confirm and extend Beth Simmons's previous research linking regional commitments to treaty ratification.

Regional contagion proved in fact to be substantially more significant than global contagion, which was associated with only two types of state behavior: leniency and political imprisonment. A close look at the diffusion of these commitments, moreover, suggests a normative dynamic. States' willingness to act with leniency was also tied to pressure from INGOs, precisely those actors equipped to link global normative commitment to state behavior.[28] And of the four human rights violations examined, political imprisonment is coincidentally the one with the weakest normative taboo, making it a stronger candidate for global diffusion.[29]

The effects of coercive sanctions on human rights behavior were in turn mixed. First, sanctions were more significant in eliciting human rights commitments than improving violations. Sanctions helped to explain all forms of state commitment, with the exception of treaty ratification.[30] And although they were associated with lower levels of disappearance and political imprisonment, these effects were rather weak. Second, the duration of multilateral sanctions was the single most important sanctions criterion. States subject to long-standing multilateral sanctions were more likely to permit human rights monitors, implement international norms, practice accountability, and at least to some extent, engage in fewer violations.[31]

On balance, these findings call into question the effectiveness of relying on economic coercion to target human rights *violations*. Not only was the impact of sanctions on violations minimal, but this influence also depended on the duration of the sanctions.[32] And as other studies have noted, duration itself can be costly for the sender, just as it can increase the risk of unintended humanitarian consequences in the target state.[33] The role of economic coercion more generally is further undermined when one considers the insignificance of national economic power: weaker states (i.e., those presumably most vulnerable to external coercion) were no more likely to accept international human rights norms than stronger ones.

It is nonetheless possible that a sanction's effects depend on a country's openness to foreign trade. Trade openness, after all, was associated predictably with lower levels of violation, across all types of abuse, just as it led to greater norm implementation and more leniency. To test the potentially mediating role of trade, I created an interaction term capturing the joint effects of sanctions and trade openness.[34] Yet in no case (except norm implementation) did trade openness magnify the impact of economic sanctions.[35] Even on its own, moreover, the effects of trade need to be put into their proper context. First, the direction of causality may not be what it appears, because more-compliant states may also be less subject to trade restrictions. Second, even if trade openness and human rights compliance are related, this still does not take into account the fuller range of conditions explaining human rights practices, as discussed later.

DOMESTIC FACTORS

According to the evidence, domestic factors can also shape state responses to human rights pressure. Regime type was associated predictably with human rights abuses, as more autocratic polities engaged in greater personal integrity violations, especially political imprisonment. Poor economic development resulted in greater violations of physical integrity too, though this effect was far less pronounced.[36] And extending Moravscik's findings about democratic lock-in, the analysis reveals that emerging democracies were more likely to undertake certain human rights commitments (accountability, implementation, and monitoring).

Additionally, armed conflict was significant in explaining all cases of abuse, except torture. Although the absence of a link between armed conflict and torture may seem striking, the case studies point to a possible explanation: national security threats provide states with a public rationale to violate human rights. Once the threat is eliminated, violations that are tied most visibly to the state's security (those depriving people of life and, to a lesser extent, freedom of movement) have diminishing returns. In this regard, the security gains associated with torture, which essentially deprives people of their human dignity, are far less clear; torture is therefore more likely to persist as a form of social control, even in the absence of armed conflict. This may also be why torture and political imprisonment remained the most widespread violations in the 1990s.[37]

The evidence further suggests that these domestic factors had differential effects, as state leaders looked to appease competing domestic and foreign constituencies. Accordingly, emerging democracies not only were more prone to making commitments but also were more likely to hold political prisoners, an internationally "palatable" abuse that could reduce domestic instability. Similar cross-cutting dynamics are evident among states experiencing armed conflict, which engaged in a high level of violations but also accepted human rights monitors and moved to implement international norms. Likewise, relatively democratic regimes were both less likely to violate human rights norms and more likely to commit to them, namely by ratifying human rights treaties.[38]

Domestic pressure itself was influential, a finding that is significant because the effects of domestic human rights NGOs have been documented almost exclusively in case studies.[39] This analysis finds a link between nonstate actors and human rights commitments (accountability, implementation, and monitoring). What remains uncertain is their causal role, because a reverse logic is also possible: state commitments create a political space in which domestic nonstate groups can mobilize. But even if state commitments facilitate social mobilization, this does not prevent NGOs from having more dynamic effects, such as exhorting states to strengthen prior commitments.[40] By defining appropriate behaviors, nonstate groups may affect what states do, even if they cannot explain fully why they do it.

What domestic NGOs do not appear to influence is the level of human rights violations, at least not directly. In fact, a closer look at the analysis reveals the possibility of more indirect effects. Countries with higher numbers of NGOs were more likely to violate human rights, especially by holding political prisoners. Perhaps this type of repressive behavior compels social groups to mobilize and challenge the state; and, in a subsequent "boomerang" effect, these activists enter into transnational alliances and lobby powerful actors to pressure their home countries further.[41]

If international human rights pressure has to compete with a countervailing set of domestic conditions, it also has to contend with the path-dependent nature of the state's past practices. As other studies have shown, prior violations can leave a strong legacy.[42] Indeed, past violations increased the future likelihood of all types of state abuse, although their role in accounting for future commitments appears more modest.[43] Whether past commitments themselves shape future behavior is a different matter, one tapping into a broader debate about the effects of human rights treaties.[44] In this analysis, states that had ratified more treaties were also more inclined to accept human rights monitors. This may be axiomatic, because treaty acceptance often entails verification procedures. More importantly, treaty acceptance was related to lower levels of political imprisonment. This might be explained by the fact that low political imprisonment is also linked closely to democratic governance, which in turn enhances the likelihood of treaty ratification.

To consider more directly the possibility that human rights pressure leads to *changes* in state violation, I reran the analysis to explain annual changes in behavior. After recoding the Physical Integrity Index based on whether the level of violations improved from one year to the next (1 = improvement, 0 = deterioration or no improvement), no form of human rights pressure was found to be statistically significant. Even when controlling for the fact that past violators have more room to improve, the only factors related to human rights improvements were armed conflict and regime type.[45] (See Table 13.) Physical integrity violations declined, therefore, only when armed conflict was absent and under relatively democratic regimes. Taken in conjunction with the case studies, the evidence strongly suggests that improving human rights practices depends on a decline in armed conflict and a rise in democratization.

POLICY LESSONS

These findings raise a related set of policy implications. First, given the impressive role of regional contagion, international actors should devise more concerted means of targeting regions, including by supporting regional institutions and mechanisms. Although regional support for human rights norms may not eradicate violations, it may compel states to commit publicly to international norms.

Second, any manipulation of international costs and benefits should be sensitive to the broader normative and domestic contexts. For example, pressure short of economic coercion can change state commitments, without incurring as many costs or exacting an unintended humanitarian toll. And when sanctions are used, multilateral sanctions are likely to be more effective than unilateral ones. Furthermore, as long as domestic instability is left unchecked, no amount of economic coercion or trade openness will eliminate countervailing pressures on states to use repression and violate human rights (e.g., armed conflict and nondemocratic rule).[46] Whether coercive sanctions are applied or free trade is fostered, international actors should concurrently promote democratization, conflict resolution, and the demilitarization of target states.

Third, because countries with robust human rights groups are more likely to undertake human rights commitments, it pays to strengthen these groups. As the case studies here and elsewhere have shown, domestic groups can be critical in mobilizing international pressure, especially by providing crucial information and symbolic testimony about violations. There should be no illusion, however, that the mere existence of such groups will reduce violations.

Fourth, the human rights commitments that often follow human rights pressure should be encouraged, even if they are not always the harbingers of sustainable change. These commitments can have indirect effects, by opening domestic political spaces, empowering activists, or mobilizing transnational networks, just as they can set a valuable precedent for future state behavior. And at a minimum, some human rights commitments (e.g., cases of leniency) may help save or at least improve individual lives.

Fifth, in evaluating the effectiveness of human rights pressure, it is crucial to disaggregate different state commitments and types of violation. Under no circumstances should observers assume a priori that a state that releases political prisoners, ratifies a treaty, or incorporates human rights norms into its domestic laws will soon improve the full range of its human rights practices. In fact, an improvement in any single response does not necessitate more pervasive or long-term reform, because different human rights behaviors can be propelled by distinct causal logics. Violations themselves can end only when the entrenched domestic conditions that give rise to them cease to exist.[47]

These findings and recommendations, despite their limitations, serve to extend the contours of human rights research. Because case studies cannot disentangle fully the effects of different types of pressure on distinct state responses, examining empirically the impact of human rights pressure on state responses helps to fill this important gap. At the same time, the analysis presented here reflects the state of the world only in the first half of the 1990s. Compared to earlier decades, human rights pressures became much more commonplace in the post-Cold War world, although states still faced pressures for compliance alongside powerful incentives to violate international norms. Forced to respond to these cross-cutting pressures, states continued to respond in multifaceted and often seemingly contradictory ways. Indeed, the first years of the new millennium, dominated by the global "war on terror" and a genocide in Darfur that the world watched silently, confirmed ongoing clashes between personal and national security.

Human Rights "Success" Stories

Two of the most dramatic human rights success stories occurred in the early 1990s: Eastern Europe and South Africa. Although both are relative achievements, they do differ in terms of the particular configuration of factors that led to a rights-protective regime.[48] Just as the decision to violate an international norm is shaped by security threats, pro-violation constituencies, and rules of exception, the decision to create a rights-protective regime is affected by a parallel set of conditions: (1) a national security threat is absent or the state is not capable of providing national security; (2) the economic interests of domestic elites are threatened by norm violations; *and* (3) the demands of pro-compliance constituencies, which define an alternative to domestic rules of exception, enjoy broad societal support. International human rights influence cannot succeed in creating rights-protective regimes until all three conditions are satisfied. Indeed, this explains why human rights reform can take so long to achieve.

EASTERN EUROPE

The nature of human rights change in Eastern Europe was more protracted than that of the Southern Cone. Whereas Chile's authoritarian regime was in place for not even two decades, the communist regimes of Eastern Europe lasted almost half a century. In recent years, observers have credited the international human rights norms embedded in the 1975 Helsinki Final Act as playing a decisive if partial role in the demise of communist rule and the nonviolent transition to rights-protective regimes across the region.[49]

Daniel Thomas in his path-breaking account, for example, has emphasized the role played by social movements and state identity. Thomas argues that international human rights norms established by the Helsinki Final Act in 1975 led ultimately to the demise of communism. If so, why did the Helsinki norms take over a full decade to elicit regime change? According to Thomas, international and domestic norms, identities, and interests clashed after 1975, leading to a protracted period of contradictory state practices. Regime change and human rights compliance were forthcoming only after a substantial number of domestic elites came to identify with the Helsinki norms. Thomas's account of human rights change in Eastern Europe is quite persuasive, especially his explanation of why domestic social actors mobilized. In terms of *state* behavior, however, this kind of identity-driven argument makes two important leaps of logic.

First, the argument assumes that state identity preceded rather than followed regime change, perhaps underestimating the influence of domestic institutions. Even if individuals within a regime identified with international society, domestic institutional structures still exerted a powerful legacy, defining appropriate courses of action and providing key constituencies with access to decision making. As long as Eastern European regimes remained nondemocratic, at least some pro-violation constituencies continued to hold formal power, and ongoing human rights violations were deemed appropriate means of social control. Despite changes in the identity of individual Eastern European elites or limited political reform, the state—as an institutional actor—may not have identified with international human rights norms until *after* the collapse of communist rule.

Second, an identity-centered approach may also underemphasize the material context, particularly the national security environment and the economic interests of domestic elites. Pro-violation constituencies in Eastern Europe may have agreed to a regime transition partly because the costs of violating international norms had risen (especially in a climate of economic decline) while the political utility of breaking them had fallen (in a context in which the state's security apparatus was also in relative global decline). Just as state elites were concerned with staying in power in the 1970s and continued to engage in repression when faced with human rights pressure, state elites in the 1980s may have accepted democratization precisely to stay in power.[50] Democratic elections were a gamble but, given domestic and international opposition, democratization may have seemed a relatively low-risk gambit with a potentially high payoff.

The positive steps taken by various Eastern European regimes in the 1980s may therefore have been human rights commitments taken publicly to appease critics, rather than signs of a gradual shift in state interests or the dismantling of the state's coercive apparatus.[51] The state's interests and institutional structures did change, but only after regime transition. At the same time that these regimes accepted foreign monitors and volunteered to host international conferences, they continued to violate human rights, including by severely restricting freedom of movement and information.[52] Even after the collapse of communism, moreover, states in the region continued to violate international human rights norms when faced with purported domestic threats. Note, for example, the deteriorating human rights climate in Russia. As Matthew Evangelista observes, post-Soviet "Russian policies have tended to reflect far less the goals of the transnational peace activists than the interests of the traditional national-security bureaucracies."[53]

Certainly, human rights pressures were influential in eliciting commitments from states in Eastern Europe, making violations more costly and empowering domestic groups to mobilize on behalf of international norms. Yet repression, or human rights abuse, was discontinued as systematic policy only when it was no longer deemed necessary, given the state's waning capacity to provide national security and the threatened economic interests of domestic elites. Thomas documents compellingly how human rights pressure played an invaluable role in defining an alternative set of norms with which to comply, but in the absence of a shifting security and economic environment, that alternative vision may not have been deemed especially desirable in the late 1980s.

SOUTH AFRICA

Of the major targets of human rights sanctions last century, South Africa was subject to pressure for longer than any other country. International bystanders witnessed for decades the systematically entrenched system of apartheid that stripped members of the black majority of their most fundamental human rights. The conventional wisdom now asserts that human rights sanctions, applied by both the United Nations and the United States, were largely successful in dismantling this oppressive system.[54] After three decades of international sanctions, the system of apartheid ended formally and democratization ensued in the early 1990s.

Most observers agree that human rights sanctions played a crucial role in this transition, even if they debate the specific mechanisms by which this occurred.[55] For some, human rights sanctions were primarily coercive, raising the economic costs of ongoing apartheid for the regime in Pretoria.[56] For others, the sanctions had an added constitutive effect, setting international standards as the touchstone of change and empowering domestic groups. Audie Klotz, for example, offers a sophisticated version of the latter argument:

Turning the spotlight on racial discrimination in South Africa successfully pressured the target state to comply with international standards; the government abolished apartheid according to the criteria established by sanctioning organizations and countries. Furthermore, multilateral and bilateral sanctions policies determined recognition of (and allocation of resources to) nonstate actors, notably the African National Congress.[57]

Whether sanctions were most influential for their social or coercive effects, state elites in South Africa eventually complied with their demands. To what extent can the sanctions be credited directly with the end of apartheid?

Human rights sanctions centered on three particularly violent episodes of repression in South Africa. Following the infamous 1960 Sharpeville massacre, the United Nations began condemning South Africa for its human rights abuses. By 1963, it initiated a first round of multilateral sanctions, including arms and oil embargoes. A second round of international pressure followed the regime's violent suppression of protests in Soweto in 1976. The Carter administration linked human rights abuses in South Africa to bilateral relations, while the United Nations imposed a mandatory arms embargo in 1979. An even more severe wave of international pressure, including the imposition of U.S. trade sanctions, met the regime's repressive response in 1986 to a two-year armed insurrection. Despite the apparently unrelenting sanctions, however, some scholars have noted the symbolic nature and contradictions implicit in international pressure.[58] In the case of the United States, for example, sanctions under the Reagan administration occurred alongside a policy of "constructive engagement." These contradictions notwithstanding, human rights sanctions were increasingly visible, partly in response to mounting repression in South Africa.

If the long-term impact of sanctions is contested, their short-term economic effects are clearer. According to Robert Price, a leading scholar of the country, "By the end of 1986 South Africa was effectively cut off from international capital markets."[59] For an economy that depended heavily on foreign trade, this was extremely costly. Foreign governments blocked South Africa's access to foreign capital, foreign firms divested, and major international private banks withdrew their capital. In addition to curtailing the country's capacity to purchase imports, trade embargoes against South Africa limited the country's ability to export goods.

The regime responded to these human rights pressures by committing partially to international norms. In the 1970s, it initiated "township upgrading" and it "deracialized" certain local administrative practices.

After 1987, the South African government undertook a series of general reforms, legally and politically implementing international norms that it continued to break. More broadly, the government launched an intensive campaign to convince domestic and international audiences that it was genuinely committed to human rights change.[60] Many observers fell for the trap, interpreting the new reforms as evidence of a dramatic policy shift, rather than a change in tactics designed to appease the regime's critics. Skeptics, however, emphasized the government's skill in defying the sanctions. More precisely, Price characterizes the consistent logic driving South African reforms: "Each core aspect of reform can be seen to be oriented to a set of three interrelated goals—the reestablishment of domestic security, the attainment of international legitimacy, and the return to a trajectory of rapid economic growth."[61]

Hypocritical responses aside, international human rights pressure did elicit domestic political change in South Africa.[62] International pressure invigorated domestic regime opponents by providing them with resources and even arms. Since 1984, foreign governments and private groups assisted South Africa's blacks directly, bolstering their ability to mobilize and confront the oppressive regime. The regime's heavy hand after 1986 certainly dissipated some of this threat, but domestic groups continued to launch armed attacks against white civilians and to challenge openly the state's authority. Only once the state's coercive apparatus seemed unable to control armed groups did many "pro-violation" constituencies relent and support regime change.

Human rights sanctions may have played an *indirect* role in this transformation. After all, domestic elites continued to support the apartheid regime even after international pressure intensified substantially and new U.S. sanctions went into effect in 1986. The regime, ironically, felt liberated by the imposition (not mere threat) of sanctions. No longer needing to devote its energies to avoiding sanctions, the regime felt free to pursue a more heavy-handed response to its internal security problem. As Price contends, "faced with an increasingly powerful insurrection and the inevitability of sanctions, influence within the South African government shifted away from those ministries most sensitive to the international repercussions of Pretoria's actions."[63] Rather than supporting regime change, the government responded to rising sanctions by restructuring its economy so that the country would be less dependent on foreign capital and trade and therefore less vulnerable to any sanctions. In the midst of an economic downturn, however, this pattern of inward industrialization failed; and it was then that the system began to crumble.

Domestic elites, facing the incapacity of the state's security apparatus on the one hand and their own dire economic straits on the other, finally withdrew their support for the system of apartheid. A regional peace agreement was signed in 1988; and the apartheid system was formally dismantled under President De Klerk in 1991, with universal-suffrage elections being held in 1994. Human rights sanctions played an essential role in this process, including by altering South Africa's security and economic landscape. Two critical turning points stand out: when international actors directly assisted the armed insurgency in the mid-1980s, affecting their capacity to continue confronting the state, and when national economic strategies to resist foreign sanctions failed miserably in a broader climate of economic downturn. Neta Crawford elucidates this broader context:

[T]he impact of sanctions on political change was complex. The many sanctions imposed from outside were only one of several forces at work in . . . forcing a negotiated end to apartheid and creating the conditions for the construction of a democratic government. The determined resistance of those who fought South African aggression . . . along with long-term structural changes in the economy and society, probably had much more to do with the character and timing of the transition than sanctions. Still, sanctions played an important role. They directly helped to pressure the regime by increasing the costs of maintaining apartheid, and sanctions also helped to promote economic changes that undermined the economic structures of apartheid.[64]

The South African case demonstrates that the process of human rights change, even when sanctions appear to succeed most impressively, remains highly contingent.[65] Indeed, the regime and its allies resisted almost to the bitter end. Even in the late 1980s, the regime responded to human rights sanctions predictably: by committing publicly to the very international norms that it continued to violate egregiously; the goal still was one of maintaining internal security and retaining power. Domestic elites did not support dismantling the apartheid state, or desisting from a high level of human rights violations, until the state's *capacities* in both the security and economic realms had virtually collapsed. Sanctions played a substantial but indirect role in this process. As others have noted, sanctions raised the economic costs of maintaining the status quo and they defined a desirable alternative. That alternative was not viable, however, until it was clear that the state was no longer capable of controlling armed groups; the resilience of these groups, in turn, was bolstered crucially by external support.

How does the South African case square with the preceding quantitative analysis? The case confirms the general findings, while revealing more precisely why sanctions succeed *when* they do. First, as in the preceding analysis, international pressure led in the short term only to human rights commitments, not violations. Second, although the ultimate success of human rights sanctions certainly depended on their economic implications, it also hinged on the role of armed conflict. In contrast to the quantitative analysis, however, South African elites agreed to negotiate the details of systemic reform amid armed conflict, not in its absence. Rather than contradicting the earlier findings, the case of South Africa joins the Southern Cone ones in helping to address the more specific question of timing: when will human rights sanctions finally succeed?

In particular, the South African case suggests that it may not always be the domestic threat posed by armed groups per se that matters for eliciting human rights change but the state's (in)capacity to control this threat. Recall that such threats must only be apparent. Even if regime survival is never in question, most capacious states will control domestic threats by repressing them. At some point, however, repression may no longer be viable. As discussed in Chapter 2, at least three scenarios can undermine states' willingness to violate human rights norms in the face of international sanctions and armed conflict: (1) armed conflict no longer exists because the conflict has been resolved, (2) armed conflict is no longer relevant because, perversely, the state has succeeded in eliminating its armed opponents, or (3) armed groups prove resilient in the face of ongoing repression. The third scenario was evident in South Africa in the 1990s, wheras the second accounts for events in the Southern Cone of the 1980s. Jack Donnelly has emphasized the centrality of state capacity for explaining regime change in South Africa: "Apartheid ultimately collapsed because of the inability of the white government either to modernize apartheid or to keep the lid on opposition through increasing repression."[66] As armed groups withstood the regime's repressive blows, due in part to external support—arms flows, financial backing, and networks of solidarity—the domestic benefits of continuing to violate personal integrity rights at last were offset by the international costs of doing so. Sanctions succeeded, but only once the state was no longer capable of controlling its armed opponents.

Human Rights "Failures"

Many other countries have been subject to long-standing international human rights pressures and yet have failed to reform substantially. The intransigent states discussed here are not the only or necessarily most onerous human rights "failures" in the world, but they have generated close international scrutiny. My objective in including them is to consider why countries that have received enormous human rights attention have nonetheless proved so resistant to change.

China is perhaps today's most high-profile human rights holdout. In the aftermath of Tiananmen Square, the regime has attempted to undertake numerous human rights commitments without improving its record of abuse. International human rights pressure, for its part, has been quite mixed. Although the Chinese case has been debated vigorously in the United States, the principal form of leverage—linking human rights compliance to most-favored-nation trade status—was eliminated in 1994 under the Clinton administration. Supporters of delinkage argued that continued trade would have a liberal effect; it would provide international actors with domestic channels of influence, including to civil society.[67] Skeptics pointed to the limited impact of sanctions, confirmed by some experts: "Economic sanctions have prompted China to release a few individual dissidents and intermittently relax repressive policies. China's leadership, however, maintains the position that threats to the regime must be quelled."[68]

According to the prevailing view, Chinese resistance reflects insufficient international pressure against this powerful state, weak domestic human rights organizations, and the absence of democracy. As Keck and Sikkink observe, "What is often missed in the debate over the apparent 'failure' of human rights policy in China is that virtually none of the classic military and economic levers exist."[69] Chinese resistance to international pressure may stem partly from its status as a powerful state, but it also reflects other factors.

Domestically rooted interests impel a nondemocratic Chinese regime to violate human rights. Groups in China who challenge the state—by demanding rights of expression, association, or belief—are labeled threats to national security and are targeted for repression. Pro-violation constituencies, in turn, continue to support this policy as long as the Chinese state is able to guarantee national security. That said, the most promising avenue for reform may be economic pressure targeting the country's elite. Although coercive economic sanctions on their own are unlikely to produce a decline in human rights violations, suspending (or threatening to suspend) preferential trade relations may be relatively more effective. Such pressures could lead to greater government concessions, gradually strengthening the role of pro-compliance constituencies and at least increasing the likelihood of eventual democratic change. Fundamental human rights change, however, still would require a decline in the state's overall capacity to provide national security, something unlikely to occur given the international power of the regime and its nondemocratic mode of governance. Without this change in national security, international human rights influence may well follow the pattern established after the Tiananmen Square massacre, as the regime undertakes some human rights commitments without improving its overall record of abuse.[70]

In contrast, Israel stands as a state having democratic structures of governance and yet intensely resisting international human rights pressures. Israel has been pressured by the world community, with the partial exception of the U.S. government, for over three decades to desist its occupation of the West Bank and Gaza. In the process, Israel has been charged with violating international human rights norms of self-determination, refugee rights, as well as rights prohibiting arbitrary detention, torture, and execution.[71] What would it take for Israel to comply fully with international human rights demands?

Despite the strength of its security apparatus, Israel has not been able to protect its citizens entirely against armed attack by Palestinian extremist groups. Thus, one of the factors shaping the decision of pro-violation constituencies to support meaningful reform—the state's incapacity to protect civilians against armed attack—may already be partially present. Another positive factor is the existence of some pro-compliance constituencies within Israel. Likewise, occupation has been economically costly for Israelis in general. More dramatic change, however, will require the economic security of Israeli elites to be at stake, especially as a direct and unequivocal consequence of the regime's human rights violations. Until then, those sectors justifying continued occupation and human rights abuses in the name of national security continue to win. It would take nothing short of concerted American economic pressure, including the threatened withdrawal of aid, to change the preferences of pro-violation constituencies. And as long as broader perceptions of U.S. security in the region do not change, the prospects for human rights reform appear grim.

Cuba stands as another resister state, albeit an internationally weak one, defying calls for regime transformation and human rights protection.[72] Indeed, the sanctions imposed by the United States since 1960 have not appeared to work, although Cuba's population has suffered economically as a direct consequence of the sanctions. This has been especially true since the mid-1990s, following the collapse of Soviet aid and a sharp economic decline.[73] Despite the longevity of the sanctions, and the apparent international vulnerability of the regime, the Cuban government continues to curtail extensive social mobilization while committing ongoing human rights abuses.[74] The nature of the sanctions themselves may have something to do with their apparent failure. By indiscriminately affecting the masses—those it purports to benefit—human rights sanctions are used by a populist leader such as Castro to support and sustain some measure of regime legitimacy.

Ironically, more international pressure may not be better for eliciting human rights reform and political change in Cuba. International human rights pressure that falls short of full-blown sanctions may instead be more effective against an aging state apparatus that, in a post-Cold War world, no longer faces an apparent national security threat. In a globalizing world, moreover, pro-violation constituencies in Cuba could increasingly shift their support to international norms. While on the face of it, the prospects for human rights success in China and Cuba—two long-standing nondemocratic regimes—may seem comparably dim, attention to the sources of state violation suggests that human rights reform would be more feasible in Cuba. Of the three cases of resistance to international pressure, human rights reform appears most likely in Cuba.

Democracy and Its Limits

Even human rights "success" stories demonstrate the difficulties that new democracies so often face in protecting human rights. When new national security threats arise, pro-violation constituencies retain access to decision making, or domestic rules of exception remain entrenched in state structures, even democratic regimes will suspend personal security. This pattern was amply evident in Latin America during the 1990s, including in the Southern Cone.

In both democratic Argentina and Chile, international human rights norms became embedded in domestic rules and laws, as well as in the standard operating procedures of the state coercive apparatus. The two countries ratified international human rights instruments, incorporated international norms into domestic law, and created government institutions to self-monitor human rights compliance. A democratic Argentina, for example, ratified the ICCPR, the American Convention on Human Rights, and the Convention against Torture, all in the 1980s. Argentina also recognized the jurisdiction of the Inter-American Court of Human Rights and created a sub-secretariat of human rights within the Ministry of the Interior. A defense law in 1988 empowered the armed forces to defend the nation only against foreign aggression. Reforms of the penal code also were made, and civilian courts began sentencing police officers for human rights abuses. In 1992, for instance, Buenos Aires province fired hundreds of police officers due to human rights violations.[75]

New regulations addressed the issue of past violations in Argentina. For example, a national genetic bank was created in 1987 to facilitate the identification of missing children; legislation was passed in 1991 that would grant financial compensation to some political prisoners; and a law in 1994 awarded compensation to relatives of the disappeared. Additionally, a new constitution created the office of an ombudsman for human rights, recognized the rights of indigenous people, and granted constitutional status to several international human rights treaties.[76]

Argentina also took unprecedented steps in the days following the collapse of military rule to confront its human rights past. Meeting the principal demand of Argentine society—state accountability for past human rights abuses—Argentina's new democratic government held a human rights trial against the former military regime in 1985. In the widely watched case, junta members were found guilty of human rights abuses during the dirty war and sentenced to prison terms.[77]

Yet in the aftermath of the trial, questions of retroactive justice increasingly became the subject of controversy. A cycle ensued wherein the judiciary took independent steps to prosecute past human rights crimes while the armed forces made veiled threats to rebel. The armed forces were clearly interested in both avoiding punishment and retaining ample resources under democracy. In a series of staged rebellions, military officers called tellingly for an end to human rights trials and better salaries. Argentine leaders, in turn, attempted to appease the armed forces. Alfonsín promoted military officers who had committed human rights violations. The president also passed legislation in 1986 and 1987 that limited future human rights trials for violations committed during the dirty war. President Carlos Menem later declared a general amnesty, in response to which large segments of Argentine society demonstrated against human rights impunity.[78] Conflicts over past human rights abuses have nonetheless continued, as society and the judiciary persist in their quest to hold former members of the armed forces accountable for the crimes of the dirty war.

Still, in democratic Argentina as elsewhere, countervailing norms of national security remained embedded in domestic institutions. States of siege could be declared for reasons of domestic instability, which in fact occurred several times in the 1980s and 1990s. New antisubversive legislation also was enacted following sporadic military rebellions. The internal structure of the armed forces itself still emphasized weaponry and forms of organization that facilitated repression. As Alison Brysk notes, the repressive apparatus was "deactivated but not dismantled."[79] This permitted human rights violations to persist. Throughout the 1990s, reports rose of torture and ill-treatment of detainees in police custody, threats against human rights workers, and even some cases of disappearance and extrajudicial executions. And despite these violations, the government remained reluctant to conduct timely and thorough investigations.[80]

Chile showed similar signs of progress and resistance. On a positive front, a series of constitutional reforms in 1989 repealed repressive legislation. Regarding past abuses, a government agency (the National Corporation for Reparation and Reconciliation) was created in 1992 to process complaints. Democratic Chile also signed or ratified several human rights treaties, including the American Convention on Human Rights, the Convention Against Torture, and a regional convention on forced disappearances. Yet pockets of national security norms remained equally pronounced in Chile. The constitution continued to allow states of legal exception to undermine constitutional rights and guarantees. Furthermore, those responsible for past violations still held power. Pinochet himself remained commander in chief until 1998 as well as senator for life, a title of which he would eventually be stripped. Within the organizational structure of both the Senate and the Supreme Court, human rights opponents were given decision-making authority. These actions were justified in terms of needing to protect Chile's armed forces against prosecutions for past human rights practices.

Although a Truth and Reconciliation Commission was established after the transitional government of Patricio Aylwin took office in 1989, the scope of even this commission remained limited.[81] From a comparative perspective, moreover, Chilean decision makers seemed to have learned from their Argentine neighbors. Just as Argentina's authoritarian government had tried to avoid Chile's international human rights pressure, under democratization Chile was intent on avoiding a repeat of the human rights trials in Argentina. In fact, Pinochet made regime change itself conditional on military impunity for past abuses.

Social conflicts remained tense in Chile. On more than one occasion, the military took to the streets to show that human rights accountability would not be tolerated. Tensions rose to the surface even further in 1999 when Spain requested Pinochet's extradition from Britain, and in subsequent years as Pinochet was placed under house arrest and his fitness to stand trial in Chile was debated. Groups on both sides of the normative divide confronted each other in street protests.[82] For their part, important segments of the military continued to be committed to national security ideology. In a Chilean military journal of the 1990s, the armed forces' mission was described as "not only defense against internal threats that affect society and the national as a whole . . . their function transcends governments, groups, and persons, responding only to the permanent interests of the national, where the principle of National Security predominates over all others."[83] Still more broadly, and eerily reminiscent of Operation Condor, former military officers from both Chile and Argentina exported their skills throughout the region. They traveled in the post–Cold War period to other countries in Latin America, including Mexico, to train paramilitary groups in counterinsurgency techniques and national security ideologies.[84] Despite ongoing advances, these democratic states and their counterparts in the region have continued to violate human rights in response to domestic threats—from rising social demands and economic crises to the global war on terror. In the process, they have catered to latent pro-violation constituencies; and they have perpetuated exclusionary rules, marginalizing groups such as the indigenous Mapuche in the name of antiterrorism and national assimilation.

Tensions aside, the end of the Cold War saw an impressive rise in the institutionalization of human rights norms, both internationally and domestically. It also reinforced processes of democratization, themselves associated with greater if imperfect human rights compliance. Both Argentina and Chile have undergone dramatic transformations from the days of military rule, encapsulated in landmark judicial decisions: Argentina's Supreme Court ruled in 2004 that no statute of limitations applied to crimes against humanity, and in 2005 it paved the way to human rights prosecutions by declaring amnesty laws unconstitutional; Chile's Supreme Court voted in 2004 and 2006 to lift Pinochet's long-held immunity, a symbolic development even if the dictator does not stand trial due to purported health concerns. In both countries, moreover, blatant rejection of international human rights norms is virtually unimaginable today, and contemporary abuses pale in comparison to the horrors of the past. These countries now enjoy vibrant civil societies, democratic governance systems, and rights-protective regimes.

The events of 11 September 2001—like those in Chile, twenty-eight years earlier to the day—raise a cautionary flag to this narrative of progress: the protection of human rights is vulnerable even in countries with democratic traditions. Although actions by the United States today may not match those instituted by the Pinochet regime, they no less constitute breaches of international law. Global dynamics after the Cold War have remained remarkably consistent with those of past authoritarian regimes, even if international human rights pressure has become far more institutionalized and technologically sophisticated. States around the world continue to deploy a two-pronged strategy of commitment and violation: as the costs of repression rise, states undertake numerous and even meaningful human rights commitments; but when faced with countervailing forces, such as national security threats, states do not hesitate to violate international norms. The scope and magnitude of rights violations may vary by time and place, but states' basic rationale for abusing human beings remains much the same.

Chapter 6

Compliance and Resistance in International Politics

Human rights issues have always been manifestly contradictory. In ancient Greece and Rome, torture was an integral aspect of the legal system. Torture of citizens was forbidden, but a slave's testimony tended to be accepted only if it had been extracted by torture.[1] Today, freedom from torture is considered part of customary international law and even *jus cogens*, a norm so basic that it cannot be derogated under any circumstances. And yet torture is routinely practiced around the world: recent Amnesty International surveys confirm systematic torture or ill-treatment in over one hundred countries. Given what is at stake, we cannot ignore that human rights norms often coexist alongside egregious abuses. The repercussions of such double standards are too serious to sweep under ideological or epistemological covers. The compliance paradox—why states sometimes support international norms and laws at the same time that they violate and resist these norms—has to be confronted squarely.

This paradox challenges popular images of globalization, which predict normative convergence. Is the world in fact becoming more interdependent normatively as well as materially? Is the influence of international norms and ideas comparable to that of the material goods and services that are transferred across national boundaries? And do states face a choice between international norms and domestic authority, as Robert Gilpin has observed with regard to the international economy?[2] The widespread nature of human rights violations that are justified in the name of ethnic conflicts and local norms seems to support this view. Yet if the pull of the local is so powerful, why do leaders everywhere increasingly claim to uphold international human rights norms? How do we reconcile these competing trends, and what do they tell us about the relationship between morality and self-interest in international relations? The role of international norms on the one hand and state sovereignty and cultural differences on the other? The connection between personal and national security? The answers to these questions, like so many state responses to human rights pressure, may lie in what Howard

Margolis has described as a "zone of ambiguity," wherein conflicting normative pressures coexist uneasily.[3]

The Logic of Account Making

Virtually every human rights conflict involves a war of images. One side launches an assault of accusations. The other side fires back in self-defense. Not surprisingly, observers sitting on the sidelines can interpret these responses very differently. For example, when a state claims to accept international human rights norms, optimists may take lip service at face value, treating it as an embryonic commitment to reform. Skeptics, on the other hand, are more circumspect about improvements in state rhetoric, seeing it as "cheap talk" intended to manipulate and deflect criticism. Although either interpretation can be accurate, each can also reflect the interests of the observer. After all, observers can be biased. They may be more inclined to believe the actions of allies but not adversaries, or they may be more willing to take credit for "positive" responses while dismissing "negative" ones.[4] In international politics, as in other areas of public life, interpreting rhetoric can be deeply problematic.

These dilemmas can be partially offset by interpreting state responses according to a different logic: the logic of account making. Despite its application to a wide variety of domains (e.g., organization theory, research on attributions, symbolic interactionism, and the study of narratives and scripts), the concept of accounts has been largely absent from the study of international relations and human rights.[5] Yet the sociological study of accounts suggests that, when actors are accused of violating a norm or committing an act that is widely considered illegitimate, they will attempt to persuade others of their innocence. They will do so through "motive talk," or by "aligning their behavior with culturally acceptable language."[6] This may entail emphasizing the facts of the accusation, their own or their accuser's intentions and values, as well as issues of responsibility. The ultimate goal of account making is always to evade responsibility and punishment for violating a norm. Accounts are thus strategic, insofar as they are externally directed, even if the language they employ is norm-laden. The logic of consequences and of appropriateness are both at work here. This is also why accounts sometimes appear to be contradictory but in fact are internally consistent.

Account making therefore offers us an analytical lens through which to study state responses to international compliance pressure. In the face of cross-cutting pressures, research on account making suggests that actors will put a positive spin on their own behavior while casting others in a negative light. As Table 14 indicates, these "positive accounts" may take various forms. Actors can insist on their own compli-

TABLE 14. A TYPOLOGY OF STATE ACCOUNTS

Category	Negative Accounts		Positive Accounts	
Responsibility	*Excuses*	They deserved it.	*Justification*	We had to do it.
Values	*Rejection*	They have no right to judge us.	*Legitimation*	Our way is valid.
Intentions	*Counterclaim*	They do worse things.	*Assurance*	We will comply.
Facts	*Denial*	Their claim is false.	*Evidence*	We do comply.

ance, ascribe legitimacy to their actions, promise future compliance, or justify their behavior. What type of response they use—evidence, assurances, legitimation, or justification—will depend partly on the argument with which they are confronted. If faced with incontrovertible proof of noncompliance, for example, actors will be hard-pressed to deny the facts. To evade responsibility and escape punishment, they are likely to justify their behavior.

As long as a state continues to violate international norms, however, it will simultaneously emphasize others' culpability. "Negative accounts" may entail denying violations, offering counteraccusations, rejecting accusations outright, or providing excuses for noncompliance.[7] Excuses imply admission of responsibility, but they do differ from justifications: to offer an excuse is to blame others, or circumstances beyond one's control, for noncompliance; to justify violating a norm is to admit one's own responsibility while absolving oneself of guilt.[8] Negative accounts—in the form of denial, counterclaim, rejection, or denial—remain ways of deflecting criticism and evading responsibility for norm violations.

These complex accounts alert us to the possibility that states engage in "strategic social construction," a term that Finnemore and Sikkink have coined to describe the work of transnational norm entrepreneurs.[9] States targeted by international pressure may practice tactics of persuasion, concurrently embracing and rejecting the language of international norms. As the case studies here amply demonstrate, states often respond to international pressure with "reverse issue linkages" and "perverse learning" alongside extensive lip service to international norms. Target states resort regularly to these complex strategies, as they seek to alter others' perceptions of them. In human rights struggles, moreover, these strategic social constructions are commonplace. While existing research has focused on their adoption by transnational human rights advocates, account making suggests that states also employ such strategies in responding to transnational pressure.

Certainly, these dynamics were evident in the Southern Cone. Despite manifest contradictions, the rhetoric of human rights compliance was internally consistent in these countries. In responding to human rights pressure, government officials refused to admit egregious violations ("denial of injuries"); they challenged the status of alleged victims by labeling them enemies ("denial of victims") and by characterizing the situation as a state of war ("appeal to situation"); they offered assurances of the regime's moral foundations ("appeal to obligation") and continually emphasized the unjust nature of accusations ("refusal to accept accusation").[10] These were all defensive strategies, or tactical communications, taken in the face of international accusations.

Critics might argue that states operating within different cultural and historical milieus may approach evasion differently. Some actors may be more willing than others to accept responsibility for their actions; others may not be as inclined to accuse outsiders of wrongdoing. In short, self-defense may not be a universal instinct. This may or may not be true. Yet the advantage of an approach that incorporates account making is precisely that it allows us to test, and not just stipulate, propositions about state motive.

The evidence presented here suggests that state actions falling under the rubric of compliance may be externally oriented "accounts" more than reflections of internal commitment. Not all states that commit publicly to international norms are hypocritical, but the reality is that sometimes they are. Even apparent improvements in violation may be attempts to shield a state from further scrutiny. As students of institutions in other fields have recognized, organizations facing conflicting demands can maintain their legitimacy for the sake of powerful actors by "adopting visible structures that conform to social norms and by decoupling those structures from less acceptable core activities or goals."[11] To use a courtroom analogy, states responding to international pressure may be more like defendants relying on a variety of strategies to protect themselves before their accusers than potential offenders deciding whether to violate or comply with a norm.

Personal Security versus State Sovereignty?

State compliance is closely related to state sovereignty. According to Beth Simmons, compliance is an aspect of sovereignty because it involves states voluntarily agreeing to give something up.[12] The very idea of human rights and personal security challenges the concept that states can do whatever they want within their own borders. Are states in fact shifting their notions of sovereignty to protect the rights of individuals, minorities, and refugees?

This study casts doubt on the extent to which state sovereignty both has changed and is likely to change dramatically as a result of human rights norms. Those who see evidence of the reconceptualization of sovereignty trace it to incremental changes in state action. These changes span a "continuum of erosion of state sovereignty": from the rejection and denial of international legitimacy to lip service and cooperation and finally to actual improvements in state practice.[13] This study's findings do not fit neatly into this continuum. In the Southern Cone cases examined, states continued to resist international human rights pressure throughout the period under review. While there was a movement to lip service, cooperation, and improved practices, this was matched by ongoing denial, rejection, and systematic abuse. These discrepancies are not traces of residual variance, or leftover remnants of an otherwise improving situation; nor do they merely mirror splits within a regime. A close look at policy debates, variations over time, differences between human rights norms, and diverse state responses evokes a different image. While human rights change can appear incremental in retrospect, the process described here emphasizes the contingent and nonteleological nature of change. The fact that both Southern Cone countries are democratic rights-protective regimes today—dramatically symbolized by the 2006 election of Michelle Bachelet, a former human rights victim and the first female president in Chile's history—rightfully vindicates the fundamental optimism of activists, but it should not obscure the lessons of the past. Quantitative and qualitative analyses suggest that the dynamics pushing and pulling states to respond to human rights pressure in seemingly contradictory ways have remained remarkably consistent over time.

The complex picture of state compliance that emerges from this study does not deny that state sovereignty has changed, but it does dispute the extent of this change. Indeed, there has been a rise in state responsibility, or recognition of international norms, with nation-states incorporating notions of personal security to a greater extent than in the past. As the graph in Chapter 1 depicting changes in human rights commitments and protection shows, despite some improvements over time, the gap between the two types of behavior has widened. Although some may interpret this finite gap as temporary, and view commitment levels as signaling greater future convergence, the compliance story presented here offers a more sober account. Changes in violation will ultimately remain contingent on the national security and economic environments, which to some extent are exogenously driven and therefore susceptible to reversal or setback.

There is further reason to interpret human rights change cautiously. To say that states are more responsible for their actions and international norms are influential is not to say that states are redefining their interests and identities in terms of these international norms, or that state sovereignty is transforming. On the contrary, because norms of all stripes coexist in the international system, state responsibility can reflect another possibility: an interest in evading the consequences of actions widely considered illegitimate.

According to a growing body of international law, a state is responsible for a "wrongful act" when the act breaches an international obligation and it is attributable to the state.[14] States consequently can alter their actions so that wrongfulness cannot be attributed to them. State resistance in the form of negative accounts, states of exception (or "rules about breaking rules"), and other evasive techniques, including using new modes of repression that hide the physical traces of abuse, can all be interpreted as attempts to influence the attributions of a broader community of liberal states.[15] Evasion may arise out of a recognition that accusations of illegitimacy can spiral into material costs. But even in the absence of significant material incentives, evasion may stem from a more basic motive of defending the self against external attack. Insights from social psychology might emphasize how actors, in the face of threats to their identity, tend to "negotiate reality" through the use of evasion and other cognitive strategies.[16]

Regardless of its origins, evasion reminds us of the deceptiveness of appearances in international politics. As long as states are subject to cross-cutting pressures, isomorphism in state compliance may be more apparent than real.[17] Compliance or resistance may appear similar over time and space but reflect different underlying dynamics. This should not alter our estimate of whether international norms are significant, but it should caution us about the degree to which they are influential. States may incur greater international obligations and even conform their behavior to international norms (i.e., act in more socially appropriate ways) in order to evade accusations of noncompliance. To repeat a point made earlier, both the logics of appropriateness and consequences undergird state compliance.

Students of international norms may have exaggerated the implications of state compliance for sovereignty. They have treated compliance and resistance, respectively, as signs of normative influence and paralysis. When we reconceptualize state compliance as a multidimensional and complex variable, however, the findings are sobering. Overall changes do indicate greater state responsibility and the influence of international norms. Yet states may also be identifying with international norms to a greater degree than in the past because they have an interest in avoiding blame (and punishment) for illegitimate acts, not because they are becoming privately committed to these norms. As long as collective beliefs, perpetuated by basic disparities of wealth and power, support the view that some human beings are less equal than others, personal security will remain under the purview of the nation-state. Just because the international system is not an anomic one does not mean that "good" or "moral" norms will prevail. The norm of state sovereignty remains strong in spite of the emergence of competing norms of personal sovereignty.

Policy Implications

The topic of compliance is clearly laden with practical implications. Compliance, after all, is central to all social regulation. Whether we are talking about compliance with Supreme Court regulations, tax codes, or arms control agreements, the basic issue is the same: how can compliance be attained most effectively? This study's findings offer recommendations about the criteria used to assess policy influence, the conditions that favor international influence, and the types and quantities of pressure that are most likely to be effective.

First, compliant and noncompliant responses to international pressure should not be treated as respective indicators of policy success or failure. Yet decision makers routinely take state responses at face value. In the cases examined, foreign governments pointed to these responses as reasons to desist from applying more pressure, arguing that such pressure was either unnecessary or would lead to greater intransigence that could undermine bilateral relations. The argument here suggests, instead, that state responses can also be attempts to influence international actors more than indicators of policy success. State hypocrisy should be a reason to apply more rather than less pressure. Likewise, the human rights commitments that often follow human rights pressure should be encouraged, even if they do not always signal long-term change. These commitments open domestic political spaces, mobilize transnational networks, and can save or at least improve individual lives.

Second, international human rights pressure should be tailored to domestic conditions. The amount of external regulatory pressure required to elicit changes in human rights violation will vary depending on a configuration of factors: apparent national threats, the strength of pro-violation constituencies, and the entrenchment of domestic rules of exception or exclusion.[18] Thus, different types and degrees of pressure may be met over time by similar levels of violation. Conversely, similar pressures over time can be associated with different human rights violations. This suggests, for example, that intervention—in terms of the use of force and the imposition of severe economic sanctions—which is most likely to be an option the more noncompliant a state is, will not necessarily be more effective than relatively less costly forms of pressure. Issue linkages that withhold or threaten to withhold the benefits of an

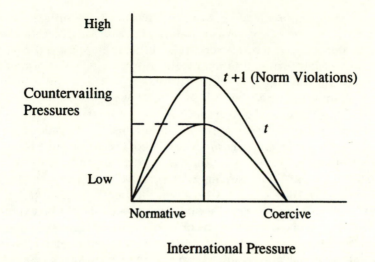

Figure 3. Dynamics of International Human Rights Influence

existing relationship may be as effective as outright coercion. Even if intervention is marginally more effective, its potentially adverse effects on domestic instability should make policy makers think twice. As Figure 3 shows, the effectiveness of applying coercive international pressure declines as the incentives to violate an international norm rise.

The fact that full human rights reform is rare, and cross-cutting pressures are prevalent, does not suggest the futility of international human rights pressure. Rather, it helps us to identify the forms of pressure that are most likely to be influential. Directly, international actors must continue to link human rights violations to the economic well-being of domestic elites, as well as to empower domestic opponents of an abusive regime. Indirectly, international actors should reinforce processes of conflict resolution and democratic rule. Equally important, international actors should refrain from assisting abusive governments and further militarizing conflict situations. Human rights pressure certainly can make noncompliance costly and define an alternative to systematic human rights violations—recasting domestic expectations—and in some cases serve as a precursor to a rights-protective regime transition. In the end, however, future human rights abuses can be prevented only by investing resources to change the structural conditions (both material and ideational) underpinning them. Although it pays to increase the material costs attached to noncompliance, more costly international human rights pressure is not necessarily better for inducing a substantial reduction in the overall level of violations.

One type of international pressure that has not been sufficiently appreciated is the use of *government* rhetoric, because language can be a powerful weapon in a state's arsenal. Rather than emphasize the moral superiority of international human rights norms, a new rhetoric of international human rights should focus on contradictions in state policy.[19] Following the lead of NGOs, who have long relied on the mobilization of "shame," governments must consistently call attention to any discrepancy between norm commitments and violations (state hypocrisy), the bankruptcy of domestic rules of exception, and concrete evidence of abuse, just as they should avoid sending "mixed signals" to repressive regimes.[20] These strategies may seem obvious, but they are no less pertinent. Likewise, any myths about the internal threat posed by members of ethnic and other discriminated groups should be exposed. International actors, especially powerful ones, should also oppose new forms of repression that are less visible but no less unacceptable according to international law. "Sanitized" and "high-tech" forms of repression and torture, which may even be a perverse side effect of international human rights pressure, should be condemned forcefully. Doing so may at least help to redefine national agendas and elicit further human rights commitments. This social context of international bargaining should not be ignored.[21] If hypocrisy is indeed "the homage that vice pays to virtue," it is also an opportunity for powerful observers to demand consistency in state action.

Final Observations

States continue to constitute both the primary violators and enforcers of international human rights norms. Observers have either highlighted this as a source of skepticism or neglected it in the face of optimism. In studying compliance with weak but principled regimes, or "soft" norms, it is no doubt tempting to blur the distinction between explanations of what tends to occur and prescriptions for what observers believe should occur. Because we often see what we want to see—like psychoanalysts who overlook the defensiveness, ambiguities, and complexities of compliance in their patients—the challenge is to confront analytically those ideas that may undermine our own normative agenda.[22] By sorting through the complexities of state action and providing empirically informed explanations, social scientists should be able to contribute to practical debates in the human rights field, an area that remains dominated by international lawyers, activists, and policy makers.

The compliance story I have told complements prior accounts. My objective has been to show, using both case studies and statistical methods, that existing approaches are incomplete. They often fail to explain why compliance differs—over time, cross-nationally, and between norms—even when human rights pressures are similar. Seeking to offer a policy relevant analysis, I have explored why human rights violations occur in the first place, thereby focusing more fully on the conditions under which human rights pressure can matter.

The dynamics I have discussed should apply even to human rights norms that are subject to more open cultural contestation, such as women's rights. For example, states that systematically abuse women's rights still undertake substantial human rights commitments. They may deny abuses, portray the treatment of women as based on a different set of moral principles, and reject external pressure at the same time that they attend international conferences, ratify international instruments, establish parliamentary committees, and permit women's groups to function. If anything, similarities across cultural contexts suggest that it is time to begin unpacking and testing empirically arguments about the cultural relativity versus universality of international human rights norms.

It may turn out that international actors are most influential simply in contesting practices that conflict with international norms. "Normative contestation," as Martha Finnemore observes, "is in large part what politics is all about."[23] The outcome of norm contestation nonetheless will depend on the creativity and ability of both the sources and targets of international pressure to adapt to changing and often unexpected conditions. Norm contestation is a highly contingent process. It takes time, is prone to accidents, and depends on actors who are constrained by their environment but have some room to maneuver. Because norm contestation both introduces uncertainty and makes change more likely, international actors cannot predict the direction of change but they can contribute to it. They can motivate domestic actors to identify with certain norms and practices at the same time that they contest competing ones.

The capacity of international and domestic actors to set norm contestation in motion should not be underestimated. It is a necessary step for any normative change. According to one student of human rights, "It is only when a concept has emerged as an explicit symbol, competing with other strong symbols . . . [that] serious social and political contests arise to seize control of the symbol and invest it with meaning."[24] In a similar vein, Peter Hall observes how policy debates over competing ideas may provide an essential step in the eventual forging of a common purpose.[25] International pressure on behalf of a norm cannot on its own lead to full and sustainable reform. But by reinforcing the public commitments that

states are willing to make, international pressure may improve individual lives and shape the social struggles that underlie all normative
change.

Despite an emphasis on strategic signaling, I have not addressed at
length how exactly state responses themselves can "feed back" to affect
international pressure.[26] If human rights commitments are sometimes
an attempt to influence others, do they work? While I have considered
this question only in passing, it would be well worth understanding
more fully the conditions under which state₁ hypocrisy and other responses affect subsequent international interactions.

In a mid-1970s study of compliance with regional norms, noncompliance was described in the following way:

the politics of noncompliance take the general form of a bargaining game
played mainly to gain time . . . The fascinating aspect of this game of bargaining
for time lies in the fact that all players . . . recognize its nature, and all play along
with full awareness of the problems which are causing delay. Yet no one raises
the real issue.[27]

The real issue in the human rights area is that it is not in most states' interests to enforce international human rights norms although it is now
in their interest to identify publicly with these norms. Many human
rights policies are an attempt to obscure this reality. Students of international norms, in turn, have often downplayed the extent to which state
compliance can be part of a larger game of conflict.

This is not to suggest that we should be cynical about the substantial
progress made in the human rights field, but it does caution us to tem-
per our optimism. As Jack Donnelly has noted, "although international
action has had, and continues to have, an impact on the realization of
human rights, its role is ultimately subsidiary. The fate of human rights
is largely a matter of national, not international action."[28]

Morality and self-interest may not coincide very often in international
politics, but this Machiavellian dichotomy has overshadowed our understanding of normative change. If human action is purposeful, strategic,
and dynamic, how actors manage any tensions between morality and
self-interest may account for political change more than either single
factor. Just as "[n]o democracy was ever born without opposition, dou-
bletalk, and self-interested calculations," compliance with some international norms may require a measure of norm contestation and even
hypocrisy.[29] The history of human rights norms, which has never been a
peaceful one, confirms this. Norms cannot be translated easily into the
language of trade, or exported and imported across space. The diffusion of one set of norms depends on their interaction with those that an
actor already holds. Deliberate international pressure alone cannot ex-

plain all changes in state compliance; but it can get states to commit publicly to international norms, and it can help to define an alternative to systematic human rights violations. Human rights issues make apparent what often is obscured in other areas of international politics: the influence of norms may be present in conflict as much as in compliance.

Appendix: Measuring Human Rights Determinants

Variable	Description	Indicators	Sources
U.S. sanctions	Economic sanctions applied by the United States and having human rights goals	Yes = 1, No = 0, lagged by one year	Institute for International Economics (http://www .iie.org)
Duration of U.S. sanctions	Amount of time sanctions have been applied	Number of years	Institute for International Economics
Multilateral sanctions	Economic sanctions applied by an IO or more than one state, having human rights goals	Yes = 1, No = 0, lagged by one year	Institute for International Economics
Duration of multilateral sanctions	Amount of time sanctions have been applied	Number of years	Institute for International Economics
Economic development	GDP per capita	Converted to 9-point index (9 = high and 1 = low)	Country Indicators for Foreign Policy, based on World Bank data (http://www .carleton.ca/cifp)
Trade openness	Trade as a percentage of GDP	Converted to 9-point index (9 = high and 1 = low)	Country Indicators for Foreign Policy, based on World Bank and OECD data
Emerging democracies	Extent to which a country is a new democracy, relative to well-established	Countries scoring over 7 on Polity's democracy scale are coded 1; all others 0; this is	Polity IV (http:// www.cidcm.umd .edu/inscr/ polity/) and

(*continued*)

Variable	Description	Indicators	Sources
Emerging democracies (*continued*)	democracies and autocratic regimes	multiplied by a "regime durability" index, whereby 9 = high and 1 = low	Country Indicators for Foreign Policy
Armed conflict	Situations in which armed force is used between two parties, one of which is the government of a state	Countries with at least 25 battle-related deaths per year are coded 1; all others 0	Conflict Data Project and SIPRI (http://www.pcr.uu.se/research/UCDP)
International human rights NGOs	Groups with head-quarters outside a country against which pressure is applied	Number of organizations	Human Rights Internet, *Masterlist*
Global contagion	Average human rights commitment/violation in the world in a given year	Mean scores are calculated separately for each dependent variable	CIRI Human Rights Data (http://ciri.binghamton.edu/) and Amnesty International annual reports
Regional contagion	Average human rights commitment/violation in a region in a given year	Mean scores are calculated separately for each dependent variable	CIRI Human Rights Data and Amnesty International annual reports
Regime type/democracy	Relative degree of democracy or	Polity Score: 21-point scale, autocracy ranging from +10 (strongly democratic) to −10 (strongly autocratic)	Polity IV
Domestic non-governmental organizations	Human rights groups operating within a country	Number of organizations, organizations in 1993, logged	Human Rights Internet, *Masterlist*
Prior human rights commitments	State commitments made before the period under review	Based on the six "core" human rights treaties, number ratified before 1992	United Nations Office of the High Commissioner for Human Rights, Human Rights Treaty Database (http://www.unhchr.ch/tbs/doc.nsf)
Past human violations	Degree of physical integrity violations in the recent past	Nine-point Physical Integrity Index, lagged by one year (combines torture, extrajudicial, political imprisonment, and disappearance, each scored between 0 and 2)	CIRI Human Rights Data

Notes

Chapter 1

1. Amnesty International, *Amnesty International Report* (London: Amnesty Publications, 1990–95).

2. See Yitan Li and A. Cooper Drury, "Threatening Sanctions When Engagement Would Be More Effective: Attaining Better Human Rights in China," *International Studies Perspective* 5, 4 (2004): 378–94; Steve Chan, "Economic Sanctions: The US Debate on MFN Status for China," in *Sanctions as Economic Statecraft: Theory and* Practice, ed. Steve Chan and A. Cooper Drury (Basingstoke: Macmillan, 2000); Ming Wan, *Human Rights in Chinese Foreign Relations: Defining and Defending National Interests* (Philadelphia: University of Pennsylvania Press, 2001); Michael A. Santoro, *Profits and Principles: Global Capitalism and Human Rights in China* (Ithaca, N.Y.: Cornell University Press, 2000); Ann Kent, *China, the United Nations, and Human Rights: The Limits of Compliance* (Philadelphia: University of Pennsylvania Press, 1999); Donald D. A. Schaefer, "U.S. Policies for Presidents Bush and Clinton: The Influence of China's Most Favored Nation Status upon Human Rights," *Social Science Journal* 35 (1998): 407–21; Alice H. Amsden, ed., "Human Rights and China: A Symposium," *Dissent* 44 (Spring 1997); and "China: United States Policy after Tiananmen Square," *Harvard Human Rights Journal* 3 (Spring 1990): 195–204.

3. See esp. Robert O. Keohane, *After Hegemony: Cooperation and Discord in the World Political Economy* (Princeton, N.J.: Princeton University Press, 1984), 98–109; Abram Chayes and Antonia Handler Chayes, *The New Sovereignty: Compliance with International Regulatory Agreements* (Cambridge, Mass.: Harvard University Press, 1995); Ronald B. Mitchell, *Intentional Oil Pollution at Sea: Environmental Policy and Treaty Compliance* (Cambridge, Mass.: MIT Press, 1994); and Edith Brown Weiss and Harold K. Jacobson, *Engaging Countries: Strengthening Compliance with International Accords* (Cambridge, Mass.: MIT Press, 1998).

4. In this regard, I follow David Forsythe's widely accepted legal-empiricist approach to human rights issues. See Forsythe, *The Internationalization of Human Rights* (Lexington, Mass.: Lexington Books, 1991), 10–11. On personal integrity, see esp. Steven C. Poe and C. Neal Tate, "Repression of Human Rights to Personal Integrity in the 1980s: A Global Analysis," *American Political Science Review* 88 (December 1994): 853–72.

5. Louis Henkin, *How Nations Behave*, 2nd ed. (New York: Columbia University Press, 1979), 235.

6. Jack Donnelly, "Human Rights: The Impact of International Action," *International Journal* (Spring 1988): 241–63; Donnelly, *International Human Rights*, 2nd ed. (Boulder, Colo.: Westview Press, 1997); David Forsythe, "Human Rights in a Post–Cold War World," *Fletcher Forum of World Affairs* 15 (Summer 1991): 64; Forsythe, *Human Rights in International Relations*, 2nd ed. (New York: Cambridge University Press, 2006); Julie A. Mertus, *Bait and Switch: Human Rights and U.S. Foreign Policy* (New York: Routledge, 2004); Lori Fisler Damrosch, "The Civilian Impact of Economic Sanctions," in *Enforcing Restraint: Collective Intervention in Internal Conflicts*, ed. Damrosch (New York: Council on Foreign Relations Press, 1993); Stephen Krasner, *Sovereignty: Organized Hypocrisy* (Princeton, N.J.: Princeton University Press, 1999); Krasner, "Sovereignty, Regimes, and Human Rights," in *Regime Theory and International Relations*, ed. Volker Rittberger and Peter Mayer (Oxford: Clarendon Press, 1993); and Andrew Moravcsik, "The Origins of Human Rights Regimes: Democratic Delegation in Postwar Europe," *International Organization* 54 (Spring 2000): 217–52.

7. Abram Chayes and Antonia Handler Chayes, "On Compliance," *International Organization* 47 (Spring 1993): 197; Oran Young, *International Governance* (Ithaca, N.Y.: Cornell University Press, 1994); Dinah Shelton, ed., *Commitment and Compliance: The Role of Non-Binding Norms in the International Legal System* (Oxford: Oxford University Press, 2000); Margaret Keck and Kathryn Sikkink, *Activists Beyond Borders: Advocacy Networks in International Politics* (Ithaca, N.Y.: Cornell University Press, 1998); Sikkink, *Mixed Signals: U.S. Human Rights Policy and Latin America* (Ithaca, N.Y.: Cornell University Press, 2004); Sikkink, "Human Rights, Principled Issue Networks, and Sovereignty in Latin America," *International Organization* 47 (Summer 1993): 411–41; Sikkink, "The Power of Principled Ideas: Human Rights Policies in the United States and Western Europe," in *Ideas and Foreign Policy: Beliefs, Institutions, and Political Change*, ed. Judith Goldstein and Robert O. Keohane (Ithaca, N.Y.: Cornell University Press, 1992); Thomas Risse, Stephen Ropp, and Kathryn Sikkink, eds., *The Power of Human Rights: International Human Rights Norms and Domestic Change* (Cambridge: Cambridge University Press, 1999); Martha Finnemore, "Constructing Norms of Humanitarian Intervention," in *The Culture of National Security: Norms and Identity in World Politics*, ed. Peter J. Katzenstein (New York: Columbia University Press, 1996); Audie Klotz, *Norms in International Relations: The Struggle Against Apartheid* (Ithaca, N.Y.: Cornell University Press, 1995); Ann Marie Clark, *Diplomacy of Conscience: Amnesty International and Changing Human Rights Norms* (Princeton, N.J.: Princeton University Press, 2001); Daniel C. Thomas, *The Helsinki Effect: International Norms, Human Rights, and the Demise of Communism* (Princeton, N.J.: Princeton University Press, 2001); and Susan Burgerman, *Moral Victories: How Activists Provoke Multilateral Action* (Ithaca, N.Y.: Cornell University Press, 2001).

8. Robert Keohane makes a similar point about international cooperation. See Keohane, *After Hegemony*, 6.

9. Oran R. Young, *Compliance and Public Authority: A Theory with International Application* (Baltimore: Johns Hopkins University Press, 1979); and Chayes and Chayes, *The New Sovereignty*. For related work, see Roger Fisher, *Improving Compliance with International Law* (Charlottesville: University Press of Virginia, 1981); Beth Simmons, "Compliance with International Agreements," *Annual Review of*

Political Science 1 (1998): 75–94; and Anne-Marie Slaughter and Kal Raustiala, "Considering Compliance," in *Handbook of International Relations*, ed. Walter Carlnaes, Thomas Risse, and Beth Simmons (Thousand Oaks, Calif.: Sage Publications, 2002).

10. Examples include Beth Simmons, "International Law and State Behavior: Commitment and Compliance in International Monetary Affairs," *American Political Science Review* 94 (December 2000): 819–35; Jeffrey T. Checkel, "Why Comply? Social Learning and European Identity Change," *International Organization* 55 (Summer 2001): 553–88; Jonas Tallberg, "Paths to Compliance: Enforcement, Management, and the European Union," *International Organization* 56 (Summer 2002): 609–43; and Xinyuan Dai, "Why Comply? The Domestic Constituency Mechanism," *International Organization* 59 (April 2005): 363–98. See note 3 for studies of compliance with international environmental regimes.

11. See John Duffield, "International Relations and Alliance Behavior: NATO Force Levels," *International Organization* 26 (Fall 1992): 819–51.

12. For example, Sikkink, "Human Rights, Principled Issue Networks, and Sovereignty in Latin America"; and Risse, Ropp, and Sikkink, eds., *The Power of Human Rights*. For a comparison of behavioral and interpretive measures of compliance, consult Gregory A. Raymond, "Problems and Prospects in the Study of International Norms," *Mershon International Studies Review* 41 (November 1997): 205–45; and Janice E. Thomson, "Norms in International Relations: A Conceptual Analysis," *International Journal of Group Tensions* 23 (1993): 67–83.

13. James M. McCormick and Neil J. Mitchell propose treating human rights violations as a multidimensional variable. See McCormick and Mitchell, "Human Rights Violations, Umbrella Concepts, and Empirical Analysis," *World Politics* 49 (July 1997): 510–25.

14. While quantitative research often differentiates between treaty ratification and state compliance, it is inattentive to other types of commitment. See, for example, Oona Hathaway, "The Cost of Commitment," *Stanford Law Review* 55, 5 (May 2003): 1821–62; Simmons, "International Law and State Behavior"; and Todd Landman, *Protecting Human Rights* (Washington, D.C.: Georgetown University Press, 2005).

15. Judith Goldstein, Miles Kahler, and Anne-Marie Slaughter, eds., *Legalization and World Politics*, Special Issue, *International Organization* 54 (Summer 2000); see esp. Miles Kahler, "Conclusion: The Causes and Consequences of Legalization," 675. Xinyuan Dai discusses the role of domestic constituencies in "Why Comply?"

16. Robert Jervis, *System Effects: Complexity in Political and Social Life* (Princeton, N.J.: Princeton University Press, 1997).

17. Friedrich Kratochwil and John Ruggie, "International Organization: A State of the Art on an Art of the State," *International Organization* 40 (1986): 768.

18. Thomas Franck popularized the phrase "compliance pull" in *The Power of Legitimacy Among Nations* (New York: Oxford University Press, 1990).

19. George W. Downs, David M. Rocke, and Peter M. Barsoom, "Is the Good News about Compliance Good News about Cooperation?" *International Organization* 50 (Summer 1996): 379–406.

20. Emphasis added. See Jon Elster, *The Cement of Society: A Study of Social Order* (New York: Cambridge University Press, 1989), 132.

21. See Risse, Ropp, and Sikkink, eds., *The Power of Human Rights*; and

Thomas Risse, "'Let's Argue!' Communicative Action in World Politics," *International Organization* 54 (Winter 2000): 1–39.

22. Louis Henkin, "International Instruments for the Protection of Human Rights," *Acta Juridica* (1979): 224.

23. See, for example, Jennifer Schirmer, *The Guatemalan Military Project: A Violence Called Democracy* (Philadelphia: University of Pennsylvania Press, 1998).

24. Rick Fawn, "Encouraging the Incorrigible? Russia's Relations with the West over Chechnya," *The Journal of Communist Studies and Transition Politics* 18 (March 2002): 3–20; Eric A. Heinze and Douglas A. Borer, "The Chechen Exception: Rethinking Russia's Human Rights Policy," *Politics* 22 (May 2002): 86–94. For relevant background, Leo Zwaak, "The Council of Europe and the Conflict in Chechnya," *Netherlands Quarterly of Human Rights* 18 (June 2000): 179–82.

25. Slaughter and Raustiala, in "Considering Compliance," differentiate between ex-post and ex-ante strategies of compliance, calling on researchers to pay greater attention to the latter.

26. Starting points for research on violations of personal integrity rights are Steven C. Poe, "The Decision to Repress: An Integrative Theoretical Approach to the Research on Human Rights and Repression," in *Understanding Human Rights Violations: New Systematic Studies*, ed. Sabine C. Carey and Steven C. Poe (Aldershot, UK: Ashgate, 2004); Poe and Tate, "Repression of Human Rights to Personal Integrity in the 1980s"; and Steven C. Poe, C. Neal Tate, and Linda Camp Keith, "Repression of the Human Right to Personal Integrity Revisited: A Global Cross-National Study Covering the Years 1976–1993," *International Studies Quarterly* 43 (June): 291–313.

27. In a similar vein, James Ron argues that methods of state violence can be altered to enhance a regime's international and domestic legitimacy. See Ron, "Varying Methods of State Violence," *International Organization* 51 (Spring 1997): 275–300.

28. Judith Goldstein and Lisa L. Martin, "Legalization, Trade Liberalization, and Domestic Politics: A Cautionary Note," *International Organization* 54 (Summer 200): 603–32.

29. Peter Gourevitch, *Politics in Hard Times: Comparative Responses to International Economic Crises* (Ithaca, N.Y.: Cornell University Press, 1986), 10.

30. Alexander L. George, "Case Studies and Theory Development: The Method of Structured, Focused Comparison," in *Diplomacy: New Approaches in History, Theory, and Policy*, ed. Paul Gordon Lauren (New York: Free Press, 1979).

31. See, in general, Todd Landman, *Studying Human Rights* (New York: Routledge, 2006); Thomas B. Jabine and Richard P. Claude, *Human Rights and Statistics: Getting the Record Straight* (Philadelphia: University of Pennsylvania Press, 1992); and Russel Lawrence Barsh, "Measuring Human Rights: Problems of Methodology and Purpose," *Human Rights Quarterly* 15 (1993): 87–121.

Chapter 2

1. Henkin, *How Nations Behave*, 47.

2. See Hans Peter Schmitz and Kathryn Sikkink, "International Human Rights," in *Handbook of International Relations*, ed. Walter Carlsnaes, Thomas Risse, and Beth A. Simmons (Thousand Oaks, Calif.: Sage Publications, 2002).

3. On norms cascades, see Martha Finnemore and Kathryn Sikkink, "International Norm Dynamics and Political Change," *International Organization* 52

(Autumn 1998): 887–917. For a general overview, see Forsythe, *Human Rights in International Relations.*

4. For example, see Jack Donnelly, "International Human Rights: A Regime Analysis," *International Organization* 40 (Summer 1986): 599–641; Sikkink, "The Power of Principled Ideas"; and Andrew Moravcsik, "Explaining International Human Rights Regimes: Liberal Theory and Western Europe," *European Journal of International Relations* 1 (Summer 1995): 157–89.

5. See esp. Risse, Ropp, and Sikkink, eds., *The Power of Human Rights.* For an early example, see Sikkink, "Human Rights, Principled Issue Networks, and Sovereignty in Latin America."

6. Margaret Levi uses a similar trichotomy to explain compliance in comparative politics. See Levi, *Of Rule and Revenue* (Berkeley: University of California Press, 1988). From the perspective of international relations, Arild Underdal, "Explaining Compliance and Defection: Three Models," *European Journal of International Relations* 4 (March 1998): 5–30.

7. See Duffield, "International Relations and Alliance Behavior." In legal studies, see Tom R. Tyler, *Why People Obey the Law* (New Haven, Conn.: Yale University Press, 1990).

8. Martha Finnemore, *The Purpose of Intervention: Changing Beliefs about the Use of Force* (Ithaca, N.Y.: Cornell University Press, 2003).

9. Thomas Risse and Kathryn Sikkink, "The Socialization of International Human Rights Norms into Domestic Practices," in *The Power of Human Rights,* 19–22.

10. Clark, *Diplomacy of Conscience.*

11. Simmons, "International Law and State Behavior"; and Beth Simmons, "Why Commit? Explaining State Acceptance of International Human Rights Obligation," University of California, Berkeley, School of Law, International Legal Studies, Working Paper Series, 02–05 (2002).

12. Ellen Lutz and Kathryn Sikkink, "International Human Rights Law and Practice in Latin America," *International Organization* 54 (Summer 2000): 633–59.

13. See esp. Alison Brysk, "From Above and Below: Social Movements, the International System and Human Rights in Argentina," *Comparative Political Studies* 26 (October 1993): 259–85.

14. Jeffrey T. Checkel, "Norms, Institutions and National Identity in Contemporary Europe," *International Studies Quarterly* 43 (March 1999): 84–114.

15. Andrew P. Cortell and James W. Davis, Jr., "How Do International Institutions Matter? The Domestic Impact of International Rules and Norms," *International Studies Quarterly* 40 (1996): 451–78.

16. See esp. Sikkink, "Human Rights, Principled Issue Networks, and Sovereignty in Latin America"; and Keck and Sikkink, *Activists Beyond Borders.* See also Shareen Hertel, *Unexpected Power: Conflict and Change Among Transnational Activists* (Ithaca, N.Y.:Cornell University Press, 2006); *Sanjeev* Khagram, James V. Riker, and Kathryn Sikkink, eds., *Restructuring World Politics: Transnational Social Movements, Networks, and Norms* (Minneapolis: University of Minnesota, 2002); Richard Price, "Reversing the Gun Sights: Transnational Civil Society Targets Land Mines," *International Organization* 52 (Summer 1998): 613–44; Patricia Chilton, "Mechanics of Change: Social Movements, Transnational Coalitions and the Transformation Processes in Eastern Europe," in *Bringing Transnational Relations Back In: Non-State Actors, Domestic Structures, and International Institutions,* ed. Thomas Risse-Kappen (New York: Cambridge University Press, 1995); and Sandra Gubin, "Between Regimes and Realism—Transnational Agenda Setting:

Soviet Compliance with CSCE Human Rights Norms," *Human Rights Quarterly* 17 (Summer 1995): 278–302.

17. Keck and Sikkink, *Activists Beyond Borders,* 12–13.

18. Harold H. Koh, "Why Do Nations Obey International Law?" *Yale Law Journal* 106 (1997): 2598–659.

19. Risse, "'Let's Argue!' Communicative Action in World Politics."

20. Thomas, *The Helsinki Effect.*

21. See Donnelly, "International Human Rights: A Regime Analysis."

22. Shelton, ed., *Commitment and Compliance.*

23. Chayes and Chayes, *The New Sovereignty.*

24. Emilie M. Hafner-Burton, "Trading Human Rights: How Preferential Trade Agreements Influence Government Repression," *International Organization* 59, 3 (July 2005): 593–629; Julie Harrelson-Stephens and Rhonda L. Callaway, "Does Trade Openness Promote Security Rights in Developing Countries? Examining the Liberal Perspective," *International Interactions* 29, 2 (2003): 143–58; and William H. Meyer, "Human Rights and MNCs: Theory versus Quantitative Analysis," *Human Rights Quarterly* 18 (May 1996): 368–97.

25. See note 2, Chapter 1. For a broad, sometimes critical, discussion of these issues, see Alison Brysk, ed., *Globalization and Human Rights* (Berkeley: University of California Press, 2002).

26. For example, see Sabine C. Zanger, "A Global Analysis of the Effect of Political Regime Changes on Life Integrity Violations, 1977–1993," *Journal of Peace Research* 37 (March 2000): 213–33; Christian Davenport, "Human Rights and the Democratic Proposition," *Journal of Conflict Resolution* 43 (February 1999): 92–116. For an emphasis on liberal regimes, see Rhoda E. Howard and Jack Donnelly, "Human Dignity, Human Rights, and Political Regimes," *The American Political Science Review* 80, 3 (1986): 801–17.

27. Moravcsik, "The Origins of Human Rights Regimes."

28. Simmons, "International Law and State Behavior."

29. For example, see Frank B. Cross, "The Relevance of Law in Human Rights Protection," *International Review of Law and Economics* 19 (March 1999): 87–98; and Eugene Cotran and Adel Omar Sherif, eds., *The Role of the Judiciary in the Protection of Human Rights* (Dordrecht: Kluwer Law International, 1997).

30. Simmons, "Why Commit?" 11.

31. Robert Keohane, Andrew Moravcsik, and Anne-Marie Slaughter, "Legalized Dispute Resolution: Interstate and Transnational," *International Organization* 54 (Summer 2000): 457–88. For an application of this logic to human rights, see Azza Salama Layton, *International Politics and Civil Rights Policies in the United States, 1941–1960* (Cambridge: Cambridge University Press, 2000).

32. Anne-Marie Slaughter, "International Law in a World of Liberal States," *European Journal of International Law* 6 (1995): 503–38.

33. See Center for the Study of Human Rights, *Capacity-Building by Human Rights Organizations: Challenges and Strategies* (New York: Center for the Study of Human Rights, Columbia University, 2002).

34. Krasner, "Sovereignty, Regimes, and Human Rights."

35. Ernst B. Haas, *When Knowledge Is Power: Three Models of Change in International Organizations* (Berkeley: University of California Press), 184.

36. See, for example, Neta C. Crawford and Audie Klotz, eds., *How Sanctions Work: Lessons from South Africa* (New York: St. Martin's Press, 1999).

37. Sikkink, "Human Rights, Principled Issue Networks, and Sovereignty in Latin America"; and Burgerman, *Moral Victories*.

38. Sonia Cardenas, "Emerging Global Actors: The United Nations and National Human Rights Institutions," *Global Governance* 9, 1 (January–March 2003): 23–42.

39. Lisa Martin and Kathryn Sikkink, "U.S. Policy and Human Rights in Argentina and Guatemala, 1973–1980," in *Double-Edged Diplomacy: International Bargaining and Domestic Politics*, ed. Peter B. Evans, Harold K. Jacobson, and Robert D. Putnam (Berkeley: University of California Press, 1993).

40. Burgerman, *Moral Victories*.

41. On combining rationalist arguments, see Tallberg, "Paths to Compliance"; for a call to fuse rationalist and constructivist approaches, see Jeffrey T. Checkel, "The Constructivist Turn in International Relations Theory," *World Politics* 50, 2 (1998): 324–48.

42. Krasner, *Sovereignty: Organized Hypocrisy*.

43. Chayes and Chayes, "On Compliance."

44. Mitchell, *Intentional Oil Pollution at Sea*.

45. See Paul Kowert and Jeffrey Legro, "Norms, Identity, and Their Limits," in *The Culture of National Security*, esp. 486–88.

46. Some of the most prominent examples include Carey and Poe, eds., *Understanding Human Rights Violations*; Poe, Tate, and Keith, "Repression of the Human Right to Personal Integrity Revisited"; Poe and Tate, "Repression of Human Rights to Personal Integrity in the 1980s"; Landman, *Protecting Human Rights*; Conway W. Henderson, "Conditions Affecting the Use of Political Repression," *Journal of Conflict Resolution* 35 (March 1991): 120–42; Christian Davenport, "Multi-dimensional Threat Perception and State Repression: An Inquiry into Why States Apply Negative Sanctions," *American Journal of Political Science* 39 (1995): 683–713; Davenport, "'Constitutional Promises' and Repressive Reality: A Cross-National Time-Series Investigation of Why Political and Civil Liberties Are Suppressed," *Journal of Politics* 58 (1996): 627–54; Henderson, "Population Pressures and Political Repression," *Social Science Quarterly* 74 (1993): 322–33; Mitchell and McCormick, "Economic and Political Explanations of Human Rights Violations"; Han S. Park, "Correlates of Human Rights: Global Tendencies," *Human Rights Quarterly* 9 (May 1987): 405–13; Davenport, ed., *Paths to State Repression: Human Rights Violations and Contentious Politics* (Lanham, Md.: Rowman and Littlefield, 2000); and Scott S. Gartner and Patrick M. Regan, "Threat and Repression: The Non-Linear Relationship between Government and Opposition Violence," *Journal of Peace Research* 33 (August 1996): 273–87.

47. In proposing an "integrative" model of human rights violations, Steven Poe categorizes variables according to the extent to which they shape perceptions of strength and threat, as well as help define alternative options and the choice among alternatives. See Poe, "The Decision to Repress." The argument I propose complements Poe's decision-making process while focusing more explicitly on the full range of international relations theories, including rationalist and normative approaches.

48. See note 46.

49. For instance, see Charles Tilly, *Coercion, Capital, and European States, A.D. 990–1992* (Cambridge, Mass.: Blackwell, 1990); and Ted Robert Gurr, "The Political Origins of State Violence and Terror: A Theoretical Analysis," in *Government Violence and Repression: An Agenda for Research*, ed. Michael Stohl and George A. Lopez (Westport, Conn.: Greenwood Press, 1986).

50. See Goldstein and Martin, "Legalization, Trade Liberalization, and Do-

mestic Politics"; and Kahler, "Conclusion: The Causes and Consequences of Legalization."

51. In addition to note 26, see Christian Davenport and David A. Armstrong, "Democracy and the Violation of Human Rights: A Statistical Analysis from 1976 to 1996," *American Journal of Political Science* 48, 3 (July 2004): 538–60; Poe, Tate, and Keith, "Repression of the Human Right to Personal Integrity Revisited"; Davenport, "Human Rights and the Democratic Proposition"; Poe and Tate, "Repression of Human Rights to Personal Integrity in the 1980s"; and Henderson, "Conditions Affecting the Use of Political Repression." Michael Goodhart presents an intriguing argument that democracy *is* human rights in *Democracy as Human Rights: Freedom and Equality in the Age of Globalization* (New York: Routledge, 2005).

52. Adam Przeworski, *Democracy and the Market: Political and Economic Reforms in Eastern Europe and Latin America* (Cambridge: Cambridge University Press, 1991), 95.

53. Kratochwil and Ruggie, "International Organization."

54. For example, see Brian Loveman, *The Constitution of Tyranny: Regimes of Exception in Spanish America* (Pittsburgh, Pa.: University of Pittsburgh Press, 1993). See also Anna-Lena Svensson-McCarthy, *The International Law of Human Rights and States of Exception* (The Hague: Martinus Nijhoff, 1998); and Joan Fitzpatrick, *Human Rights in Crisis: The International System for Protecting Rights during States of Emergency* (Philadelphia: University of Pennsylvania Press, 1994).

55. Tilly, *Coercion, Capital, and European States.*

56. Anthony W. Marx, *Making Race and Nation: A Comparison of the United States, South Africa, and Brazil* (Cambridge: Cambridge University Press, 1998), 25.

57. See Jack Donnelly, "Unfinished Business," *PS Political Science and Politics* 31 (September 1998): 530–36.

58. For relevant examples, see, respectively, Margaret E. Crahan, "National Security Ideology and Human Rights," in *Human Rights and Basic Needs in the Americas,* ed. Crahan (Washington, D.C.: Georgetown University Press, 1982); and David Pion-Berlin, *The Ideology of State Terror: Economic Doctrine and Political Repression in Argentina and Peru* (Boulder, Colo.: Lynne Rienner, 1989). More recently, see Michael Ignatieff, ed., *American Exceptionalism and Human Rights* (Princeton, N.J.: Princeton University Press, 2005).

59. Jack Snyder, *Myths of Empire* (Ithaca, N.Y.: Cornell University Press, 1991), 1–2.

60. Snyder, *Myths of Empire,* 17.

61. See Jeffrey W. Legro, *Rethinking the World: Great Power Strategies and International Order* (Ithaca, N.Y.: Cornell University Press, 2005).

62. On rights-protective regimes, see Jack Donnelly, *International Human Rights* (Boulder, Colo.: Westview Press, 1993), 145–49.

63. Chayes and Chayes, "On Compliance," 175–76.

64. Shelton, ed., *Commitment and Compliance,* 17.

65. See Slaughter and Raustiala, "Considering Compliance." For attempts to measure state compliance, as an indicator of international legal influence, see Eric Neumayer, "Do International Human Rights Treaties Improve Respect for Human Rights?" *Journal of Conflict Resolution* 49, 6 (2005): 925–53; Oona A. Hathaway, "Do Human Rights Treaties Make a Difference?" *Yale Law Journal* 111, 8 (June 2002): 1935–2042; Douglass Cassel, "Does International Human Rights Law Make a Difference?" *Chicago Journal of International Law* 2, 1 (Spring 2001): 121–35; and Linda Camp Keith, "The United Nations International Covenant

on Civil and Political Rights: Does It Make a Difference in Human Rights Behavior?" *Journal of Peace Research* 36 (1999): 95–118.

66. CIRI Human Rights Data are available at http://ciri.binghamton.edu/. This database, which is highly correlated with the PTS, covers 13 internationally recognized human rights for 162 countries between 1981 and 2004. See David L. Cingranelli and David L. Richards, "Measuring the Level, Pattern, and Sequences of Government Respect for Physical Integrity Rights," *International Studies Quarterly* 43 (1999): 407–17.

67. For a call to disaggregate human rights violations, see McCormick and Mitchell, "Human Rights Violations, Umbrella Concepts, and Empirical Analysis."

68. CIRI Coding Guide, available at http://ciri.binghamton.edu/documentation.asp.

69. I inverted this scale so that 2 would equal the highest level of violations and 0 would indicate no violations.

70. Though it disaggregates human rights violations, this index is cumulative and scaled (i.e., one-dimensional). C.f.. McCormick and Mitchell, "Human Rights Violations."

71. For a relevant methodological discussion, see George Lopez and Michael Stohl, "Problems of Concept and Measurement in the Study of Human Rights," in *Human Rights and Statistics.*

72. All state commitments are coded using Amnesty International annual reports, which document consistently the principal instances of state action in these areas. In the case of monitoring, I determined whether Amnesty International, or other international organizations reported in Amnesty International's annual report, visited a country in a given year. Binary coding certainly does not capture the subtleties of human rights commitments such as accountability. For example, Amnesty International may discuss cases of accountability alongside impunity. As a first-cut indicator of commitment, however, any state accountability can be significant in comparative terms.

73. Following Simmons's lead in "Why Commit?" I code treaty ratification as follows: ratification (2), signature (1), no action (0).

74. See, for example, Gennady M. Danilenko, "Implementation of International Law in CIS States: Theory and Practice," *European Journal of International Law* 10, 1 (1999): 51–69.

75. In total, 172 countries were examined over the 1992 to 1996 period. For the purposes of this chapter, I measured human rights commitments on a six-point scale, depending on how many of the five types of state commitment (ratification, monitoring, leniency, implementation, and accountability) were present in a given year. This required treating ratification as a dummy variable, where 1 signifies either signature or ratification. To facilitate comparison, moreover, the nine-point Physical Integrity Index was scaled to a six-point score.

76. Lumping refers to adding commitments and respect for personal integrity, which can range from 0 to 12.

Chapter 3

1. See, for example, Forsythe, *Human Rights in International Relations.*

2. Paul E. Sigmund, *The Overthrow of Allende and the Politics of Chile, 1964–1976* (Pittsburgh, Pa.: University of Pittsburgh Press, 1977), 253; and Jinny Arancibia, Marcelo Charlín, and Peter Landstreet, "Chile," in *International Handbook of Hu-*

man *Rights*, ed. Jack Donnelly and Rhoda Howard (New York: Greenwood Press, 1987), 54. Ascanio Cavallo Castro, Manuel Salazar Salvo, and Oscar Sepúlveda Pacheco, *La historia oculta del régimen militar: Chile, 1973–1988* (Santiago: Editorial Antártica, 1989). A good overview of the use of arbitrary arrests and detentions during military rule is provided in Inter-American Commission on Human Rights (IACHR), *Report on the Situation of Human Rights in Chile* (Washington, D.C.: Organization of American States/OAS, 1985), esp. 112–24, OEA/Ser. LV/II, 66, Doc. 17 (27 September 1985).

3. Chile had ratified the International Covenants on Civil and Political Rights and on Economic, Social, and Cultural Rights in 1972. It also had accepted the following international human rights instruments: Convention on the Prevention and Punishment of the Crime of Genocide, Geneva Conventions, Convention Relating to the Status of Refugees, International Convention on the Elimination of All Forms of Racial Discrimination, as well as several relevant International Labor Organization instruments. Chile had signed, but not ratified, the American Convention on Human Rights.

4. In the Inter-American human rights system, the Chilean case has been described as a "turning point." Cecilia Medina Quiroga, *The Battle of Human Rights: Gross, Systematic Violations and the Inter-American System* (Dordrecht: Martinus Hijhoff, 1988), 261. For how Chile influenced the institutionalization of human rights in the United States, see Paul E. Sigmund, *The United States and Democracy in Chile* (Baltimore: Johns Hopkins University Press, 1993), 101. On the overwhelming attention paid by the United Nations to the Chilean case, see Jack Donnelly, "Human Rights at the United Nations 1955–85: The Question of Bias," *International Studies Quarterly* 32 (1988): esp. 291–92.

5. "El Proceso de Reorganización Nacional [Process of National Reorganization]," *Boletín Oficial* (Buenos Aires) (29 March 1976). See also Helio Juan Zarini, *Historia e instituciones en la Argentina* (Buenos Aires: Editorial Astreda de Alfredo y Rocardo Depalma, 1981), 362–66.

6. *Official Journal of the European Community: Debates of the European Parliament 1978–1979 Session,* Report of Proceedings from 8 to 12 May 1978, no. 230 (Luxembourg: Office for Official Publications of the European Communities, May 1978); and Patrick J. Flood, "U.S. Human Rights Initiatives Concerning Argentina," in *The Diplomacy of Human Rights,* ed. David D. Newsom (Lanham, Md.: University Press of America, 1986).

7. Proponents of the view that international human rights pressure against Chile was effective include Alan Angell, "International Support for the Chilean Opposition, 1973–1989: Political Parties and the Role of Exiles," in *The International Dimensions of Democratization: Europe and the Americas,* ed. Laurence Whitehead (Oxford: Oxford University Press, 1996); Sigmund, *The United States and Democracy in Chile,* and John A. Detzner, "De l'efficacité des mécanismes internationaux de protection des droits de la personne: Le cas du Chili," *Annuaire canadien des droits de la personne* 5 (1988): 145–65. Examples of skeptics are Wolfgang S. Heinz, "The Military, Torture and Human Rights: Experiences from Argentina, Brazil, Chile and Uruguay," in *The Politics of Pain: Torturers and Their Masters,* ed. Ronald D. Crelinsten and Alex P. Schmid (Boulder, Colo.: Westview Press, 1995); and Susan Kaufman Purcell, "Chile: The Limits of U.S. Leverage," in *Chile: Prospects for Democracy,* ed. Mark Falcoff, Arturo Valenzuela, and Susan Kaufman Purcell (New York: Council on Foreign Relations, 1988). A more nuanced argument is offered by Darren Hawkins, who emphasizes the regime's quest for legitimacy. See Hawkins, *International Human Rights and Authoritarian Rule in Chile* (Lincoln: University of Nebraska Press, 2002); and Hawkins, "State

Responses to International Pressures: Human Rights in Authoritarian Chile,"
European Journal of International Relations 3 (December 1997): 403–34.

8. Carlos Escudé, "Argentina: The Costs of Contradiction," in *Exporting Democracy: The United States and Latin America*, ed. Abraham F. Lowenthal (Baltimore: Johns Hopkins University Press, 1991); and Gracia Berg, "Human Rights Sanctions as Leverage: Argentina, a Case Study," *Journal of Legislation* 7 (1980): 93–112.

9. See Kathryn Sikkink, "The Effectiveness of US Human Rights Policy 1973–1980," in *The International Dimensions of Democratization: Europe and the Americas*; Sikkink, "Human Rights, Principled Issue Networks, and Sovereignty in Latin America"; Martin and Sikkink, "U.S. Policy and Human Rights in Argentina and Guatemala"; Brysk, "From Above and Below"; David Weissbrodt and María Luisa Bartolomei, "The Effectiveness of International Human Rights Pressures: The Case of Argentina, 1976–1983," *Minnesota Law Review* 75 (February 1991): 1009–35; Maria Luisa Bartolomei, *Gross and Massive Violations of Human Rights in Argentina: 1976–1983* (Lund, Sweden: Institute of International Law, 1991); Emilio F. Mignone, *Derechos humanos y sociedad. El caso argentino* (Buenos Aires: Centro de Estudios Legales y Sociales, 1991); and Iain Guest, *Behind the Disappearances: Argentina's Dirty War Against Human Rights and the United Nations* (Philadelphia: University of Pennsylvania Press, 1990).

10. Roberta Cohen, "Human Rights Diplomacy: The Carter Administration and the Southern Cone," *Human Rights Quarterly* 9 (1982): 212–42.

11. Alvaro de Arce, MªPaz Martínez Nieto, and Alberto Sepúlveda Almarza, *Cuba y Chile: La cuestión de los derechos humanos*, no. 39 (Madrid: Instituto de Cuestiones Internacionales, October 1988): 46. For a list of the principal decrees, see *100 primeros decretos: Leyes dictados por la junta de gobierno de la república de Chile* (Santiago: Editorial Jurídica de Chile, 1973). See also Comisión Andina de Juristas, *Perú y Chile: Poder judicial y derechos humanos* (Lima, Peru: Comisión Andina de Juristas, 1988), 227; and National Commission for Truth and Reconciliation, *Report of the Chilean National Commission on Truth and Reconciliation*, trans. Phillip E. Berryman (Notre Dame, Ind.: University of Notre Dame Press, 1993), 76 [hereafter, *Rettig Report*].

12. U.S. Department of State, briefing memorandum from Jack B. Kubisch to the secretary of state on the subject of "Chilean Executions," 16 November 1973. Available through the National Security Archive: http://www.gwu.edu/~nsarchiv/NSAEBB/NSAEBB8/ch10–01.htm.

13. *Rettig Report*, 470–81. An organigram of DINA and a list of detention sites are provided in Cavallo, Salazar, and Sepúlveda, *La historia oculta del regimen militar*, 50 and 37.

14. Interview in *Le Monde*, quoted in *Chile Informativo* (Mexico City) (13–26 March 1976). See also Jac Forton, *20 ans de résistance et de lutte contre l'impunité au chili 1973–1993* (Geneva: Editions de CETIM, 1993), 22–26.

15. Lars Schoultz, *Human Rights and United States Policy Toward Latin America* (Princeton, N.J.: Princeton University Press, 1981), 12.

16. *Rettig Report*, 118–19; and Comisión Andina de Juristas, *Perú y Chile*, 231–32. On the behavior of the courts during military rule, see *Rettig Report*, chap. 4.

17. Medina Quiroga, *The Battle of Human Rights*, 277; Comisión Andina de Juristas, *Perú y Chile*, 295; IACHR, *Report on the Status of Human Rights in Chile, Findings of "on the Spot" Observations in the Republic of Chile, July 22–August 2, 1974* (Washington, D.C.: OAS, 1974), OEA/Ser. L/V/II, 34, Doc. 21 (25 October

1974) [hereafter, *First Chile Report*]; *Chile-America*, no. 10–11 (Rome, 1975): 119–20; and *Rettig Report*, 75.

18. *Chile Informativo*, no. 78 (1975).

19. See María Seoane and Héctor Ruíz Nuñez, *La noche de los lápices*, 3rd ed. (Buenos Aires: Editorial Contrapunto, 1986); Claudio Trobo, *¿Quién mató a Michelini y Gutiérrez Ruíz?* (Buenos Aires: Ediciones Teoría y Práctica, 1986); CONADEP, *Nunca Más: The Report of the Argentine National Commission for the Disappeared* (New York: Farrar Straus Giraux, 1986), 236–37 and 349–53; and Carlos Gabetta, *Todos somos subversivos* (Buenos Aires: Editorial Bruguera, 1983), 209–48. For Solari Yrigoyen's case, see IACHR, *Diez Años de Actividades 1971–1981* (Washington, D.C.: Organization of American States, 1982), 174–77 (Case 2088).

20. Amnesty International, *Amnesty International Report 1975–76* (London: Amnesty International Publications, 1977); Pion-Berlin, *The Ideology of State Terror*, 112–16; and Paul G. Buchanan, "State Terror as a Complement of Economic Policy: The Argentine Proceso, 1976–1981," in *Dependence, Development, and State Repression*, ed. George A. Lopez and Michael Stohl (New York: Greenwood Press, 1989), 48. For the general legal structure of the military regime, see Frederick Snyder, "State of Siege and the Rule of Law in Argentina," *Lawyer of the Americas* 15 (Winter 1984): 503–20.

21. Amnesty International, *The Amnesty International Report 1975–76*. On the junta's interest in maintaining the appearance of legal continuity, Mark J. Osiel, "Dialogue with Dictators: Judicial Resistance in Argentina and Brazil," *Law and Social Inquiry* 20 (Spring 1995): 481–560.

22. United Nations Economic and Social Council, *Study of the Impact of Foreign Economic Aid and Assistance on Respect for Human Rights in Chile*, report prepared by Antonio Cassesse, E/CN.4/Sub.2/412 (26 October 1978), 10–29.

23. For example, see Jonathan Kandell, "Private U.S. Loans in Chile up Sharply," *New York Times* (12 November 1973).

24. IACHR, *First Chile Report*.

25. *Chile Informativo* (Mexico City), multiple issues, 1976–78.

26. U.S. Congress, House, Subcommittee on International Organizations of the House Committee on International Relations, *Human Rights in Argentina*, 94th Cong., 2d sess., 1976. On bureaucratic infighting, see Stephen B. Cohen, "Conditioning U.S. Security Assistance on Human Rights Practices," *American Journal of International Law* 76 (1980): 259. For an argument that many of the U.S. military credits could in fact be used for counterinsurgency purposes, see *Human Rights and the U.S. Foreign Assistance Program: Fiscal Year 1978, Part I—Latin America* (Washington, D.C.: Center for International Policy, n.d.), 19.

27. On the role of the UNHCR, see Guest, *Behind the Disappearances*, 464, n. 1; and Amnesty International, *The Amnesty International Report 1976–77*. Europe's role is discussed in *Official Journal of the European Communities: Informations and Notices*, 19, no. C 178/65 (Luxembourg: Office for Official Publications of the EC, 2 August 1976).

28. Amnesty International, *Report of an Amnesty International Mission to Argentina, 6–15 November 1976* (London: Amnesty International Publications, 1977); and Guest, *Behind the Disappearances*, 49.

29. Hugo Fruhling, "Resistance to Fear in Chile: The Experience of the Vicaría de la Solidaridad," in *Fear at the Edge: State Terror and Resistance in Latin America*, ed. Juan E. Corradi, Patricia Weiss Fagen, and Manuel Antonio Garretón (Berkeley: University of California Press, 1992), 123. More generally, see Cristián Parker, "La Iglesia y los derechos humanos en Chile (1973–1989)," *Re-*

vista chilena de los derechos humanos 12 (April 1990); and Gutiérrez Funete and Juan Ignacio, *Chile: La Vicaría de la Solidaridad* (Madrid: Alianza Editorial, 1986).

30. Amnesty International, *Report of an Amnesty International Mission to Argentina*, 27.

31. See esp. Sigmund, *The United States and Democracy in Chile.*

32. United Nations, Economic and Social Council (ECOSOC), *Study of the Impact of Foreign Economic Aid*, 21. For British human rights pressure, see Walter Little, "Britain, Chile and Human Rights, 1973–1990," in *The Legacy of Dictatorship: Political, Economic and Social Change in Pinochet's Chile*, ed. Alan Angell and Benny Pollack, Monograph Series, no. 17 (Liverpool: University of Liverpool, Institute of Latin American Studies, 1993).

33. Mennot Kamminga, *Inter-State Accountability for Violations of Human Rights* (Philadelphia: University of Pennsylvania Press, 1992), 94.

34. United Nations General Assembly Resolution 3448 (9 December 1975).

35. Chile's principal lenders were the United States, Argentina, and Brazil; its major creditors included Western Europe, Japan, and Canada. U.N. ECOSOC, *Study of the Impact of Foreign Economic Aid*, 46.

36. U.S. Congress, Senate, Committee on Appropriations, *Foreign Assistance and Related Programs Appropriations Fiscal Year 1978*, 95th Cong., 1st sess., 1977.

37. Subsequent observations about Derian's visits are based on her testimony in the 1985 trial against the junta. See "Argentina, Cámara Nacional de Apelaciones en lo Criminal y Correccional de la Capital Federal," *El Libro de El Diario del Juicio* (Buenos Aires: Perfil, 1985), 85–101.

38. Berg, "Human Rights Sanctions as Leverage," 110; and *Human Rights and the U.S. Foreign Assistance Program*, 22.

39. Martin and Sikkink, "U.S. Policy and Human Rights in Argentina and Guatemala," 348.

40. The amendment, which became known as the Kennedy-Humphrey amendment after Senator Hubert Humphrey proposed a one-year grace period, nonetheless permitted Argentina to renew military export licenses issued before September 1978. See Berg, "Human Rights Sanctions as Leverage," 104; and Guest, *Behind the Disappearances*, 173.

41. In particular, the Catholic Church founded the *Academia de Humanismo Cristiano* in 1975 to assist expelled academics. See Angell, "International Support for the Chilean Opposition," 188. See also Brian H. Smith, "Old Allies, New Enemies: The Catholic Church as Opposition to Military Rule in Chile, 1973–1979," in *Military Rule in Chile: Dictatorship and Opposition*, ed. J. Samuel Valenzuela and Arturo Valenzuela (Baltimore: Johns Hopkins University Press, 1986), 282.

42. *Rettig Report*, 627–31.

43. Guest, *Behind the Disappearances*, 167–68. On the role of U.S. diplomatic contacts, see Flood, "U.S. Human Rights Initiatives Concerning Argentina," 134–35. For the role of the grandmothers, see Rita Arditti, *Searching for Life: The Grandmothers of the Plaza de Mayo and the Disappeared Children of Argentina* (Berkeley: University of California Press, 1999). Regarding *Las Madres*, see, for example, Marguerite Guzmán Bouvard, *Revolutionizing Motherhood: The Mothers of the Plaza de Mayo* (Wilmington, Del.: Scholarly Resources, 2002).

44. Amnesty International, *The Amnesty International Report, 1978–79* (London: Amnesty International Publications, 1980); and Guest, *Behind the Disappearances*, 51.

45. For example, the *Asamblea Permanente por los Derechos Humanos* (APDH).

46. Sigmund, *The United States and Democracy in Chile*, 104.

47. Sigmund, *The United States and Democracy in Chile*, 103–5.

48. Interview with *La Repubblica* (22 September 1976), cited in *Chile Informativo* (Mexico City) (16–29 October 1976).

49. Sigmund, *The United States and Democracy in Chile*, 110.

50. *Chile Informativo* (Mexico City), multiple issues, 1977.

51. See Sigmund, *The United States and Democracy in Chile*.

52. U.S. Congress, Senate, Subcommittee on Western Hemisphere Affairs of the Senate Committee on Foreign Relations, *Latin America*, 95th Cong., 2d sess., 1978 (Statement of Thomas E. Skidmore).

53. Even Andrew Young sent a letter to National Security Adviser Zbigniew Brzezinski holding Derian personally responsible for "denying jobs to U.S. workers." Guest, *Behind the Disappearances*, 172. See also "Human-Rights Zeal That Costs U.S. Jobs," *Washington Post* (18 September 1978), A23.

54. Lars Schoultz, *Human Rights and United States Policy Toward Latin America* (Princeton, N.J.: Princeton University Press, 1981), 331–32.

55. U.S. human rights policy toward Argentina had been contradictory since the postwar period, reflecting interbureaucratic rivalry more than changing circumstances in Argentina. See Escudé, "Argentina: The Costs of Contradiction." Escudé attributes inconsistencies in U.S. policy to Argentina's salient but geostrategically marginal role.

56. Schoultz, *Human Rights and United States Policy Toward Latin America*, 349, n. 8; Guest, *Behind the Disappearances*, 174–75; and Flood, "U.S. Human Rights Initiatives Concerning Argentina."

57. *Chile Informativo*, no. 141 (April 1978); and no. 157 (November 1978). Within the IACHR, the decision to hold the next General Assembly meeting in Santiago served as a point of contention, as did the IACHR's refusal to issue an official report condemning repression in Chile; the latter led in March 1976 to the largest group resignation within the organization in seventeen years. *Chile Informativo* (Mexico City) (27 March–9 April 1976).

58. *Yearbook of the United Nations* (New York: United Nations, 1978), 704–5 and 710. See also *Chile Informativo*, no. 147 (July 1978); and Detzner, "De l'efficacité des mécanismes internationaux de protection des droits de la personne," 148. In contrast to other U.N. bodies, voting in ECOSOC remained mostly constant. See *Yearbook of the United Nations* (New York: United Nations, 1974–78).

59. Bartolomei, *Gross and Massive Violations of Human Rights in Argentina*, 189–92.

60. *Official Journal of the European Communities: Debates of the European Parliament 1977–1978 Session*, Report of Proceedings from 16 to 20 January 1978, no. 225 (Luxembourg: Office for Official Publications of the EC, 1978): 190–91.

61. For the debate, see the *Official Journal of the European Communities: Debates of the European Parliament 1978–1979 Session*, Report of Proceedings from 8 to 12 May 1978, no. 230 (Luxembourg: Office for Official Publications of the EC, 1978): 172–86.

62. Inter-American Commission on Human Rights, *Report on the Situation of Human Rights in Argentina*, OEA/Ser. L/V/II, 49 (11 April 1980).

63. Other groups in civil society called for a return to democratic freedoms and rights. In August 1977, the Group of Ten (10 prominent centrist members of the labor movement) issued an open letter to the junta, signed by over 850 trade union officials representing close to 500 organizations; three hundred youths issued a similar document. In 1978, the Group of 24, representing ideologically diverse sectors of the opposition, formed to oppose the regime's self-

institutionalization. *Chile Informativo*, no. 124 (September 1977); and Manuel Antonio Garretón, "Party Opposition under the Chilean Authoritarian Regime," in *Military Rule in Chile*, 172.

64. Hugo Fruhling, *Nonprofit Organizations as Opposition to Authoritarian Rule: The Case of Human Rights Organizations and Private Research Centers in Chile* (New Haven, Conn.: Institutions for Social and Policy Studies, Yale University, April 1985), 36 and 126; and *Chile Informativo* (30 April–13 May 1977).

65. See the account by Chilean poet Marjorie Agosín, *Ashes of Revolt* (Fredonia, N.Y.: White Pine Press, 1996).

66. Fruhling, *Nonprofit Organizations as Opposition to Authoritarian Rule*, 30–36.

67. Fruhling, *Nonprofit Organizations as Opposition to Authoritarian Rule*, 28 and 90; and Fruhling, "Resistance to Fear in Chile," 30 and 35.

68. Timerman was the director and founder of *La Opinión* newspaper. Jacobo Timerman, *Prisoner Without a Name, Cell Without a Number*, trans. Toby Talbot (New York: Random House, 1981).

69. Arancibia, Charlín, and Landstreet, "Chile." For the role of DINA during this period, see *Chile Informativo* (13–26 November 1976), Supplement.

70. *Chile Informativo*, no. 135 (February 1978).

71. Amnesty International, *The Amnesty International Report 1978–79*; and Guest, *Behind the Disappearances*, 51.

72. Military writings are reproduced in Héctor Riesle Contreras, "La legitimidad de la junta de gobierno," in *Fuerzas armadas y seguridad nacional*, ed. Pablo Baraona Urzúa, Ricardo Cox, K. Juraj Domic, et al. (Santiago: Ediciones Portada, 1973).

73. Speech at the Escuela Militar marking Pinochet's second year as commander-in-chief of the army. Augusto Pinochet Ugarte, *Camino Recorrido, Memorias de un soldado* (Santiago: Talleres Gráficos del Instituto Geográfico Militar, 1990), 111.

74. *Observations of Chile (Chapters I-XII) on report of Ad Hoc Working Group*, transmitted by letters of October 18, 20, 21, 25, and 26, 1976, from Chile, U.N. Doc. A/C.3/31/6 and Add. 1.

75. Medina Quiroga, *The Battle of Human Rights*, 280.

76. Comisión Andina de Juristas, *Perú y Chile*, 280, n. 24; and *Chile Informativo* (13–26 March 1976); and (2–15 October 1976).

77. U.S. State Department spokesperson John King, 2 October 1973. Quoted in Nathaniel Davis, *The Last Two Years of Salvador Allende* (Ithaca, N.Y.: Cornell University Press, 1986), 377.

78. *Chile Informativo* (22 May–4 June 1976); and no. 119 (June 1977). Also *Rettig Report*, 51.

79. *Clarín* (Buenos Aires), 31 March 1976. Quoted in Marcelo Cavarozzi, *Autoritarismo y democracia, 1955–1983* (Buenos Aires: Centro Editor de América Latina, 1983), 134.

80. Closing speech at governors' convocation in Buenos Aires, 30 July 1976. Quoted in García, *La Doctrina de seguridad nacional* (Buenos Aires: Centro Editor de Américâ Latina, 1991), 176.

81. Guest, *Behind the Disappearances*, 64.

82. Amnesty International, *The Amnesty International Report 1975–76*.

83. *Wall Street Journal* (29 October 1978).

84. Guest, *Behind the Disappearances*, 367–74; and Bartolomei, *Gross and Massive Violations of Human Rights in Argentina*, 195.

85. In the second half of 1976, for example, mutilated bodies washed up on riverbanks and Chilean beaches. *Rettig Report,* 502.

86. *Chile Informativo,* no. 124 (September 1977): 16. Prior to this, the government had admitted only that certain legal rights were suspended under the state of siege. For example, see *Observaciones Formuladas por el Gobierno de Chile sobre el Según Informe Elaborado por la Comisión Interamericana de Derechos Humanos acerca de la situación de los derechos humanos en dicho país,* OEA/Ser. P AG/Doc. 667/76 (25 May 1976).

87. Raquel Correa, Malú Sierra, and Elizabeth Subercaseaux, *Los generales del régimen* (Santiago: Editorial Aconagua, 1983), 88.

88. Medina Quiroga, *The Battle of Human Rights,* 265–69.

89. *Chile Informativo,* no. 145 (June 1978): 42. INGO visits in 1976 included the AFL-CIO (March), the International Investigatory Commission on the Crimes of the Chilean Military Junta (March), the Center for Constitutional Rights and the International League for Human Rights (June), UNESCO (July), and ICRC president (December). *Chile Informativo,* multiple issues, 1976.

90. *Chile Informativo,* multiple issues, 1978.

91. Amnesty International, *The Amnesty International Report 1978–79.* See also Lawyers Committee for International Human Rights, *Violations of Human Rights in Argentina, 1976–1979: A Report* (New York: Lawyers Committee for International Human Rights, 1979); and Association of the Bar of the City of New York, *Report of the Mission of Lawyers to Argentina, April 1–7, 1979* (New York: Association of the Bar of the City of New York, 1979).

92. Medina Quiroga, *The Battle of Human Rights,* 268; and *Rettig Report,* 632.

93. Angell, "International Support for the Chilean Opposition," 177; and Cavallo, Salazar, and Sepúlveda, *La historia oculta del régimen militar,* 75.

94. *Chile Informativo* (22 May–4 June 1976); and (18 September–10 October 1976); as well as Heraldo Muñoz, *Las relaciones exteriores del gobierno militar chileno* (Santiago: Ediciones del Ornitorrinco, 1986), 25.

95. *Chile Informativo* (31 January–13 February 1976); and (22 May–4 June 1976); Sigmund, *The United States and Democracy in Chile,* 108; and Heraldo Muñoz, "Chile's External Relations under the Military Government in *Military Rule in Chile,*" 308. On Corvalán's release, see letter to the U.N. secretary-general from the Chilean government on 20 December 1976, U.N. Doc. A/31/461.

96. Amnesty International, *The Amnesty International Report 1977–78;* and *The Amnesty International Report 1975–76.*

97. Amnesty International, *The Amnesty International Report 1978–79;* Amnesty International, *The Amnesty International Report 1979–80;* and Jana Bennett and John Simpson, *The Disappeared and the Mothers of the Plaza* (New York: St. Martin's Press, 1985), 274.

98. Amnesty International, *Report of an Amnesty International Mission to Argentina,* 27.

99. *Chile Informativo* (January 26–February 18, 1986). See Chilean government report of the status of human rights in Chile, U.N. Doc. A/10285 (October 1975).

100. *Rettig Report,* 85. Extracts from the text of the Chacarillas speech are reprinted in *Chile Informativo,* no. 124 (September 1976): 17.

101. *Cauce* (Santiago), no. 2 (6 December 1983). See also *Rettig Report,* 636–37; and Amnesty International, *The Amnesty International Report 1977–78.*

102. Amnesty International, *The Amnesty International Report 1978–79*; and *Chile Informativo*, no. 139 (April 1978).

103. Mary Helen Spooner, *Soldiers in a Narrow Land: The Pinochet Regime in Chile* (Berkeley: University of California Press, 1999), 97; and Genaro Arriagada Herrera, "The Legal and Institutional Framework of the Armed Forces in Chile," in *Military Rule in Chile*, 132.

104. Pinochet interview with Rosenda Fraga, cited in Heinz, "The Military, Torture, and Human Rights," 77.

105. The U.S. Justice Department filed suit against the Marvin Liebman public relations firm in 1975 for not disclosing its activities on behalf of a foreign government. Spooner, *Soldiers in a Narrow Land*, 97; and Schoultz, *Human Rights and United States Policy Toward Latin America*, 80.

106. Smith, "Old Allies, New Enemies," 283.

107. *Chile Informativo* (Mexico City) (15–27 December 1975).

108. Argentina and Brazil apparently declined the invitation to join "Operation Lighthouse," so a common front was never formed. *Chile Informativo*, no. 119 (June 1977).

109. Muñoz, *Las relaciones exteriores del gobierno militar chileno*, Appendix, Table 5, 140–41.

110. Pinochet, *Camino Recorrido*, 340.

111. Muñoz, "Chile's External Relations under the Military Government," 307; U.N. ECOSOC, *Study of the Impact of Foreign Economic Aid*, 4.

112. Pinochet, *Camino Recorrido*, 361.

113. Air Force General Fernando Matthei in interview, *Cosas*, no. 52 (28 September 1978): 14. Quoted in Muñoz, *Las relaciones exteriores del gobierno militar chileno*, 201–2.

114. Muñoz, *Las relaciones exteriores del régimen militar chileno*, 47–48 and 294–95. The continued need for foreign borrowing was evident in the enactment of the *tablita* exchange rate policy in 1978, which, by assuring a declining rate of devaluation, was meant to combat inflation and encourage foreign borrowing. Nonetheless, as domestic and world inflation failed to converge and the dollar appreciated, Chilean exports became globally uncompetitive. Despite the costs involved in maintaining the *tablita*, dominant economic groups supported its continued use. Karen Remmer, *Military Rule in Latin America* (Boston: Unwin Hyman, 1989), 166.

115. *La Prensa* and *La Nación* (Buenos Aires) (2 June 1976). Cited in José Antonio Ocampo, *Política exterior argentina (1973–1983)* (Buenos Aires: CEAL, 1989), 187.

116. Quoted in Guest, *Behind the Disappearances*, 105.

117. Guest, *Behind the Disappearances*, 70 and 466, n. 18; and Schoultz, *Human Rights and United States Policy Toward Latin America*, 50–52.

118. Quoted in Guest, *Behind the Disappearances*, 101.

119. Guest, *Behind the Disappearances*, 417.

120. Quoted in Spanish in Guest, *Behind the Disappearances*, 417–18.

121. Guest, *Behind the Disappearances*, 178.

122. Guest, *Behind the Disappearances*, 178–79 and 489, n. 11.

123. Sikkink, "Human Rights, Principled Issue Networks, and Sovereignty in Latin America," 427.

124. Foreign Ministry memorandum, quoted in Guest, *Behind the Disappearances*, 496, n. 1.

125. Borrowing from international lenders increased during the first two

years of military rule, when the junta followed a traditional, orthodox stabilization program that reduced real wages; this was part of Argentina's agreements with the IMF (August 1976–September 1978). See Larry A. Sjaastad, "Argentine Economic Policy, 1976–81," in *The Political Economy of Argentina, 1946–83*, ed. Guido Di Tella and Rudiger Dornbusch (Pittsburgh, Pa.: University of Pittsburgh, 1989); Pion-Berlin, *The Ideology of State Terror*, chap. 5; and David Rock, *Argentina, 1516–1987: From Spanish Colonization to Alfonsín* (Berkeley: University of California, 1987), 368–74.

126. The Eximbank denial, moreover, covered only an early stage of the project. See Flood, "U.S. Human Rights Initiatives Concerning Argentina," 133; and Pion-Berlin, *The Ideology of State Terror*, 121.

Chapter 4

1. Amnesty International, *The Amnesty International Report 1977–78*.

2. The number of people arrested in 1976 was 552; this number rose to 606 in 1977 and 1,612 in 1978. See IACHR, *Report on the Situation of Human Rights in Chile* (1985), 113.

3. Lisa Martin and Kathryn Sikkink ask a similar question: Why did human rights practices improve significantly in 1978 although international pressure had been applied since the onset of the dirty war? Martin and Sikkink, "U.S. Policy and Human Rights in Argentina and Guatemala."

4. Tilly, *Coercion, Capital, and European States*; and Michel Foucault, *Discipline and Punish: The Birth of the Prison*, trans. Alan Sheridan (New York: Vintage Books, 1995 trans. ed.).

5. Schoultz, *Human Rights and United States Policy Toward Latin America*, 12.

6. See John Dinges, *The Condor Years: How Pinochet and His Allies Brought Terrorism to Three Continents* (New York: New Press, 2003).

7. Political arrests in 1976 numbered 552; 606 in 1977; and 1,612 in 1978. Broader trends, described here, suggest that these figures are not simply the result of higher reporting rates. IACHR, *Report on the Situation of Human Rights in Chile* (1985), based on reports of the *Vicaría de la Solidaridad*.

8. Lawyers Committee for International Human Rights, *A Critique of the United States Department of State Country Reports on Human Rights Practices for 1980: Argentina, Chile, Paraguay and Uruguay* (New York: Lawyers Committee for International Human Rights, July 1981); and *Chile Informativo* (19 June–2 July 1976).

9. Medina Quiroga, *The Battle of Human Rights*, 293; and *Rettig Report*, 636. See also *Annual Report of the Inter-American Commission on Human Rights 1979–1980*, OEA/Ser. L/V/II, 50, Doc. 13, rev. 1 (2 October 1980).

10. Spooner, *Soldiers in a Narrow Land*, 112; and Muñoz, *Las relaciones exteriores del gobierno militar chileno*, 171.

11. *Cauce*, no. 12 (Santiago, 1983): 33. More generally, see *Rettig Report*, chap. 4.

12. Representative histories of human rights abuses during this period are provided in Amnesty International, *Report of an Amnesty International Mission to Argentina*, Appendix 5, 63–69; Argentine Information Service Center, *Argentina Today: A Dossier on Repression and the Violation of Human Rights*, 2nd ed. (Buenos Aires: Argentine Information Service Center, 1977); and CONADEP, *Nunca Más*.

13. U.S. Department of State, "Memorandum on Torture and Disappear-

ances in Argentina," 31 May 1978, 1. Available from the National Security Archive: http://www.gwu.edu/~nsarchiv/NSAEBB/NSAEBB73/780531dos.pdf.

14. Amnesty International, *The Amnesty International Report 1977–78*. New directives for continuing the struggle against subversion included Order No. 504/77 (April 1977) and Operational Order No. 9 (June 1977). *El Diario del Judicio* 31 (Buenos Aires) (1985): 583–85.

15. Contreras's task force was part of the 601 Army Intelligence Unit. See U.S. Department of State, "Memorandum of Conversation," 7 August 1979, 2. Available from the National Security Archive: http://www.gwu.edu/~nsarchiv/NSAEBB/NSAEBB73/790807dos.pdf.

16. Due to the negative reaction that these measures engendered, the junta rarely implemented them. See Amnesty International, *The Amnesty International Report 1979–80*; and Guest, *Behind the Disappearances*, 209.

17. Amnesty International, *The Amnesty International Report 1983–84*.

18. *Chile Informativo*, multiple issues, 1978.

19. Alison Brysk, *The Politics of Human Rights in Argentina: Protest, Change, and Democratization* (Palo Alto, Calif.: Stanford University Press, 1994), 56; Amnesty International, *The Amnesty International Report 1980–81*; Amnesty International, *Report of an Amnesty International Mission to Argentina*; and Guest, *Behind the Disappearances*, 176. See also U.S. Department of State, "Memorandum of Conversation," American Embassy in Buenos Aires, 7 August 1979, 2. Available from the National Security Archive: http://www.gwu.edu/~nsarchiv/NSAEBB/NSAEBB73/790807dos.pdf.

20. For systematic examples, see Amnesty International annual reports, multiple years.

21. Comisión Andina de Juristas, *Perú y Chile*, 224.

22. *Rettig Report*, 85.

23. *Rettig Report*, 636–37; Amnesty International, *The Amnesty International Report 1977–78*; and *Cauce* (Santiago), no. 2 (6 December 1983).

24. Amnesty International, *The Amnesty International Report 1978–79*; and *Chile Informativo*, no. 139 (April 1978).

25. Garretón in *Military Rule in Chile*, 173; Brian Loveman, "Regimes of Exception in Chile," in *The Constitution of Tyranny: Regimes of Exception inb Spanish America* (Brian Loveman, Pittsburgh: University of Pittsburgh Press, 1993); Comisión Andina de Juristas, *Perú y Chile*, 230–33; and Remmer, *Military Rule in Latin America*, 162.

26. Risse, "'Let's Argue!' Communicative Action in World Politics."

27. International Documentation and Communication Centre (IDOC), *Chile* (New York: IDOC, North America, 1973), 16.

28. United Press International, 3 October 1973. Quoted in Davis, *The Last Two Years of Salvador Allende*.

29. Rafael Valdivieso Ariztía, *Crónica de un rescate (Chile: 1973–1988)* (Santiago: Editorial Andrés Bello, 1988), 14; and Muñoz, "Chile's External Relations under the Military Government," 314.

30. *Cauce* (Santiago) (6 December 1983). The government also denied human rights violations in its reply to a 1974 telegram from the U.N. Commission on Human Rights. See U.N. Economic and Social Council, Letter of 7 March 1974 to the chairman of the Commission on Human Rights from the permanent representative of Chile, U.N. Doc. E/CN.4/1153.

31. *Rettig Report*, 118.

32. *Observaciones formuladas por el Gobierno de Chile sobre el segundo informe elabo-*

rado por la Comisión Interamericana de Derechos Humanos acerca de la situación de los derechos humanos en dicho país, OEA/Ser. P AG/Doc. 667/76 (25 May 1976). See also Medina Quiroga, *The Battle of Human Rights*, 279–83.

33. Kamminga, *Inter-State Accountability for Violations of Human Rights*, 95–98.

34. Muñoz, *Las relaciones exteriores del gobierno militar chileno*, 40.

35. Pinochet, *Camino Recorrido*, 107 and 111–17; Kamminga, *Inter-State Accountability for Violations of Human Rights*, 106; *Chile Informativo* (4–17 September 1976); *Chile Informativo*, no. 123 (August 1977); and *Chile Informativo*, no. 136 (February 1978).

36. Author's translation. See *Chile Informativo*, no. 102 (November 1976).

37. Reported by the Associated Press on 1 July 1977. See also *Chile Informativo*, no. 120 (July 1977). For an example of state responses during this period, see letter of 17 November 1978 from the Chilean government to the U.N. secretary-general regarding its observations on the report of the special rapporteur, U.N. Doc. A/C.3/33.7.

38. *Chile Informativo*, no. 157 (November 1978).

39. Guest, *Behind the Disappearances*, 197.

40. Guest, *Behind the Disappearances*, 116.

41. Amnesty International, *The Amnesty International Report 1975–76*, 49. For how Argentina's junta used language as a form of violence, see Marguerite Feitlowitz, *A Lexicon of Terror: Argentina and the Legacies of Torture* (Oxford: Oxford University Press, 1998).

42. Amnesty International, *The Amnesty International Report 1976–77*.

43. Originally in *Gente* magazine (22 December 1977), quoted in CONADEP, *Nunca Más*, 53. For further examples of denial, see Weissbrodt and Bartolomei, "The Effectiveness of International Human Rights Pressures," 1018; and Horacio Verbitsky, *Civiles y militares: Memoria secreta de la transición*, 3rd ed. (Buenos Aires: Editorial Contrapunto, 1987), 25.

44. U.N. Doc. E/CN.4/R.68/Add 3 (24 December 1980). Quoted in Bartolomei, *Gross and Massive Human Rights Violations in Argentina*, 193.

45. Argentina's last grant from the U.S. Agency for International Development (USAID) had been in 1971; and as a food exporter, it had never received assistance from the Food for Peace program. See Berg, "Human Rights Sanctions as Leverage," 104.

46. Internal Foreign Ministry memo, quoted in Guest, *Behind the Disappearances*, 164–65.

47. See "Enérgico rechazo del documento de la CIDH," *El Cronista comercial* (Buenos Aires) (21 April 1980).

48. Quoted in Guest, *Behind the Disappearances*, 502, n. 6. The Argentine government also drew a parallel between international pressure against itself and the Soviet Union when Adolfo Pérez Esquivel, an Argentine human rights activist, was awarded the Nobel Peace Prize in 1980. "The decision of the Nobel Peace committee is further proof of the intensity of the international campaign . . . . This serves to unite both governments and subject them to the same criticism." In issuing the award, the Nobel Peace Prize Committee itself had drawn a comparison between Esquivel and Sakharov, the 1975 recipient. Foreign Ministry analysis, quoted in Guest, *Behind the Disappearances*, 239.

49. In meeting with General Andrew Goodpaster, Argentine government officials referred explicitly to the deterioration in bilateral relations due to human rights. *El Cronista Comercial* (Buenos Aires) (1 February 1980).

50. Argentine Foreign Ministry cable, quoted in Guest, *Behind the Disappear-*

ances, 182. Although it did not concede to join the U.S.-led grain embargo against the Soviet Union, Argentina agreed not to increase its exports to the Soviet Union; in exchange, Goodpaster offered modest military assistance and cooperation. See Guest, *Behind the Disappearances*, 241; and Vázquez Ocampo, *Política exterior argentina*, 98–99.

51. Loveman, *The Constitution of Tyranny*. See also Simon Collier and William F. Sater, *A History of Chile, 1808–1994* (New York: Cambridge University Press, 1996); and Alain Rouquié, *The Military and the State in Latin America* (Berkeley: University of California Press, 1987), esp. 226–28. For human rights in Chile in historical perspective, see Arzobispado de Santiago, *Vicaría de la Solidaridad, Derechos Humanos*, Estudios no. 1 (Santiago: Arzobispado de Santiago, 1978).

52. Christian Anglade and Carlos Fortín, eds., *Monetarism and Liberalization: The Chilean Experiment* (Chicago: University of Chicago Press, 1991).

53. Especially after the 1960s, both Chile and Argentina were two of the principal recipients of U.S. military assistance. See Brian H. Smith, "U.S.-Latin American Military Relations since World War II: Implications for Human Rights"; and Crahan, "National Security Ideology and Human Rights."

54. On the use of repression by the armed forces during this period, see also Pío García, *Las fuerzas armadas y el golpe de estado en Chile* (Mexico City: Siglo Veintuno Editores, 1974), sec. V.

55. Raquel Correa, Malú Sierra, and Elizabeth Subercaseaux, *Los generales del régimen* (Santiago: Editorial Aconagua, 1983), 88; Pamela Constable and Arturo Valenzuela, *Nation of Enemies: Chile under Pinochet* (New York: W. W. Norton, 1991), 128; and *Rettig Report*, 757–58. For "terrorist" acts during this period and figures on related death tolls, see *Rettig Report*, Appendix.

56. Loveman, *The Constitution of Tyranny*, 334.

57. Sigmund, *The United States and Democracy in Chile*, 85.

58. Pinochet, *Camino Recorrido*, 70. In a 1973 *White Book*, the Chilean government also published "Plan Z," which included a list of opponents that the government reportedly was planning to eliminate. *White Book of the Change of Government in Chile: 11ᵗʰ of September 1973* (Santiago: Empresa Editora Nacional Gabriela Mistral, 1973).

59. Emphasis added. U.S. Department of State, "Briefing Memorandum" from Jack Kubisch to the secretary of state, 1973, 2.

60. A Chilean internal intelligence document ("Breve Reseño de la Creación del MIR") stated that in the second half of the 1970s, fewer than 50 members of the MIR remained in Chile. See Spooner, *Soldiers in a Narrow Land*, 193. For an excellent discussion of the "disappearance" of the MIR, see Mark Ensalaco, *Chile under Pinochet: Recovering the Truth* (Philadelphia: University of Pennsylvania Press, 2000), 69–84.

61. *Rettig Report*, 635–37 and 640–41.

62. *Decreto de seguridad individual*, 23 November 1811. Cited in Loveman, *The Constitution of Tyranny*, 268.

63. Even civilian president Arturo Frondizi (1958–62), in pursuing goals of economic nationalism and political liberalization, acquiesced to the military's view that austerity necessitated internal security. In exchange for an IMF-negotiated stabilization program, Frondizi approved an army-sponsored internal security plan, *Conintes*, which was the basis of subsequent civil rights violations. On Frondizi's economic program, see Kathryn Sikkink, *Ideas and Institutions: Developmentalism in Brazil and Argentina* (Ithaca, N.Y.: Cornell University Press, 1991), chap. 3; for human rights violations, see Ricardo Rodríguez Molas, *Histo-*

ria de la tortura y el orden represivo en la Argentina (Buenos Aires: EUDEBA, 1984), 202–9.

64. Since the 1950s, the curricula of the leading war colleges and institutes, as well as U.S.-sponsored training programs, instructed Argentina's military officers in this regard. See Smith, "U.S.-Latin American Military Relations Since World War II: Implications for Human Rights"; and Lesley Gill, *The School of the Americas: Military Violence and Political Training in the Americas* (Durham, N.C.: Duke University Press, 2004).

65. On the *cordobazo,* see William C. Smith, *Authoritarianism and the Crisis of the Argentine Political Economy* (Stanford, Calif.: Stanford University Press, 1989), chap. 6.

66. Rock, *Argentina,* 352–55. According to an Amnesty International survey, 461 politically motivated murders occurred between mid-1974 and mid-1975, almost two-thirds of which were committed by death squads. Amnesty International, *The Amnesty International Report 1975–76.*

67. In May 1971, for example, Lanusse created a Federal Chamber for Special Crimes relating to subversion (*Cámara Federal en lo Penal Especial*), which was known as the "Chamber of Terror" until its closure in 1973. See Foro de Buenos Aires por la Vigencia de los Derechos Humanos, *Proceso a la explotación y represión en la Argentina* (Buenos Aires, May 1973), 125; and Mignone, *Derechos humanos y sociedad,* 51. Perón introduced changes in the Penal Code that increased the scope of "subversive" offenses (Law 20,462), a broad definition that would be used in the dirty war. Rock, *Argentina,* 360; and Amnesty International, *The Amnesty International Report 1975–76.* An annotated chronology of political repression in 1973 and 1974 is provided in Centro de Estudios Latinoamericanos, *La represión en Argentina, 1972–1974: Documentos,* 1st ed. (Mexico City: Universidad Autónoma de México, 1978).

68. An analysis of the antiterrorism measures passed by Isabel Perón's government is provided in International Commission of Jurists, *The Situation of Defense Lawyers in Argentina* (Geneva: ICJ, 1975). For the relationship between economic policy and state repression during this period, see Guido di Tella, "Argentina's Economy under a Labour-based Government, 1973–76," in *The Political Economy of Argentina;* and Smith, *Authoritarianism and the Crisis of the Argentine Political Economy,* 225–31. Isabel Perón's government also declared an unlimited state of siege and issued a series of decrees ordering the armed forces to "annihilate" subversion. Even in their 1985 trial for human rights abuses committed during the dirty war, the armed forces relied on the 1975 decrees; see Alicia S. García, ed., *La doctrina de la seguridad nacional (1958–1983)* (Buenos Aires: Centro Editor de America Latina, 1991), 162–64. The 1985 defense is reprinted in "Las Defensas de los acusados," in *El Libro de El Diario del Judicio* (Buenos Aires: Editorial Perfil, 1985), 331–69.

69. Eight secret detention centers were functioning by the end of 1975, and even the Navy Mechanics School (*Escuela Superior de Mecánica de la Armada,* ESMA), the leading clandestine center in Buenos Aires during the dirty war, had its first recorded case of a disappearance in February 1976. See Mittelbach, *Informe sobre desaparecedores,* based on Centro de Estudios Legales y Sociales (CELS), *692–Culpables del terrorismo de estado* (Buenos Aires: CELS, 1986). Over 3,000 suspected "subversives" were arrested, and more than 4,000 people were held in preventive detention; about 1,000 disappearances occurred between 1974 and early 1976. Amnesty International, *Report of an Amnesty International Mission to Argentina,* 8.

70. Brigadier General Antonio Domingo Bussi in *La Opinión* (Buenos Aires)

(17 October 1976); quoted in Daniel Frontalini and Maria Cristina Caiati, *El mito de la "guerra sucia"* (Buenos Aires: Centro de Estudios Legales y Sociales, 1984), 25.

71. In the *Ideology of State Terror*, David Pion-Berlin argues that political repression in Latin America reflects the role of ideology more than a response to dissent. My argument is that both ideas and armed dissent are significant.

72. General Luciano Benjamín Menéndez in June 1976. Amnesty International, *Report of an Amnesty International Mission to Argentina*, 49.

73. Frontalini and Caiati, *El mito de la "guerra sucia"*; and Martin Edwin Andersen, *Dossier Secreto: Argentina's Desaparecidos and the Myth of the "Dirty War"* (Boulder, Colo.: Westview Press, 1993).

74. "Report on the Subversive Situation" (3 June 1977), 2, 4, and 5. This is a translated document obtained by the U.S. Embassy in Argentina in mid-1977. Available from the National Security Archive: http://www.gwu.edu/~nsarchiv/NSAEBB/NSAEBB73/770603dos.pdf.

75. Pion-Berlin, *The Ideology of State Terror*, 5.

76. A meeting of the Instituto para el Desarrollo de Ejecutivos en la Argentina (IDEA). See María Laura San Martino de Dromi, *Historia política argentina (1955–1988)* (Buenos Aires: Editorial Astrea de Alfredo y Ricardo Depalma, 1988), 332.

77. Cf. Lutz and Sikkink: "Although by the military's admission 90 percent of the armed opposition had been eliminated by April 1977, their defeat did not lead to an immediate change in human rights practices." See Lutz and Sikkink, "International Human Rights Law and Practice in Latin America."

78. Amnesty International, *The Amnesty International Report 1978–79*.

79. *Clarín* and *La Prensa* (Buenos Aires) (6 July 1979), quoted in Frontalini and Caiati, *El mito de la "guerra sucia,"* 19. See also Amnesty International, *The Amnesty International Report 1975–76*.

80. *La Prensa* (Buenos Aires) (24 May 1978), quoted in Frontalini and Caiati, *El mito de la "guerra sucia,"* 19.

81. *The Times* (London) (4 January 1978). Quoted in Amnesty International, *The Amnesty International Report 1977–78*.

82. Guest, *Behind the Disappearances*, 453, n. 24.

83. Smith, *Authoritarianism and the Crisis of the Argentine Political Economy*, 233.

84. U.S. Department of State, telegram from U.S. Embassy in Buenos Aires, Subject: "More on PST Disappearances," 14 May 1980. Available from the National Security Archive: http://www.gwu.edu/~nsarchiv/NSAEBB/NSAEBB73/800514dos.pdf.

85. The implications of the economic model for state repression are discussed in Carlos Fortín, "The Political Economy of Repressive Monetarism," in *Monetarism and Liberalization*.

86. Emphasis added. See U.N. Economic and Social Council, *Study of the Impact of Foreign Economic Aid and Assistance on Respect for Human Rights in Chile*, prepared by Rapporteur Antonio Cassese, 94, U.N. Doc E/CN.4/ Sub. 2/412/Corr. 1 (26 October 1978).

87. Decree Law 521, discussed in *Rettig Report*, 473.

88. Felipe Aguero, "Autonomy of the Military in Chile: From Democracy to Authoritarianism," in *Democracy under Siege: New Military Power in Latin America*, ed. Augusto Varas (New York: Greenwood Press, 1989).

89. Fruhling, *Nonprofit Organizations as Opposition to Authoritarian Rule*, 46.

90. Muñoz, *Las relaciones exteriores del gobierno militar chileno*, 41–42. For details of the economic policy, see Alejandro Foxley, "The Neoconservative Economic

Experiment in Chile"; and Ricardo French-Davis, "Import Liberalization: The Chilean Experience, 1973–82," in *Military Rule in Chile.*

91. Sheila Cassidy, *Audacity to Believe* (1977), as quoted in Mario Terrazas Guzmán, *¿Quien se acuerda de Sheila Cassidy? (Cronica de un conflicto religioso-político-diplomático)* (Santiago: Ediciones Emete, 1992), 379.

92. See editorial, "Ahora Bolivia," in the pro-government magazine *Qué Pasa* (Santiago) (23–29 March 1978). See also "Ni pesimismo ni oportunismo," *Qué Pasa,*(30 March–5 April 1978). Cited in Fruhling, *Nonprofit Organizations as Opposition to Authoritarian Rule,* 93–94.

93. Cavallo, Salazar, and Sepúlveda, *La historia oculta del régimen militar,* 236 and 271; and Sigmund, *The United States and Democracy in Chile,* 115.

94. In 1976, the largest single employer in Argentina was the army enterprise Fabricaciones Militares. See Guest, *Behind the Disappearances,* 12–13.

95. *Clarín* (Buenos Aires) (24 October 1975), quoted in Frontalini and Caiati, *El mito de la "guerra sucia,"* 25. The soft-liners were represented by Generals Videla and Roberto Eduardo Viola; hard-liners included Generals Carlos Suárez and Mario Menéndez.

96. *El Libro de El Diario del Judicio,* 90–91.

97. Timerman, *Prisoner Without a Name, Cell Without a Number.* The rebellion also was related to hard-liners' opposition to new trade union legislation (Professional Association Law) in 1979, which they perceived to be insufficiently aggressive. See Buchanan, "State Terror as a Complement of State Policy," 49.

98. Quoted in Guest, *Behind the Disappearances,* 242–43.

99. Stephan Haggard and Robert R. Kaufman, *The Political Economy of Democratic Transitions* (Princeton, N.J.: Princeton University Press, 1995), 38–44; and Remmer, *Military Rule in Latin America.* Pion-Berlin and Arcenaux examine the role of decision-making structures in explaining human rights reforms in *democratic* Chile and Argentina. They rely on two indicators: the independence of the executive from the armed forces and the number of actors involved in decision making. David Pion-Berlin and Craig Arcenaux, "Tipping the Civil-Military Balance: Institutions and Human Rights Policy in Democratic Argentina and Chile," *Comparative Political Studies* 31 (October 1998): 633–61.

100. Cavallo, Salazar, and Sepúlveda, *La historia oculta del régimen militar,* 28 and 64–65.

101. Arturo Valenzuela, "The Military in Power: The Consolidation of One-Man Rule," in *The Struggle for Democracy in Chile, 1982–1990,* ed. Paul W. Drake and Ivan Jaksic (Lincoln: University of Nebraska Press, 1991), 61; Remmer, *The Military in Latin America,* 129; Herrera, "The Legal and Institutional Framework of the Armed Forces in Chile," 132; Constable and Valenzuela, *A Nation of Enemies,* 66; and Cavallo, Salazar, and Sepúlveda, *La historia oculta del régimen militar,* 30–32.

102. Alejandro Foxley, "The Neoconservative Economic Experiment in Chile," 17–26; and Remmer, *The Military in Latin America,* 139.

103. *Rettig Report,* 482; and Herrera, "The Legal and Institutional Framework of the Armed Forces in Chile."

104. In a linguistic analysis, Giselle Munizaga characterizes the frequent contrast that Pinochet made between Chileans and non-Chileans, and his description of human rights proponents as aggressors, as an "us–them" worldview. See Munizaga, *El discurso publico de Pinochet: Un análisis semiológico* (Santiago: CESOC/CENECA, 1988), 27.

105. Pinochet, *Camino Recorrido,* 111.

106. Remmer, *The Military in Latin America,* 131. See also *Rettig Report,* 478–82;

and U.S. Department of State, document from Embassy in Chile on "Directorate of National Intelligence (DINA) Expands Operations and Facilities," 15 April 1975. Available from the National Security Archive: http://www.gwu.edu/~nsarchiv/NSAEBB/NSAEBB8/ch25–01.htm.

107. Cavallo, Salazar, and Sepúlveda, *La historia oculta del régimen militar*, 80 and 146; and Muñoz, *Las relaciones exteriores del gobierno militar chileno*, 41–45.

108. The moderate sector included both the minister of defense, General Herman Brady, and armed sectors that were concentrated in the northern security zone of the country. *Chile Informativo*, no. 135 (January 1978).

109. *Chile Informativo*, no. 135 (February 1978); and Cavallo, Salazar, and Sepúlveda, *La historia oculta del régimen militar*, 185.

110. Garretón in *Military Rule in Chile*, 156.

111. Pinochet, *Camino Recorrido*, 200.

112. On the various options considered by the regime, see Fruhling, *Nonprofit Organizations as Opposition to Authoritarian Rule*, 10–11. See also *Chile Informativo*, no. 120 (July 1977).

113. *Chile Informativo*, no. 139 (April 1978); and *Rettig Report*, 757.

114. *Chile Informativo*, no. 136 (February 1978); and Muñoz, *Las relaciones exteriores del gobierno militar chileno*, 45. See interview by Foreign Minister Cubillos in *El Mercurio* (Santiago) (7 May 1978).

115. Fruhling, *Nonprofit Organizations as Opposition to Authoritarian Rule*, 12. In practice, the Labor Plan placed new restrictions on union bargaining, which led to even greater labor opposition. See Manuel Barrera and J. Samuel Valenzuela, "The Development of Labor Movement Opposition to the Military Regime," in *Military Rule in Chile*, 232.

116. *Chile Informativo*, no. 157 (November 1978).

117. Muñoz, *Las relaciones exteriores del gobierno militar chileno*, 47–48.

118. Leigh broke ranks with the junta to criticize the slowness of institutionalization, although his interest appears to have been in perpetuating the regime rather than in a democratic opening; he was dismissed in July. See Herrera, "The Legal and Institutional Framework of the Armed Forces in Chile," 133; and Cavallo, Salazar, and Sepúlveda, *La historia oculta del régimen military*, 222.

119. For how international human rights norms, in general, served to redefine Chilean state interests in domestic institutional change, see Hawkins, *International Human Rights and Authoritarian Rule in Chile*.

120. For organizational flowcharts, see Mittelbach, *Informe sobre desaparecedores*. See also U.S. Department of State, memorandum from James J. Blystone, Embassy in Buenos Aires, 6 February 1980, 2. Available from the National Security Archive: http://www.gwu.edu/~nsarchiv/NSAEBB/NSAEBB73/800207dos.pdf.

121. While the navy oversaw the Foreign Ministry and the Ministry of Social Welfare, the army was charged with the Ministries of the Interior and of Labor, and the air force led the Ministries of Defense and of Justice; the Ministries of Education and Finance were in civilian hands. See Guest, *Behind the Disappearances*, 24 and 38. This differs from Brazil, for example, where intelligence organizations had separate chains of command. Pion-Berlin, *The Ideology of State Terror*, 103. See also U.S. Department of State, "Memorandum of Conversation," 7 August 1979, esp. 6–9. Available from the National Security Archive: http://www.gwu.edu/~nsarchiv/NSAEBB/NSAEBB73/790807dos.pdf.

122. See CONADEP, *Nunca Más*, 239.

123. Guest, *Behind the Disappearances*, 61, 71, and 507, n. 6; Juan Gasparini, *La pista suiza* (Buenos Aires: Editorial Legasa, 1981), 188; CONADEP, *Nunca Más*,

254–63; Vázquez Ocampo, *Política exterior argentina*, 195–97; and CELS, *Uruguay/Argentina: Coordinación represiva* (Buenos Aires: CELS, 1984).

124. Guest, *Behind the Disappearances*, 65.

125. This was evident in all meetings between Derian and government officials in 1977. *El Libro de El Diario del Judicio*, 91–93.

126. Claudio Uriarte, *Almirante Cero: Biografía no autorizada de Emilio Eduardo Massera* (Buenos Aires: Planeta, 1992), 207; and Bennett and Simpson, *The Disappeared*, 274.

127. Cable by the U.S. Embassy in Argentina in November 1980. Quoted in Guest, *Behind the Disappearances*, 240.

128. Quoted in Emilio F. Mignone, "Beyond Fear: Forms of Justice and Compensation," in *Fear at the Edge*, 250.

129. Guest, *Behind the Disappearances*, 175. For how the Videla-Viola moderate faction came to control the Foreign Ministry, see Lutz and Sikkink, "Human Rights Law in Latin America," 649.

130. Alfred Stepan, "State Power and the Strength of Civil Society in the Southern Cone of Latin America," in *Bringing the State Back In*, ed. Peter B. Evans, Dietrich Rueschemeyer, and Theda Skocpol (Cambridge: Cambridge University Press, 1985), 329.

131. The idea was Massera's, who wanted to pave his own way to power. In exchange for Massera's retirement from the junta, Videla agreed to retire as head of the army and become president. See Zarini, *Historia e instituciones en la Argentina*, 365–66; Uriarte, *Almirante Cero*, 189 and 197; Rock, *Argentina*, 371; and Roberto Russell, "Argentina y la política exterior del régimen autoritario (1976–1983): Una evaluación preliminar," in *Argentina en el mundo (1973–1987)*, ed. Rubén M. Perina and Roberto Russell (Buenos Aires: Editorial Latinoamericano, 1988), 103, n. 9.

132. Smith, *Authoritarianism and the Crisis of the Argentine Political Economy*, 232.

133. The navy chief of staff (Vice Admiral Juan Lombardo) explicitly linked the maneuver to human rights pressure. See Guest, *Behind the Disappearances*, 337.

134. Comisión Andina de Juristas, *Perú y Chile*, 249; Arce, Nieto, and Sepúlveda Almarza, *Cuba y Chile*, 20; and Ensalaco, *Chile under Pinochet*, chap. 7.

135. Sigmund, *The United States and Democracy in Chile*, 108, 133, and 150.

136. Sigmund, *The United States and Democracy in Chile*, 151.

137. *Rettig Report*, 768. On protest during this period, see, for example, Martínez, "Fear of the State, Fear of Society: On the Opposition Protests in Chile," in *Fear at the Edge: State Terror and Resistance in Latin America*, ed. Juan E. Corradi, Patricia Weiss Fagan, and Manuel Antonio Garretón (Berkeley: University of California Press, 1992); Fruhling, *Nonprofit Organizations as Opposition to Authoritarian Rule*; and *Rettig Report*. Human rights violations are discussed in the *Annual Report of the Inter-American Commission on Human Rights 1983–1984*, OEA/Ser. L/V/II, 63, Doc. 10 (24 September 1984), 24.

138. In his memoir, Pinochet details purported attacks by "subversive" groups between 1981 and 1985. See Pinochet, *Camino Recorrido*, Appendix.

139. *Rettig Report*, 641.

140. Emphasis added. Memorandum for director of Central Intelligence Agency regarding visit of Juan Manuel Contreras, 23 August 1975. Available from the National Security Archive: http://www.gwu.edu/~nsarchiv/news/20001113/750823.pdf.

141. Guest, *Behind the Disappearances*, 85 and 469, n. 13. And after Amnesty In-

ternational's report was published, the same Foreign Ministry official noted, "The dialogue is now finished. We must seek other ways." See Guest, *Behind the Disappearances*, 85.

142. For example, Hugo Fruhling argues that international human rights pressure was less effective against Argentina than Chile. See Fruhling, *Nonprofit Organizations as Opposition to Authoritarian Rule*, 17.

143. Robert R. Kaufman, "Democratic and Authoritarian Responses to the Debt Issue: Argentina, Brazil, Mexico," in *The Politics of International Debt*, ed. Miles Kahler (Ithaca, N.Y.: Cornell University Press, 1986). On Argentine-Soviet relations, see Eusebio Mujal-León, ed., *The USSR and Latin America: A Developing Relationship* (Cambridge: Cambridge University Press, 1989).

144. Sikkink, "Human Rights, Principled Issue Networks, and Sovereignty in Latin America," 426.

145. *Official Journal of the European Communities: Debates of the European Parliament 1976–1977 Session*, Report of Proceedings from 5 to 9 July 1976, no. 205, 137.

Chapter 5

1. Risse and Sikkink, "The Socialization of International Human Rights Norms into Domestic Practices," 19–22.

2. Relevant methodological issues are discussed in Chapter 2. Data availability limits the quantitative analysis of human rights compliance before 1980. Regardless, if this quantitative analysis yields findings similar to those of the earlier cases—despite the different time periods—it should bolster the argument.

3. For an argument that economic sanctions can improve human rights conditions, see Sarah H. Cleveland, "Norm Internalization and U.S. Economic Sanctions," *Yale Journal of International Law* 26 (2001): 1–102. A skeptical account of sanctions as foreign policy tools is provided in Robert Pape, "Why Economic Sanctions Do Not Work," *International Studies* 22, no. 2 (Fall 1997): 90–136.

4. Gary Clyde Hufbauer and Jeffrey J. Schott, *Economic Sanctions Reconsidered: History and Current Policy* (Washington, D.C.: Institute for International Economics, 1985), 2.

5. David Cortright and George A. Lopez, *The Sanctions Decade: Assessing UN Strategies in the 1990s* (Boulder, Colo.: Lynne Rienner, 2000).

6. For example, see Tony Evans, *US Hegemony and the Project of Universal Human Rights* (London: Macmillan, 1996). On the unilateral–multilateral distinction, see William H. Kampfer and Anton D. Lowenberg, "Unilateral Versus Multilateral International Sanctions: A Public Choice Perspective," *International Studies* Quarterly 43 (1999): 37–58.

7. I also included an interaction variable to see whether sanctions were more influential when they were applied both unilaterally and multilaterally. Because it was statistically insignificant, however, I dropped this term.

8. These measures are adequate in a broad sense; though they do not differentiate between types of sanction, such as arms embargoes, technological sanctions, trade sanctions, or targeted financial sanctions. I am indebted to George Lopez for this point. Furthermore, these measures do not differentiate between the threat and actual deployment of sanctions, which some scholars (e.g., Irfan Nooruddin, "Modeling Selection Bias in Studies of Sanctions Efficacy," *International Interactions* 28 [2002]: 59–75) have linked to a selection bias, insofar as excluding threats may obscure some of a sanction's most powerful effects.

9. On the question of duration, see Sean Bolks and Dina Al-Sowayel, "How Long Do Economic Sanctions Last? Examining the Sanctioning Process through Duration," *Political Research Quarterly* 5, 2 (2000): 241–65.

10. See Simmons, "Why Commit?" and, more broadly, "International Law and State Behavior." While material calculations may underlie interstate contagion, a possibility that I control for in the subsequent analysis, I accept Simmons's claim in "Why Commit?" that regional diffusion may be partly ideational.

11. Like Simmons, I measure the mean regional score for each type of state response in a given year (Simmons, "International Law and State Behavior"). For global contagion, I examine the mean score for any given state response throughout the world in a given year.

12. Human Rights Internet, *Human Rights Internet Reporter: Masterlist* (Ottawa: Human Rights Internet, 1994).

13. Logging this number is important because the distribution of these groups across different countries is skewed, partly reflecting differences in population size. See Human Rights Internet, *Human Rights Internet Reporter: Masterlist.* Although this database reflects only one point in time (1993), it offers a representative measure of human rights NGOs for the particular period under review, because the overall number of NGOs in a country is unlikely to change substantially from year to year. The third edition of this publication (2000) is titled *The List.*

14. For those state commitments that are binary (monitoring, implementation, leniency, and accountability), I use standard probit analysis; for all other state responses, coded as ordinal, I use ordered probit analysis. Although a duration or hazard model may seem more appropriate for explaining human rights commitments, in practice, treaty ratification is the area in which states are most likely to make enduring commitments. However, even in the case of treaty ratification, a probit model can be appropriate, because I am examining state acceptance of *any* major human rights treaty, not single treaties. This measurement minimizes the danger of temporal autocorrelation. Additionally, I include as a control variable the total number of major human rights treaties that a state had accepted by 1992, further offsetting any intertemporal bias. Nor will states generally back out of an entire *category* of commitments, which would make a switching (Markov) model more appropriate.

15. More specifically, incorporating robust standard errors adjusts for in-country clustering. See Nathaniel Beck and J. Katz, "What to Do (and Not to Do) with Time-Series—Cross Section Data in Comparative Politics," *American Political Science Review* 89 (1995): 634–47; and Beck and Katz, "Taking Time Seriously: Time-Series—Cross-Section Data with a Binary Dependent Variable," *American Journal of Political Science* 42 (1998): 1260–88.

16. According to the widely used Conflict Data Project (CDP) at Uppsala University, twenty-five is the minimum number of deaths that constitutes an armed conflict. CDP data on armed conflicts between 1946 and 2001 can be obtained from http://www.prio.no/cwp/ArmedConflict/.

17. Although armed conflict should lead to greater human rights violations, its expected effects on state commitments are unclear. Thus, I use a two-tailed test of statistical significance in assessing the effects of armed conflict on human rights commitments.

18. Data on trade openness (trade as a percentage of GDP) are based on a nine-point global rank index prepared by Country Indicators for Foreign Policy,

based on data from the World Bank Development Indicators. For the purposes of this analysis, I inverted the scale so that 9 = highest trade dependence.

19. Accordingly, I conduct a two-tailed test of significance when evaluating the relationship between economic development and state compliance. Economic development is measured in terms of GDP per capita (converted to a nine-point index); see Appendix for details.

20. Moravcsik, "The Origins of Human Rights Regimes."

21. In contrast to my measurement of emerging democracy, Landman uses a dummy variable to code countries depending on whether they underwent a democratic transition during various global democratic "waves." He finds a positive relationship between emerging democracy and treaty acceptance. Landman, *Protecting Human Rights*. C.f. Simmons, "Why Commit?"

22. Christian Davenport, "The Weight of the Past: Exploring Lagged Determinants of Political Repression," *Political Research Quarterly* 49 (June 1996): 377–403.

23. Major human rights treaties consist of the six treaties widely considered to constitute the "core" of the international human rights regime: the International Covenant on Civil and Political Rights; the International Covenant on Economic, Social, and Cultural Rights; the Convention on the Rights of the Child; the Convention on the Elimination of All Forms of Racial Discrimination; the Convention on the Elimination of All Forms of Discrimination against Women; and the Convention against Torture. Ratification data are available at: http://www.ohchr.org/english/law/index.htm.

24. None of the variables were intercorrelated.

25. I created interaction terms to assess whether the effects of human rights pressure (either U.S. or multilateral sanctions) depended on any of the other major variables examined: armed conflict, regime type, trade dependence, NGOs, and economic development.

26. The percentage of cases in which violations were "frequent" is as follows: torture (42 percent), political imprisonment (31 percent), extrajudicial killings (20 percent), and disappearances (10 percent).

27. Material calculations may not be discounted, because states that were more open to foreign trade were also more likely to implement international norms and act with leniency.

28. Interestingly, the role of INGOs was related to those state commitments that domestic activists did not appear to affect: ratification and leniency.

29. Yet political imprisonment was not the most prevalent type of abuse. Mean scores for human rights violations were as follows: torture (1.23), political imprisonment (.88), extrajudicial killing (.72), and disappearances (.35).

30. Sanctions may not affect treaty ratification for a simple reason: ratifiers are closely associated with democratic regimes, which are not as likely to face sanctions in the first place.

31. As Table 12 indicates, U.S. sanctions were associated in the short term with greater accountability and norm implementation and in the long term with more leniency. Multilateral sanctions also led in the short term to greater leniency. These variations may reflect in part the demands made of states. For example, monitoring may have been associated only with multilateral sanctions, because non-U.S. actors are more likely to request access for international organizations such as Amnesty International or the United Nations.

32. Sanctions were related somewhat to a lower probability of disappearance and political imprisonment. This may reflect the state of the world in the 1990s.

In the post–Cold War period both the prohibition against disappearance and the idea of democracy—linked to lower levels of political imprisonment—attained widespread support. See Lutz and Sikkink, "International Human Rights Law and Practice."

33. On the humanitarian consequences of sanctions, see Damrosch, "The Civilian Impact of Economic Sanctions"; and David Cortright and George Lopez, *Economic Sanctions: Panacea or Peacebuilding in a Post–Cold War World?* (Boulder, Colo.: Westview Press, 2000), esp. 23–26. According to Secretary-General Kofi Annan (1998, 64), "Humanitarian and human rights policy goals cannot easily be reconciled with those of a sanctions regime." See Annan, *Annual Report of the Secretary-General on the Work of the Organization* (New York: United Nations, 27 August 1998), A/53/1, cited in Cortright and Lopez, *Economic Sanctions*, 23.

34. I assigned a 1 to countries that were subject to either U.S. or multilateral sanctions and a 0 to all others; this term was then multiplied by "trade openness." See note 25.

35. Sanctions may lead to greater implementation—aligning domestic rules and institutions with international norms—if states perceive this form of commitment as being least costly: in contrast, ratification carries high "sovereignty costs" (Moravscik, "The Origins of Human Rights Regimes," 228); monitoring requires giving external actors access to territory and people; leniency involves altering an existing violation; and accountability entails uncertain risks and potential instability. This may explain why the worst violators were also more likely to implement international norms.

36. The fact that economic development was unrelated to specific types of abuse confirms previous human rights studies, which have found that economic development has only modest effects (e.g., Poe, Tate, and Keith, "Repression of the Human Right to Personal Integrity Revisited").

37. For states experiencing armed conflict, and therefore engaging in greater human rights violations, monitoring and implementation may prove relatively less costly than other state commitments. See note 35. Compared to other responses, monitoring and implementation may be more readily manipulated: highly controlled visits by outsiders and limited changes in domestic rules and institutions.

38. Neumayer, "Do International Human Rights Treaties Improve Respect for Human Rights?"; Hathaway, "The Cost of Commitment"; and Landman, *Protecting Human Rights*.

39. One exception is Patrick Ball, "State Terror, Constitutional Traditions, and National Human Rights Movements: A Cross-National Quantitative Comparison," in *Globalizations and Social Movements: Culture, Power, and the Transnational Public Sphere*, ed. John A. Guidry, Michael D. Kennedy, and Mayer N. Zald (Ann Arbor: University of Michigan Press, 2000).

40. For similar communicative dynamics, see Risse, "'Let's Argue!' Communicative Action in World Politics."

41. Christian Davenport, Hank Johnston, and Carol Mueller, eds., *Repression and Mobilization* (Minneapolis: University of Minnesota Press, 2005); Keck and Sikkink, *Activists Beyond Borders*, esp. 12–13; and Risse, Ropp, and Sikkink, *The Power of Human Rights*.

42. For example, Davenport, "The Weight of the Past"; and Davenport, *Paths to State Repression*; Poe, Tate, and Keith, "Repression of the Human Right to Personal Integrity Revisited"; and Poe and Tate, "Repression of Human Rights to Personal Integrity in the 1980s."

43. Past violations were related only to norm implementation. According to

Hathaway, violations among nondemocracies help to explain treaty acceptance, a proposition that I do not examine. See Hathaway, "The Cost of Commitment."

44. See Landman, *Protecting Human Rights*; Hathaway, "Do Human Rights Treaties Make a Difference?"; Ryan Goodman and Derek Jinks, "Measuring the Effects of Human Rights Treaties," *European Journal of International Law* 14, 1 (February 2003): 171–83; and Keith, "The United Nations International Covenant on Civil and Political Rights."

45. Both NGO pressure and past abuses were related to improvements in violation, but the direction of influence was the opposite of that predicted. In the case of NGO pressure, this confirms that human rights violations may influence NGO activism. The role of past abuses is probably intrinsic to the data, as greater past abuses leave more room for improvement.

46. For the limitations of using coercive measures against "global prohibition regimes," see Ethan Nadelman, "Global Prohibition Regimes: The Evolution of Norms in International Society," *International Organization* 44 (1990): 479–526.

47. Similarly Chayes and Chayes ("On Compliance") note that a time lag exists between underlying social and economic conditions and states' compliance with international human rights treaties.

48. The notion of a rights-protective regime is discussed in Donnelly, *International Human Rights* (1993), 145–49.

49. I have drawn heavily in this section from Thomas, *The Helsinki Effect*. See also Peter Juviler, *Freedom's Ordeal: The Struggle for Human Rights and Democracy in Post-Soviet States* (Philadelphia: University of Pennsylvania Press, 1997).

50. Thomas, *The Helsinki Effect*, 195–219.

51. Cf. Thomas, *The Helsinki Effect*, 241–44.

52. See annual reports of Amnesty International.

53. Evangelista, *Unarmed Forces: The Transnational Movement to End the Cold War* (Ithaca, N.Y.: Cornell University Press, 1999), 390–91.

54. Newell M. Stultz, "Evolution of the United Nations Anti-Apartheid Regime," *Human Rights Quarterly* 13, no. 1 (1991): 1–24; Donnelly, "Human Rights at the UN"; and Margaret P. Doxey, "International Sanctions: A Framework for Analysis with Special Reference to the UN and South Africa," *International Organization* 26 (Summer 1972): 527–50.

55. See Crawford and Klotz, eds., *How Sanctions Work*; for a more economistic view, see P. I. Levy, "Sanctions on South Africa: What Did They Do?" *The American Economic Review* 89, no. 2 (May 1992): 415–20.

56. For example, see Charles M. Becker, "Economic Sanctions against South Africa," *World Politics* 39 (January 1987): 147–73.

57. Klotz, *Norms in International Relations*, 163–64.

58. Donnelly, *International Human Rights* (1993), 121–23.

59. Richard M. Price, *The Apartheid State in Crisis: Political Transformation in South Africa, 1975–1990* (Oxford: Oxford University Press, 1991), 225.

60. Price discusses these reforms. See Price, *The Apartheid State in Crisis*, 101–46.

61. Price, *The Apartheid State in Crisis*, 145.

62. For example, see David Black, "The Long and Winding Road: International Norms and Domestic Political Change in South Africa," in *The Power of Human Rights*; J. Davis, "Sanctions and Apartheid: The Economic Challenge to Discrimination," in *Economic Sanctions: Panacea or Peacebuilding in a Post–Cold War World?* ed. David Cortright and George Lopez (Boulder, Colo.: Westview Press, 1995); Anthony Marx, *Lessons of Struggle: South African Internal Opposition, 1960–1990* (New York: Oxford University Press, 1992); Price, *The Apartheid State*

in Crisis; James Barber and John Barratt, *South Africa's Foreign Policy: The Search for Status and Security, 1945–1988* (Cambridge: Cambridge University Press, 1990); and Stephen Greenberg, "Economic Growth and Political Change: The South African Case," *Journal of Modern African Studies* 19 (December 1981): 667–704.

63. Price, *The Apartheid State in Crisis*, 251–52.

64. Neta C. Crawford, "The Humanitarian Consequences of Sanctioning South Africa: A Preliminary Assessment," in *Political Gain and Civilian Pain: Humanitarian Impacts of Economic Sanctions*, ed. Thomas G. Weiss, David Cortright, George A. Lopez, and L. Minear (Lanham, Md.: Rowman and Littlefield, 1997), 58.

65. For example, according to Hufbauer, Schott, and Elliott (*Economic Sanctions Reconsidered*), the impact of international economic sanctions in dismantling the apartheid regime was at best modest.

66. Donnelly, *International Human Rights* (1993), 125.

67. On the Chinese case, see note 2, Chapter 1.

68. Hufbauer, Schott, and Elliott, *Economic Sanctions Reconsidered*.

69. Keck and Sikkink, *Activists Beyond Borders*, 118.

70. Wan, *Human Rights in Chinese Foreign Relations*; Kent, *China, the United Nations, and Human Rights*; and Amsden, "Human Rights and China."

71. See, for example, National Lawyers Guild, *International Human Rights Law and Israel's Efforts to Suppress the Palestinian Uprising: Report of the National Lawyers Guild* (New York: National Lawyers Guild, 1989); and regular reports by Amnesty International and Human Rights Watch.

72. See Mayra Gómez, *Human Rights in Cuba, El Salvador and Nicaragua: A Sociological Perspective on Human Rights Abuse* (New York: Routledge, 2003). See also Kathleen C. Schwartzman, "Can International Boycotts Transform Political Systems? The Cases of Cuba and South Africa," *Latin American Politics and Society* 43, no. 2 (Summer 2001): 115–46; and Darren Hawkins, "Explaining the Lack of Institutional Change in Cuba," in *Altered States: International Relations, Domestic Politics, and Institutional Change*, ed. Andrew P. Cortell and Susan Peterson (Lanham, Md.: Lexington Books, 2002).

73. Carollee Bengelsdorf, *The Problem of Democracy in Cuba: Between Vision and Reality* (New York: Oxford University Press, 1994).

74. For example, Amnesty International, *The Situation of Human Rights in Cuba* (London: Amnesty International, May 2002).

75. Amnesty International, annual reports, multiple years.

76. Brysk, *The Politics of Human Rights in Argentina*, 111; and Amnesty International, annual reports, multiple years.

77. See Carlos Santiago Nino, *Radical Evil on Trial* (New Haven, Conn.: Yale University Press, 1997).

78. In December 1986, the *Punto Final* document limited future human rights trials. Then, in May 1987, the Law of Due Obedience granted immunity to all members of the armed services except the most senior officers, accepting the justification from lower-ranking officers that they were following orders. Largely in protest over human rights trials, military uprisings took place in 1987, 1988, and 1990. In October 1989, Menem pardoned thirty-nine senior military officers, followed by all other high-ranking officers in December 1990. In general, see Human Rights Watch, *Truth and Partial Justice in Argentina: An Update, April 1991, America's Watch Report* (New York: Human Rights Watch, 1991), 69. See also Brysk, *The Politics of Human Rights in Argentina*; and Mignone, *Derechos humanos y sociedad*, 168.

79. Brysk, *The Politics of Human Rights in Argentina*, 94 and 103.

80. Brysk, *The Politics of Human Rights in Argentina*, 167; Elizabeth Jelin, "The Politics of Memory: The Human Rights Movement and the Construction of Democracy in Argentina," *Latin American Perspectives* 21 (Spring 1994): 38–58; and annual reports of Amnesty International.

81. For a critique of the *Rettig Report*, see "Informe Rettig quedó corto," *Punto Final*, no. 235 (25 March 1991): 1 and 3. Reproduced in Terrazas Guzmán, *¿Quién se acuerda de Sheila Cassidy?*, 542–44.

82. Roger Burbach, *The Pinochet Affair: State Terrorism and Global Justice* (London: Zed Books, 2003); and Naomi Roht-Arriaza, *The Pinochet Effect: Transnational Justice in the Age of Human Rights* (Philadelphia: University of Pennsylvania Press, 2005).

83. Juan M. Gallardo Miranda and Edmundo O'Kuingttons Ocampo, "El rol de las fuerzas armadas en la sociedad: Doctrina militar en el acontecer político de Sudamérica," *Military Review*, Edición Hispanoamericana (November–December 1992), 14. Quoted in Brian Loveman and Thomas M. Davis, eds., *The Politics of Antipolitics: The Military in Latin America* (Wilmington, Del.: Scholarly Resources, 1997), 387.

84. Conference attended by the author, "Violence, Politics, and Human Rights in Mexico" (San Cristobal de las Casas, Chiapas, Mexico), 8 August 1996.

Chapter 6

1. See Edward Peters, *Torture*, rev. ed. (Philadelphia: University of Pennsylvania Press, 1996).

2. Robert Gilpin, *The Political Economy of International Relations* (Princeton, N.J.: Princeton University Press), 389.

3. Howard Margolis, "Equilibrium Norms," in "Symposium on Norms in Moral and Social Theory," *Ethics* 100 (July 1990): 827.

4. Jon Mercer, *Reputation in International Politics* (Ithaca, N.Y.: Cornell University Press, 1996).

5. "Accounts" are discussed in Terri L. Orbuch, "People's Accounts Count: The Sociology of Accounts," *Annual Review of Sociology* 23 (1997): 455–78. See also Michael J. Cody and Margaret L. McLaughlin, eds., *The Psychology of Tactical Communication* (Clevedon, England: Multilingual, 1990); and Dennis Brissett and Charles Edgley, eds., *Life as Theater: A Dramaturgical Sourcebook*, 2nd ed. (New York: Aldine de Gruyter, 1990). Classic works in this area include Marvin B. Scott and Stanford Lyman, "Accounts," *American Sociological Review* 33 (1968): 46–62; Erving Goffman, *The Presentation of Self in Everyday Life* (Garden City, N.Y.: Doubleday-Anchor, 1959); and C. Wright Mills, "Situated Actions and Vocabularies of Motive," *American Sociological Review* 5 (1940): 904–13.

6. Orbuch, "People's Accounts Count," 463. On "motive talk," see Mills, "Situated Actions and Vocabularies of Motive."

7. For a study of how states respond to human rights accusations rhetorically, see Stanley Cohen, *States of Denial: Knowing about Atrocities and Suffering* (Cambridge, UK: Polity Press, 2001).

8. On the distinction between excuses and justifications, see J. L. Austin, *Philosophical Papers* (London: Oxford University Press, 1961).

9. Finnemore and Sikkink, "International Norm Dynamics and Political Change," 910.

10. These terms are used by Cody and McLaughlin in their introduction to *The Psychology of Tactical Communication.*

11. K. D. Elsbach and R. I. Sutton, "Acquiring Organizational Legitimacy through Illegitimate Actions: A Marriage of Institutional and Impression Management Theories," *Academy of Management Journal* 35 (1992): 699–738.

12. Simmons, "Compliance and International Agreements." See also Richard A. Falk, *Human Rights and State Sovereignty* (New York: Holmes and Meier, 1981).

13. Sikkink, "Human Rights, Principled Issue Networks, and Sovereignty in Latin America"; and Lutz and Sikkink, "International Human Rights Law and Practice in Latin America."

14. For primary and secondary sources relating to "state responsibility," see State Responsibility Project, Lauterpacht Research Centre for International Law, University of Cambridge (http://lcil.law.cam.ac.uk/ILCSR/Statresp.htm).

15. James Ron, "Varying Methods of State Violence," *International Organization* 51 (Spring 1997): 275–300. On "rules about breaking rules," see Robert B. Edgerton, *Rules, Exceptions, and Social Order* (Berkeley: University of California Press, 1985).

16. For example, see Barry R. Schlenker and Michael F. Weigold, "Interpersonal Processes Involving Impression Regulation and Management," *Annual Review of Psychology* 43 (1992): 142; and C. R. Snyder and Raymond L. Higgins, "Excuses: Their Effective Role in the Negotiation of Reality," *Psychological Bulletin* 104 (1988): 23–35.

17. On how institutional isomorphism in international relations can be a matter of appearances, see Hendrik Spruyt, *The Sovereign State and Its Competitors: An Analysis of Systems Change* (Princeton, N.J.: Princeton University Press, 1994).

18. For the ineffectiveness of coercive measures against "global prohibition regimes," see Nadelman, "Global Prohibition Regimes."

19. A relevant critique of the assumptions underlying contemporary international human rights pressures appears in M. Anne Brown, *Human Rights and the Borders of Suffering: The Promotion of Human Rights in International Politics* (Manchester: Manchester University Press, 2002).

20. Sikkink, *Mixed Signals.* See also Robert F. Drinan, S.J., *The Mobilization of Shame: A World View of Human Rights* (New Haven, Conn.: Yale University Press, 2002).

21. See Leonard J. Schoppa, "The Social Context in Coercive International Bargaining," *International Organization* 53 (Spring 1999): 307–42.

22. Robert Jervis makes a similar point about the role of normative agendas and political analysis. See Jervis, "Realism in the Study of World Politics," *International Organization* 52 (Autumn 1998): 974. For an intriguing parallel with psychoanalysis, see Howard B. Levine, ed., "Clinical Aspects of Compliance," Special Issue, *Psychoanalytic Inquiry* 19 (1999).

23. Finnemore, *National Interests in International Society,* 135.

24. Kevin Dwyer, *Arab Voices: The Human Rights Debate in the Middle East* (London: Routledge, 1991), 213.

25. See Peter Hall, *The Political Power of Economic Ideas: Keynesianism Across Nations* (Princeton, N.J.: Princeton University Press, 1989).

26. On feedback, see Paul Pierson, "When Effect Becomes Cause: Policy Feedback and Political Change," *World Politics* 45 (July 1993): 595–628.

27. Donald Puchala, "Domestic Politics and Regional Harmonization in the European Communities," *World Politics* 27 (July 1975): 517.

28. Jack Donnelly, "Human Rights: The Impact of International Action," *International Journal* (Spring 1988): 241.

29. Giuseppe Di Palma, "Comment: Democracy, Human Rights, and the U.S.

Index